Reln

Available in the Master Class Series

Also available in the MasterClass Series

MasterClass in Drama Education, Michael Anderson

MasterClass in Music Education, edited by John Finney and Felicity Laurence

Also available from Bloomsbury

Effective Teaching and Learning in Practice, Don Skinner

Conducting Research in Educational Contexts, Tehmina N. Basit

Inquiring in the Clasroom: Asking the Questions That Matter about Teaching and Learning, edited by Nick Mitchell and Joanne Pearson

Educational Research and Inquiry: Qualitative and Quantitative Approaches, Dimitra Hartas

Teaching Religious Education: Researchers in the Classroom, Julian Stern

MasterClass in Religious Education

Transforming Teaching and Learning

Liam Gearon

MasterClass

B L O O M S B U R Y

LONDON · NEW DELHI · NEW YORK · SYDNEY

Bloomsbury Academic

An imprint of Bloomsbury Publishing Plc

50 Bedford Square	175 Fifth Avenue
London	New York
WC1B 3DP	NY 10010
UK	USA

www.bloomsbury.com

First published 2013

British Library Cataloguing-in-Publication Data
A catalogue record for this book is available from the British Library.

ISBN: PB: 9781441154224
     HB: 9781441153753

Library of Congress Cataloging-in-Publication Data
A catalogue record for this book is available from the Library of Congress

Typeset by Newgen Imaging Systems Pvt Ltd., Chennai, India
Printed and bound in Great Britain

Contents

Series Editor's Foreword

This is a book which will challenge and provoke thinking about Religious Education. In locating this volume within a context which positions the development of religion and religions within an historical and political narrative, Liam Gearon compellingly draws us into a critical engagement with the place of Religious Education in the modern world. Drawing extensively on national and international research, this book is both an intellectual exploration of key issues, which invites teachers to once again take delight in the notion of debate and exploration, and a pragmatic lens through which to consider teaching, learning and assessment in the Religious Education classroom, and across the wider curriculum.

The volume is structured around six major themes: Religion, Politics and Education: Modern World, Ancient Disputes; Religion in Education: Contemporary UK, European and USA Research Perspectives; Religious Education and the Religious Life: Theology and Faith Schools; Religious Education and Secularity: Issues of Cohesion, Diversity, Pluralism; Pedagogies of Religious Education: Teaching, Learning and Assessment; Religion across the Curriculum: Arts, Humanities, Sciences which separately and together explore key themes in the debates surrounding Religious Education. A strong and cogent thread permeates each chapter, drawing together Liam Gearon's key argument on contexts and influences, and presents the reader with an energetic and insistent thesis which demands the reader enter into a dialogue of ideas; there is no sitting back and coasting with this MasterClass: we are required to think and argue, and as a result our own thinking is sharpened and invigorated.

As Series Editor I am delighted to be able to include this eloquent and elegantly argued volume, and to have such a distinguished author as Liam Gearon as a major contributor to the MasterClass series.

Sue Brindley, Senior Lecturer in Education
University of Cambridge, UK

Introduction: Context, Aims and Limitations

Bede's *Ecclesiastical History of the English People* records a notable incident from the life of an Anglo-Saxon king prior to his conversion. King Edwin, deliberating over his decision, seeks advice from his noblemen. One of them renders the following account of earthly life:

> This is how the present life of man on earth, King, appears to me in comparison with that time which is unknown to us. You are sitting feasting with your elders and nobles in winter time; the fire is burning on the hearth in the middle of the hall and all inside is warm, while outside the wintry storms of rain and snow are raging; and a sparrow flies swiftly through the hall. It enters in at one door and quickly flies out through the other. For the few moments it is inside, the storm and wintry tempest cannot touch it, but after the briefest moment of calm, it flits from your sight, out of the wintry storm and into it again. So this life of man appears but for a moment; what follows or indeed what went before, we know not at all. (Bede, 1999: 95–6)

The nobleman adds, 'If this new doctrine brings us more information, it seems right that we should accept it.' The king, contemplating ultimately life-changing conversion, 'used to sit alone for hours at a time, earnestly debating within himself what he ought to do and what religion he should follow' (Bede, 1999: 94). Religion mattered. There was an existential *urgency* to conversion. Indeed, the decision was of greater import than transient, political affairs.

Christianity had featured for several centuries before Bede's eighth-century *History*. Britannia was named by Roman historians after the tribe of Britons who, inhabitants of what was then the westerly Atlantic edge of the known world, had a Christian presence from the earliest centuries of Christianity itself. Christians were certainly numerous enough in these islands to be persecuted in the second and third centuries under the reigns of Marcus Aurelius and Diocletian. As a result of such persecution, Christianity thrived, particularly in those Celtic tribal lands, *beyond* the borders of Roman rule. Celtic monks were the first missionaries through Ireland and Wales, and particularly to the southwest of England, in centres of early Christianity such as Glastonbury. From the early fourth-century reign of Constantine, Christianity became widely established in Britain. With the fall of Rome, fifth-century Britain, unprotected by Roman legions and within easy reach of the tribes of northern Europe, witnessed war and political instability to the point of anarchy.

Archaeological evidence portrays a land in anarchy and lawless destruction. From limited *written* records of this 'Dark Age', we know the extent of the chaos from one near contemporaneous, sixth-century source, Gildas's *Concerning the Ruin of Britain*. Gildas opens with self-abnegation as well as recrimination against the nation: 'Whatever in this my epistle I may write in my humble but well-meaning manner, rather by way of lamentation than for display, let no one suppose that it springs from contempt of others, or that I foolishly esteem myself as better than they; for, alas! the subject of my complaint is the general destruction of everything that is good, and the general growth of evil throughout the land; but that I would condole with my country in her distress and rejoice to see her revive therefrom: for it is my present purpose to relate the deeds of an indolent and slothful race' (Fordham, 2012). Gildas is not writing what modern historians would call reliable historical narrative. Written in the midst of calamity, Gildas writes in a prophetic apocalyptic style, seeing in the destruction warnings to a land fallen from the path of God. Yet, for all its prophetic intent, Gildas's *Ruin of Britain* presents the kernel of a chaos left after the fall of Rome.

Composed in a relatively more tranquil eighth century, and borrowing at times from Gildas, Bede's *The Ecclesiastical History of the English People* records the centuries' long conversion of warring tribes and the history of an emergent Christian nation. With Gildas, Bede's *History* is one of the key historical sources of the period. Yet, even Bede, one of the originators of English history, with his studied documentary corroboration of historical facts, freely incorporates hagiography with historical narration. With Bede, the lives of saints are generally more important than the lives of kings. The histories of Gildas and Bede share then a view of history which is meant to be morally instructive. They are accounts written to remind readers of the critical significance of faith and conversion of life in that short window of time which mortality affords. Earthly life is important only insofar as it offers opportunity for conversion. Temporal history is ultimately insignificant in the light of the eternal. Neither Gildas nor Bede then is, strictly speaking, writing simply national histories – though Britain and the emergent English people are their focus. *The Ecclesiastical History*, for example, sets national history around the events of first-century Palestine, and what for Bede as well as Gildas is the incarnational fulcrum of all human history.

The same central historiographical approach to the interpretation of history is clear from *The Anglo-Saxon Chronicle*, initiated by King Alfred in the ninth century. From this vantage point, Alfred viewed as a golden age the relative peace a hundred and fifty years earlier in which Bede wrote *The Ecclesiastical History*. This is because the Viking raids which preceded and preoccupied Alfred's reign disrupted and threatened his kingdom. They particularly decimated the monastic life whose scholarship had charted its rise. Victory over Alfred's Viking enemies was achieved, as in previous centuries, through conversion to Christianity. Indeed, so central is Christianity to the *Chronicle* that it begins its history (as does Bede) not in ninth-century England, but first-century Palestine.

We see in all of these documents – from Gildas, Bede and *The Anglo Saxon Chronicle* – a view of human political history, the rise and fall of earthly kingdoms, written in the light of salvation history. Aside from whether we accept their interpretation of history, as a religious narrative it forms a good part of a thousand years of national history. Most early English history is religious history. These early works remain foundational for subsequent English history. In the twentieth century, written after his surprise award for the Nobel Prize for

Literature in 1953, Winston Churchill's four-volume *A History of the English-Speaking Peoples* (Churchill, 1999) is a conscious mirroring of Bede.

In Alfred's time, during the emergence of a largely unified England, education played a formative if incipient role too in the maintaining of the nation and its Christian identity. We know from Asser's (1908) *Life of Alfred*, that Alfred interpreted Viking raids as God's punishment for waywardness from Christian faith. Alfred's answer was martial but also educational. Alfred conceived of schools as playing an important line of defence against moral and religious laxity. Though there is no archaeological evidence of Alfred's schools, and *The Anglo Saxon Chronicle* is concerned with regal rather than social history, we know Alfred saw learning as a means to reform his kingdom. It is no coincidence that a scholarly king, who set as great store by scholarship as by sword, has to this day, in his Wessex heartland (the south and southwest of England), numerous schools named after him.

National religious history is also inevitably local. It is so for students and teachers alike as it literally surrounds their school. I once taught, for example, in Somerset, in a community school in Glastonbury. The longer historical perspective was evident more clearly than it might be in larger towns and cities, but the history is always there. So Glastonbury, the way national history is layered, is close not only to the heart of Alfred's Wessex, but viscerally represents in the stone ruins of Glastonbury Abbey, the political–religious conflicts of sixteenth-century English and European Reformation. And the Reformation is the point in English and European history where Catholic–Protestant division marks the fracture in the medieval view of history which had been evident in British history from Gildas onwards.

Over subsequent centuries, to the eighteenth-century Enlightenment and beyond, where we are today, different, rational and secular histories would proliferate. Enlightenment history in particular began to look not simply at alternatives to the divine within history, but seeing the divine as absent from it. An Enlightenment historian like Edward Gibbon in *The History of the Decline and Fall of the Roman Empire* saw Christianity ultimately accounting for the decline of Roman imperial power itself. Christianity made secular history – of political rule and power – seem unimportant in comparison to salvation history. Enlightenment historians and philosophers confirm this interpretation but lament it. In *The Social Contract*, Rousseau's penultimate chapter, on civil religion, openly castigates Christianity: 'Christianity preaches only servitude and dependence. Its spirit is so favourable to tyranny that it always profits by such a regime. True Christians are made to be slaves, and they know it and do not much mind: this short life counts for too little in their eyes' (Rousseau, 1968 [1762]: 144 ff.). Such views offered what were then radical alternatives to the hegemony of a Christian view of history; but they were also a blueprint for the ascendancy of secular power over ecclesiastical authority which would follow, and helped shape the modern world.

The rise of secular alternatives to Christianity is the story of modernity (Habermas and Ratzinger, 2007). There have of course been nuanced readings which challenge simple views of the hegemony of modernity, a particularly important one being Eisenstadt's (2000) notion of 'multiple modernities'. Enlightenment was of course itself diverse, as Himmelfarb (2005) has shown in looking at the different ways its intellectual and political ideas played out in England or France or America, but even in Himmelfarb's view all roads led one way or the other to modernity. Other views, like Eisenstadt's, take the multiple modernities model and question the hegemony of modernity in outcome and origins. Hefner (1998), for example, examines the global historical and contemporary political influence of Hinduism and Islam in relation to Christianity and Western Enlightenment.

Models which challenge modernity in such ways also tend to challenge the secularization which is often seen as integral to it. Such alternatives have also been vigorously challenged. Schmidt (2006) asks, for example, whether 'the continued significance of religion in most parts of the world, except perhaps in some northwestern European countries, undermine the proposition that modernization leads to secularization': 'It does not of course. For secularization does not necessarily imply the complete vanishing or disappearance of religion. It only implies its gradual separation from other spheres of society in which its views cannot claim paramount importance anymore because the spheres (i.e. the economy, politics, the law, science, etc.) become structurally autonomous from religion and increasingly follow their own norms' (Schmidt, 2006: 90; also Schmidt, 2010; for consideration of the secularization and counter-secularization debates in relation to European religious education, see Gearon, 2012a). Such debates are not always or even obviously central to religious education. Yet because of the continued importance of religion itself in the modern world, they form an intellectual backdrop to religious education, some understanding of which at the very least sheds light on the subject's current aims and assumptions.

Whatever side of whichever of these debates we might be on, we can certainly note unequivocally that religion clearly persists in education. In fact it seems to be marked by an accelerated interest in it worldwide. But we may also note that religion in education internationally is more and more open to secular influences, even in countries where religious education has not historically been a part of the curriculum in state-funded schools. Indeed, one of the marks of secular influence is the separation of religious education from the religious life. Where religious education is separated from the religious life – as is required when the state provides an inclusive religious education in contexts of cultural diversity and religious plurality – the rationale for religious education today often finds strongest warrant not from religious but political aims. We learn about the world's religions in order that we can understand those who might hold these views, and, so the arguments goes, understanding them will contribute to a more harmonious, less conflict-ridden world. The *risk* of such justifications is that we lose sight of the fact that religions present perspectives other than, even if it does incorporate, history and political life. While history and politics are elements in religion, and thus *in*nate to religious education, neither religion nor religious can be reduced to the historical or *the* political.

While it cannot hope to be a comprehensive guide on 'how to teach religious education', this book shows how religious education has been shaped by such conflicting histories. Chapter 1 thus examines the relationship between religion, politics and education being as much an aspect of antiquity as of modernity. Chapter 2 demonstrates how the political importance of religion in education has come to dominate international research agendas in the UK, Europe and the United States of America. Chapter 3 explores the origins and interconnectedness of religious education with the religious life, and the continuation of this in faith schools. Chapter 4 takes a closer look at the origins and influence of secularity on religious education, particularly through rationales related to cohesion, diversity and plurality. Chapter 5 identifies the emergence of religious education pedagogies which seek to answer the questions around teaching, learning and assessment when religious education has become separated from the religious life. Chapter 6 examines the role of religion across the curriculum, framing its presence as a reflection of wider currents in the history of the arts and the sciences, with particular reference to C. P. Snow's conceptualization of the 'two cultures'.

The Venerable Bede would not recognize such notions or contexts of religious education *as religious* education. Modern-day religious educators themselves of course might well not recognize Bede's thinking as a basis for religious education. Some philosophers of education go further, arguing that 'religious' and 'education' are mutually incompatible. Bede arguably wrote all his many historical and other works as religious instruction, as edification, education in the broadest sense: What education was more important than education in religion? And such a task is pervaded by that sense of existential urgency which marks the *Ecclesiastical History*. It is plain in the nobleman's allegory of the sparrow and the feasting hall as an image of the short span of human life; and limits the significance of mere political activity, infinitesimally unimportant in the light of the eternal.

Religion, Politics and Education: Modern World, Ancient Disputes

1

Chapter Outline

Introduction

'Descending from Judaism, Christianity's central belief maintains Jesus of Nazareth is the promised messiah of the Hebrew Scriptures, and that his life, death, and resurrection are salvific for the world.' So reads a source on the history and development of Christianity. 'Christianity', it continues, 'is one of the three monotheistic Abrahamic faiths, along with Islam and Judaism, which traces its spiritual lineage to Abraham of the Hebrew Scriptures. Its sacred texts include the Hebrew Bible and the New Testament.' The text proceeds:

> Catholicism (or Roman Catholicism) is the oldest established western Christian church and the world's largest single religious body. It is supranational, and recognizes a hierarchical structure with the Pope, or Bishop of Rome, as its head, located at the Vatican. Catholics believe the Pope is the divinely ordered head of the Church from a direct spiritual legacy of Jesus' apostle Peter . . . The Catholic Church has a comprehensive theological and moral doctrine specified for believers in its catechism, which makes it unique among most forms of Christianity.

Orthodox Christianity, the text notes, is 'the oldest established eastern form of Christianity':

> The Holy Orthodox Church, has a ceremonial head in the Bishop of Constantinople (Istanbul), also known as a Patriarch, but its various regional forms (e.g., Greek Orthodox, Russian Orthodox,

Serbian Orthodox, Ukrainian Orthodox) are autocephalous (independent of Constantinople's authority, and have their own Patriarchs). Orthodox churches are highly nationalist and ethnic. The Orthodox Christian faith shares many theological tenets with the Roman Catholic Church, but diverges on some key premises.

The same text outlines sixteenth-century Protestant attempts 'to reform Roman Catholicism's practices, dogma, and theology'. Protestantism 'encompasses several forms or denominations which are extremely varied in structure, beliefs, relationship to state, clergy, and governance. Many protestant theologies emphasize the primary role of scripture in their faith, advocating individual interpretation of Christian texts without the mediation of a final religious authority.'

The source also presents details about other world faiths. Buddhism, it notes, is a 'religion or philosophy', 'inspired by the 5th century B.C. teachings of Siddhartha Gautama, (also known as Gautama Buddha "the enlightened one")': 'Buddhism focuses on the goal of spiritual enlightenment centred on an understanding of Gautama Buddha's Four Noble Truths on the nature of suffering, and on the Eightfold Path of spiritual and moral practice, to break the cycle of suffering of which we are a part. Buddhism ascribes to a karmic system of rebirth. Several schools and sects of Buddhism exist, differing often on the nature of the Buddha, the extent to which enlightenment can be achieved – for one or for all, and by whom – religious orders or laity.' Identifying Theravada and Mahayana Buddhism as the two major divisions, of the former it states that 'the oldest Buddhist school': 'Theravada is practiced mostly in Sri Lanka, Cambodia, Laos, Burma, and Thailand, with minority representation elsewhere in Asia and the West. Theravadans follow the Pali Canon of Buddha's teachings, and believe that one may escape the cycle of rebirth, worldly attachment, and suffering for oneself; this process may take one or several lifetimes. Within Mahayana Buddhism, it identifies "subsets" of Zen and Tibetan Buddhism, and forms of Mahayana Buddhism as 'common in East Asia and Tibet, and parts of the West': 'Mahayanas [*sic*] have additional scriptures beyond the Pali Canon and believe the Buddha is eternal and still teaching. Unlike Theravada Buddhism, Mahayana schools maintain the Buddha-nature is present in all beings and all will ultimately achieve enlightenment.'

Other listed traditions include Hinduism, Islam, Judaism and Sikhism. Information provided includes a worldwide list of countries with percentage break-ups of religious populations by nation-state. In the present-day educational context which sets high store on 'religiously literacy' – including Harvard's School of Divinity, see Moore (2012) – the above outline of religious traditions might be regarded as a good starting point in countering religious illiteracy.

The source which mentions all the above is the United States' Central Intelligence Agency (CIA, 2012a). We can see that there is significant *political* as well as educational currency in religious literacy. Why though is the CIA interested in religion? The CIA, for obvious reasons, has a particular post-9/11 interest in political forms of Islam. Since 2004, this has been focused on through its 'Political Islam Strategic Analysis Program (PISAP)'. This is in recognition of the fact 'that forces that have not traditionally been studied, in a comprehensive manner, by the Intelligence Community needed to be examined as they affect the national security interests of the United States' (CIA, 2012b). The CIA is careful to point out that the 'effort does not focus on Islam as a religion or on the worldwide Muslim community; rather, it examines those movements and organizations that use religion for political purposes and use religious ideology to attempt to change the existing political, social, or economic order'. Its remit 'relies on regional and functional expertise to promote, consolidate, and integrate multidisciplinary analysis on worldwide developments of interest to the US policy community' (CIA, 2012; and for the reinvention of American–Muslim relations, see Nakhleh, 2008). The information provided *across* traditions shows, however, that religion per se is of geopolitical and security interest, which I have defined elsewhere and with other examples, as the 'securitization of religion in education' (Gearon, 2012; also Gearon, 2013a; 2013b). This chapter elaborates further on how the political interest manifest in religion has impacted on education. The question to consider throughout is, how far or to what extent should religious education be influenced by political aims? And how, or by what criteria, would we be able to judge the educational value of such political impact?

Religion, politics, education: modern world

The eighteenth-century Enlightenment in Europe and America marked a fulcrum point in the history of ideas in which reason and empiricism gained the intellectual foreground over theology and revelation. In the shortest of his works, it was the philosopher Immanuel Kant who provided pithy expression of the fundamentals of this comprehensively radical idea, in *Was ist Äufklarung? – What Is Enlightenment?*: 'Enlightenment is man's release from his self-incurred tutelage. Tutelage is man's inability to make use of his understanding without direction from another. Self-incurred is this tutelage when its cause lies not in lack of reason but in lack of resolution and courage to use it without direction from another. *Sapere aude!* "Have courage to use your own reason!" – that is the motto of enlightenment' (Kant, 1784: 1). Without explicitly referring to the Bible, it is the Bible's revelation and the authority which this bestowed upon the Christian churches – fractured in their authority since the sixteenth-century Reformation – which is the target of Kant's statement when he declares: 'If I have a book which understands for me, a pastor who has a conscience for me and so forth, I need not trouble myself. I need not think, if I can only pay – others will easily undertake the irksome work for me' (Kant, 1784: 1).

The autonomy of reason from religious authority would characterize modernity (Bird, 2006). And in Kant's sense, modernity is therefore 'secular'. In this context, the potency of secular rationality, science and the technology that emerged in its wake makes discussion of Eisenstadt's (2000) 'multiple modernities', touched on above, a mere nuance of a secular-driven modernity. Rationalism in philosophy and technology in science would define social and political life and, as a consequence, the educational systems which would maintain the outlook and enterprise of modernity – in other words, the world in which we now live.

These Enlightenment hopes would take different forms and have different impacts, some more immediate and dramatic than others, along what Himmelfarb (2005) calls the 'roads to modernity'. In all cases, the rational autonomy of the individual in the matter of intellect was paramount. Along with scientific and related developments, the great impact of this was political, not only on church but on monarchy as well: Enlightenment would instigate in some cases a gradual and in others wholesale and immediate impact on the authority of 'throne' and 'altar' (e.g. Rahe, 2008).

Kant's excursus on Enlightenment was written in the aftermath of the American Revolution and just prior to the French Revolution. In the short term, the French Revolution would fail, where the American would seemingly succeed. In the 1830s, the young Frenchman Alexis de Tocqueville in *Democracy in America* would cross the Atlantic to try to find out why the French Revolution failed. Tocqueville remains of contemporary as well as historical significance: not only for insights into early American democracy, of its separations of religion and state, but also for insights into how religion remained important, and how absence from public education did not hamper religion.

However, as the Marxist historian Eric Hobsbawn states in *The Age of Revolution: 1789–1848*, it was the events of 1789 in France which would ultimately have greater long-term historical effects: 'The French Revolution is a landmark in all countries' (Hobsbawn, 1962: 75). In this, he details the violent overthrow of colonial power in nineteenth-century Latin America. However, as he would elaborate in subsequent works – *The Age of Capital: 1848–1875*; *The Age of Empire: 1875–1914*; and *The Age of Extremes: 1914–1991* (Hobsbawn, 1988, 1989, 1995) – the eighteenth-century French Revolution would provide a blueprint for revolution in subsequent centuries, including Communism and Nazism in the twentieth.

When religion is so easily associated with extremism, Hobsbawn's *Age of Extremes* is a reminder that for much of modernity, political theory has been concerned not with religious but political extremes. The founding of the United Nations (UN) at the end of the Second World War is a case in point. The notion then that religion could exert any meaningful political threat would have been laughable. Indeed, it was in 1935 the French foreign minister sought Soviet assistance as Hitler's power grew informing Stalin that the support of the Pope would be essential. Stalin is reported to have joked: 'The Pope? How many divisions has he got?'

To the UN the Holocaust was gave stark demonstration of the susceptibility of cultural, ethnic or religious difference confronted with dictatorial governance. The UN thus emphasized universal values over particularities of difference. In the light of such events, the UN's Universal Declaration of Human Rights (UDHR, 1948) was an attempt to prevent future generations from being subjected to 'the barbarous acts' of totalitarianism. To do so, the UDHR emphasized what was shared by diverse cultures rather than what divided them, what was 'universal'. Education was seen as contributing to legal and political frameworks from the UN's inception, especially through the United Nations' Educational, Scientific and Cultural Organization (UNESCO). The Preamble to the UDHR stresses 'teaching and learning' as key to the promotion of rights and freedoms after the eighteenth-century model.

The Cold War was not, however, the ideal political milieu to engender such ideals. The Soviets and North Atlantic Treaty Organisation (NATO) may have shared scientific and technological goals – the arms and space race holding the prestige – but political difference still shaped respective education systems (e.g. Bronfenbrenner, 1972; Kirkpatrick, 2002). Although 'the forty-five years from the dropping of the atom bombs to the end of the Soviet Union do not form a single homogenous period in world history' (Hobsbawn, 1994: 225), with the Cold War, education lessened as a UN priority and religion surfaced little in large-scale geopolitics.

Though ideas of 'progress' differed, there seemed to be a shared sociological analysis that modernity also meant secularization, that religion would become increasingly marginalized not only in public life, restricted to a private sphere, certainly in politics, but also in intellectual life across academic disciplines (e.g. Berger and Luckmann, 1967; Bruce, 2002, 2003; Fenn, 1978; Martin, 1978; Wilson, 1966). Yet even prior to 9/11 at least one leading theorist of secularization was renouncing his formerly held sociological faith (Berger, 1999; also Berger et al., 2008). As Casanova's (1994) *Public Religions in the Modern World* would demonstrate from Cold War case studies (especially from Latin America and Eastern Europe), secularization theory left unexplained the persistent political impact of religion on global politics. No sympathizer with religion, even Hobsbawn, would admit to (though he was dismayed by) religion's enduring presence: 'Fundamentalist religion as a major force of successful mass mobilization belongs to the last decades of the twentieth century, which have even witnessed a bizarre return to fashion among some intellectuals of what their educated grandfathers would have described as superstition and barbarism' (Hobsbawn, 1994: 202). Two significant volumes by Michael Burleigh (2006, 2007) – respectively *Earthly Powers: Religion and Politics in Europe from the Enlightenment to the Great War* and *Sacred Causes: The Clash of Religion and Politics from the Great War to the War on Terror* – show the pervasive role of religion in world politics *throughout* a modern age which had supposedly marginalized it.

In political terms, however, the early 1990s were marked by a Western liberal democratic triumphalism, epitomized by an 'end of history' thesis that declared the ideological battle decisively won by liberal democracy (Fukuyama, 2002). The retort to Fukuyama came from his former university teacher Samuel Huntington (2002) in *The Clash of Civilizations*. Huntington vigorously disputed Fukuyama's position. For one, China remained more than an insignificant ideological remnant of the Cold War. Tiananmen Square testified more than any other immediate post-Cold War event that liberal democratic triumphalism, if in part warranted, needed to be nuanced. More important was Huntington's main counter-thesis: that even if ideological conflict was less important in global politics than it had been, future international tensions would centre on the contested grounds of culture and religion, and the unresolved historical tensions between 'civilizations'. Criticized for a naive and essentialist dividing of the world into such civilizational blocks, Huntington wrote *The Clash of Civilizations* in the early 1990s when such conflict seemed a remote possibility. From September 2001, his thesis seemed prescient.

It is in this broad, necessarily simplistic sketch that we need to see present-day political interest around religion in education. Thus, in the aftermath of the Cold War, education took on renewed political urgency, centring on shared political principles – democracy, freedom, rights – through the UN's International Decade of Human Rights Education (1995–2004) and the subsequent World Programme for Human Rights Education (2004–). Though the UN would continue to focus on these secular political ideals, the post-Cold War period was marked by increasing attention to religion, particularly through the newly created office of the Special Rapporteur for Freedom of Religion or Belief. The UN's educational organ, UNESCO, would also begin explicitly to focus on religion through its historic attention to 'culture' (UNESCO, 2006, 2011). The end of the Cold War, then, saw UN efforts to establish political values through pedagogical means. The aftermath saw UN efforts targeting terrorism through legal–political policy initiatives (Boulden and Weiss, 2004; Chesterman et al., 2007; Weiss and Daws, 2008). Both these post-Cold War and post-9/11 contexts would increasingly see governmental and intergovernmental bodies such as the UN attend to religion in both political and educational contexts, often justified through security concerns (Gearon, 2012a; Philips et al., 2011).

In this geopolitical setting, there has emerged a burgeoning theoretical subdiscipline of politics and theology, alternately known as public theology or political theology. Scott and Cavanaugh (2004) provide case studies of Protestant and Catholic political theology in all its historical and contemporary complexity. Others engaged in the same debates of political theology provide warnings against the over-politicization of religion: to paraphrase, they warn, in shorthand, as does Paul's Letter to the Hebrews, that here is no abiding city (Vries and Sullivan, 2006).

Political theology as a discipline is of recent origin, though its antecedence is ancient. In modernity, its genealogy can be traced to Schmitt's (2005) *Political Theology: Four Chapters on the Concept of Sovereignty*. Emden (2006) has described the latter as 'one of the most important texts in modern political thought'. Originally published in the 1920s Germany, a time of crisis for European liberal democracy, in *Political Theology* Schmitt argued that 'All significant concepts of the modern theory of the state are secularized theological concepts.' This marks in other words the shift of power of long-held ecclesiastical authority to the secular state. This notion – that 'all significant concepts of the modern theory of the state are secularized theological concepts' – is the case 'not only because of their historic development – in which they were transferred from theology to the theory of the state, whereby, for example, the omnipotent God became the omnipotent lawgiver – but also because of their systematic structure': 'The idea of the modern constitutional state triumphed with deism [over] a theology and metaphysics' (Schmitt, 2005: 32). Schmitt above all theorists thus demonstrates how the political becomes 'theological'. Eric Voegelin's conception of totalitarianism as a form of political religion conveyed much the same (Henningsen, 2000). In *Black Mass: Apocalyptic Religion and the Death of Utopia*, Gray puts it pithily: 'Modern politics is a chapter in the history of religions' (Gray, 2007: 1).

If Kant saw autonomy as critical to Enlightenment, the search for the grounds of political legitimacy in the absence of religious authority was the engine behind modern democracy as much as the extremes of totalitarianism (for instance, Friedrich and Brzezinski, 1967; Roberts, 2006; Talmon, 1961). In political moderation and extremes, religion has been separated from political power as well as repressed by it (again, Burleigh, 2006, 2007). If religious extremism today is a form of resistance to liberal democratic governance, religious pluralism has become the dominant problem of political liberalism:

> Political liberalism addresses two fundamental questions. The first question is: what is the most appropriate conception of justice for specifying the fair terms of social cooperation between citizens regarded as free and equal? . . . The second question is: what are the grounds of toleration understood in a general way, given the fact of reasonable pluralism as the inevitable result of the powers of human reason at work within enduring free institutions? Combining these two questions into one we have: how is it possible for there to exist over time a just and stable society of free and equal citizens who still remain profoundly divided by religious, philosophical, and moral doctrines? (Rawls, 2005: 3–4)

In *The Law of Peoples*, Rawls (1996) deals with the presently vexing question of how liberal democracies should relate to those religious traditions which not only do not share such standpoints but actively seek ultimately to destroy them. Post-Cold War and post-9/11, political agencies have increasingly looked in part to education to make a contribution.

The resurgent interdisciplinary strength of political theology is *but one* bridge between the arts and humanities and the social and political sciences. Political theology is neither a new nor an undisciplined hybridity. Its disciplinary roots lie in antiquity, while its theoretical frameworks seem readymade for the modern world. It is for this reason, that it offers a multiplicity of approaches, not a limited theological or political interpretation, and hence Vries and Sullivan's (2006) collection is entitled *Political Theologies*.

In the examples that follow, we see how the unresolved issues of political and religious authority in modernity are of pressing, pragmatic rather than simply theoretic concern. Often, we note religion in education emerging as a significant aspect of a longer-term resolution to a long-standing, that is, historical political problem.

The United States

The 9/11 Commission Report

We begin with the United States, because 9/11 still provides, arguably, the defining image of the new millennium. The *9/11 Commission Report* 'provides a full and complete account of the circumstances surrounding the September 11th, 2001, terrorist attacks, including preparedness for and the immediate response to the attacks. It also includes recommendations designed to guard against future attacks.' It consists of 13 chapters, from the earliest recorded notification that a terror attack was about to take place (chapter 1) through chapter 2 ('The Foundation of the New Terrorism'), the subsequent evolution of counter-terrorism (chapter 3), intricate detail of the plot and its manifestation (chapters 4–10), the subsequent 'war on terror' and the war in Afghanistan (chapter 10) and chapters of general reflection on global strategy for countering terrorism (chapter 11), with recommendations for government, the security services and *education* (chapter 12) and a final chapter on implications for governance. The Report shows more than any other single document in recent international relations, the political, religious and, when we look at the recommendations, the potential *educational* implications of the events and aftermath of 9/11 (*The 9/11 Commission*, 2004; *The 9/11 Commission*, 2011, published without the recommendations but a new Afterword).

A key recommendation is that the US government 'must identify and prioritize actual or potential terrorist sanctuaries. For each, it should have a realistic strategy to keep possible terrorists insecure and on the run, using all elements of national power. We should reach out, listen to and work with other countries that can help. Education is seen as one arguably new element in international relations. The Report describes 'An Agenda of Opportunity' which combines '*educational* and economic opportunity'. Including addressing goals 'to cut the Middle East region's illiteracy rate' particularly 'targeting women and girls and supporting programs for adult literacy', 'vocational education . . . in trades and business skills'. There is too, the report declares, 'unglamorous help' needed 'to support the basics, such as textbooks that translate more of the world's knowledge into local languages and libraries to house such materials', critical since 'education about the outside world, or other cultures, is weak'. A recommendation here is that the US government 'should offer to join with other nations in generously supporting a new International Youth Opportunity Fund. *Funds will be spent directly for building and operating primary and secondary schools in those Muslim states that commit to sensibly investing their own money in public education*' (*The 9/11 Commission*, 2004: 396, emphasis added). A vital area is 'education that teaches tolerance, the dignity and value of each individual, and respect for different beliefs is a key element in any global strategy to eliminate Islamist terrorism' (The 9/11 Commission, 2004: 395 ff.).

Aside from its stated intentions, *The 9/11 Commission Report* in itself is a useful source for religious education, for it provides not only information about 9/11, but also a historical analysis of colonial and postcolonial resentments in the Muslim world and how this might account for the rise of 'fundamentalist' Islam. If *The 9/11 Commission Report* presents a portrait of legitimate Western liberal freedoms under threat from Islamic fundamentalist sources, there are alternate views and voices, particularly prominent being those which see in such perspectives a move towards a dominant, hegemonic power in military as well as cultural terms (Chomsky, 2003, 2006, 2007). This can be seen as part of a far pre-9/11 wider literature on postcolonial theory from critics such as Cesaire, Fanon and Said (for a selection of primary texts, Moore-Gilbert et al., 1997; also Loomba, 2005; Ashcroft et al., 2005; in religious education, Gearon, 2002a,b, also 2008). This literature, academic and activist, has had an impact on cultural and political thinking, characterizing and critiquing Western imperialism and colonialism in a range of domains. It invariably neglects the dominant imperialism and colonialism of the then Soviet Union and the People's Republic of China, and such alternative perspectives in security terms portray a 'western state terrorism' (Alexander, 1991; also Jackson et al., 2010; Zizek, 2004).

More widely it provides evidence, in the report's recommendations, of widening the political role and also the security role of religion in education (Sayed et al., 2011), in what I have elsewhere characterized as 'the securitization of religion in education' (Gearon, 2012a). There are nevertheless many further US exemplars of policy initiatives which integrate religion in education towards the buttressing of liberal democratic political goals.

The US Commission on International Religious Freedom

The United States Congress created the US Commission on International Religious Freedom (USCIRF) in the International Religious Freedom Act of 1998 (IRFA) as 'an independent, bipartisan, federal government entity, USCIRF monitors the status of freedom of religion or belief abroad'. It provides policy recommendations to the president, the secretary of state and Congress. The IRFA 'requires the President, who has delegated this function to the Secretary of State', to designate 'countries of particular concern' (CPCs). These countries are defined as those which 'commit systematic, ongoing, and egregious violations of religious freedom'. USCIRF has previously recommended that the following countries be designated as CPCs: Burma, China, Eritrea, Iran, Iraq, Nigeria, North Korea, Pakistan, Saudi Arabia, Sudan, Turkmenistan, Uzbekistan and Vietnam. In addition, the USCIRF has a closely monitored watch list. The following countries have previously been monitored: Afghanistan, Belarus, Cuba, Egypt, India, Indonesia, Laos, Russia, Somalia, Tajikistan, Turkey and Venezuela.

The USCIRF identifies three themes to guide commissioners' discussions on priority countries with severe violations of religious freedom: (1) state-sponsored hostility to and repression of religion; (2) state-sponsored extremist ideology and education; and (3) state failure to prevent and punish religious freedom violations (impunity) elaborated thus:

(1) *State-sponsored hostility and repression of religion*: The framework of state hostility towards and repression of religion captures many of the worst violators of religious freedom including China, Iran, North Korea, Sudan and Vietnam. These countries exhibit strong opposition to freedom of thought, conscience, religion or belief, either towards individual members, leaders or entire communities, and take steps to forcefully curtail and penalize such freedoms, such as the sharing of religious beliefs or the undertaking of basic practices.

(2) *State-sponsored extremist ideology and education*: This threat to religious freedom highlights countries that sponsor education systems and materials that teach hatred of and intolerance and violence

towards other religious groups. Two key countries fall into this category: Saudi Arabia and Pakistan. Considering the links between ideologies that motivate individuals to undertake acts of violence and the violent act themselves, the national security implications for the United States are clear.

(3) *State failure to prevent and punish religious freedom violations (impunity)*: In addition to religious persecution directly conducted by governments, another egregious threat to religious freedom occurs when governments systematically fail to punish violence committed against religiously identified individuals and their communities. USCIRF has confronted this breakdown in justice – known as impunity – in many places, and has seen the effects of such impunity firsthand – particularly on vulnerable minority religious groups – during fact-finding trips to Egypt, Nigeria and Sudan. The absence of accountability breeds lawlessness, which encourages individuals to attack, and even kill, others who dissent from or fail to embrace their own religious views, including members of minority religious communities. Countering impunity and promoting respect for the rule of law are among the greatest challenges the US government faces as it develops policies to effectively promote and protect freedom of thought, conscience, religion or belief around the world (USCIRF, 2012).

The USCIRF thus declares itself an 'advocate for ensuring that freedom of religion and belief are an integral part of the United States' foreign policy and national security agendas'.

The USCIRF's commitment is that the 'First Freedom', the constitutional First Amendment guaranteeing religious freedom through separation of state from religion, 'extends to all corners of the globe'. It defends itself against the accusation that the USCIRF is 'trying to impose American values or the American conception of separation of church and state on other countries', justifying its global remit by reference to international human rights:

> USCIRF monitors religious freedom through the lens of international human rights standards, such as those found in the Universal Declaration of Human Rights and the International Covenant on Civil and Political Rights. Article 18 of the Universal Declaration of Human Rights provides that 'everyone has the right to freedom of thought, conscience and religion; this right includes freedom to change his religion or belief, and freedom, either alone or in community with others and in public or private, to manifest this religion or belief in teaching, practice, worship and observance.' By relying on international human rights standards as specified in IRFA, USCIRF is not attempting to impose American values on other nations, but rather examines the actions of foreign governments against these universal standards and by their freely undertaken international commitments. (USCIRF, 2012)

The commission seeks 'to advance the visibility of and serious thinking about how the United States can best address the challenges of religious extremism, intolerance, and repression throughout the world', including 'religion-based violence and terrorism':

> Developments of the past decade have strengthened attention to the importance of freedom of thought, conscience, religion or belief, as the U.S. government navigates a world threatened by religion-based extremism and religion-imbued conflict. The issue of religious freedom has had a profound impact on America's political and national security interests, as well as on stability throughout the world. Whether in the Middle East, Africa, South and East Asia, Europe or elsewhere, religion and the striving for religious freedom have often been explicit or implicit factors in civil strife. (USCIRF, 2012)

In addition, the USCIRF thus makes recommendations on US foreign and security policy to the United Nations and the Organization for Security and Cooperation in Europe (OSCE), the latter responsible as we shall see for the *Toledo Guiding Principles on Teaching about Religions and Beliefs in Public Schools*. As with the OSCE, the USCIRF shows increasing interest in education. USCIRF's annual reports show exponential growth in references to education – 33 in the 2003, over 200 in 2011 (USCIRF, 2012).

The United Kingdom and Europe

Many European political institutions have in the past decade have developed policy initiatives on religion in education, underscoring the importance of teaching and learning about religion as a means of encouraging understanding of and between religions in Europe (Jackson, 2007). Among the most influential of these initiatives, in terms of growing global impact, is the OSCE. Closely aligned with the NATO and the Council of Europe throughout the Cold War to counter the Soviet threat, one of OSCE's post-Cold War and post-9/11 interest is to see how culture and religion can be harnessed for harmony rather than conflict. The teaching of religion in education is now regarded as a priority, as is most evident in the *Toledo Guiding Principles on Teaching about Religions and Beliefs in Public Schools* (OSCE, 2007).

The *Toledo Guiding Principles* contextualize their remit within contemporary geopolitics, and the changing culture of the OSCE itself:

> Recent events across the world, migratory processes and persistent misconceptions about religions and cultures have underscored the importance of issues related to tolerance and non-discrimination and freedom of religion or belief for the Organization for Security and Co-operation in Europe (OSCE). In the OSCE region, and indeed in many other parts of the world, it is becoming increasingly clear that a better understanding about religions and beliefs is needed. Misunderstandings, negative stereotypes, and provocative images used to depict others are leading to heightened antagonism and sometimes even violence. (OSCE, 2007: 9)

But it is in Toledo's past that the document finds symbolic justification, in the city's cultural blend of Christian, Jewish and Islamic art and architecture, through histories of (particularly) Muslim–Christian conflict and times of peaceful coexistence. Toledo is the city displaying 'not only visual reminders of interwoven civilizations' but 'also remnants of civilizations alternatively fighting each other, living together under tension, prospering together, suffering together, as well as exhibiting examples of tolerance and intolerance' (OSCE, 2007: 9).

In this history, the *Toledo Guiding Principles* downplay the conflict – the 'political situation in Spain was complex and volatile throughout the medieval period', not mentioning the Crusades – stressing 'well known *"golden ages"* emerged in medieval Spain, when religious tolerance was accepted by rulers, and some of the great accomplishments and precursors of models of peoples learning from each other with respect were achieved' (OSCE, 2007: 3, emphasis added). These 'golden ages', however, came to an end,

> when the Christian 'reconquest' of Spain was completed, the new emerging and powerful Christian Kingdom of Spain imposed a uniform religious rule in the territory ushering in a period of religious intolerance, mirroring what was taking place across many parts of Europe. Muslims and Jews were given the alternative of conversion or exile, and later Protestants were persecuted. The very country that had provided significant and progressive models of tolerance turned towards religious intolerance, as many other European countries in those times. (OSCE, 2007: 3)

Its reading of history is one which seeks to match the golden ages of the past as a model for ameliorating present-day conflicts. So: 'Toledo is thus a reminder of the flourishing that is possible when religions live together with understanding, and a reminder of how easily this flourishing can be lost, if mutual understanding and respect are not passed on to successive generations.' The *golden ages* are those models which modern-day religious education should learn from.

The OSCE's Office for Democratic Institutions and Human Rights (ODIHR) and the advisory council of its panel of experts on freedom of religion or belief thus developed the *Toledo Guiding Principles* look to historical models for contemporary coexistence, where it is 'important for young people to acquire a better understanding of the role that religions play in today's pluralistic world': 'The need for such education will continue to grow as different cultures and identities interact with each other through travel, commerce, media or migration. Although a deeper understanding of religions will not automatically lead to greater tolerance and respect, ignorance increases the likelihood of misunderstanding, stereotyping, and conflict' (OSCE, 2007: 9).

In short, the *Toledo Guiding Principles* were 'prepared in order to contribute to an improved understanding of the world's increasing religious diversity and the growing presence of religion in the public sphere'. Their primary purpose is thus 'to assist OSCE participating States whenever they choose to promote the study and knowledge about religions and beliefs in schools' (OSCE, 2009: 11–2).

The *Toledo Guiding Principles* are divided into five chapters. Chapter 1 makes the legal-political focus plain, identifying 'the particular contribution of the ODIHR and its Advisory Council in examining teaching about religions and beliefs *through the lens of religious freedom and a human rights perspective that relies on OSCE commitments and international human rights standards*' (emphasis added). Chapter 2 reiterates this approach providing an overview of relevant human rights and related legal frameworks. Chapter 3 'discusses the need for curricula to respect several principles': 'to adhere to recognized professional standards; to be inclusive and to pay particular attention to key historical and contemporary developments pertaining to religion and belief issues; to be sensitive to different interpretations of reality and the principle of multi-perspectivity'. This 'multi-perspectivity' is presumably part of being 'responsive to different local manifestations of religious and secular plurality found in schools and the communities they serve', where different 'types of curriculum and approaches to teaching about religions and beliefs' are presented which are 'subject-specific, integrated, and cross-curricular' (OSCE, 2009: 13). These, of course, are not different approaches, simply different modes of curriculum delivery.

Chapter 4 examines teacher education and underlines the importance in teaching about religions and beliefs, 'the high demands such a curriculum places on a teacher's knowledge, attitudes and competences'. It must also presuppose an unambiguous *political* commitment. The importance of 'assessment and evaluation of teacher presentation is also noted' (OSCE, 2009: 13). Given the macro-political goals of the *Toledo Guiding Principles*, the process of assessing or evaluating is left (perhaps understandably) ambiguous.

The political framework of the *Toledo Guiding Principles* is however unequivocal. Chapter 5 thus looks 'at the practical application of the general human rights framework to teaching about religions and beliefs'. It 'focuses on a number of key legal issues that may arise in the process of implementing programmes for teaching about religions and beliefs once they have been developed'. These legal issues will invariably relate to long-standing, preexisting constitutional relations between religion and state across the OSCE membership. The OSCE Guidance therefore suggests that 'teaching about religions and beliefs may be adapted to take into account the needs of different national and local school systems and traditions' (OSCE, 2009: 13).

The *Toledo Guiding Principles*, it is claimed, are '*supported by a growing consensus among lawyers and educators*' (OSCE, 2007: 19, emphasis added). This 'educational and *legal* consensus' – about the role of religion in education in relation to public and political life – is expressed in these premises. The following are exemplars: 'Knowledge about religions and beliefs can reinforce appreciation of the importance of respect for everyone's right to freedom of religion or belief, foster democratic citizenship, promote understanding of societal diversity and, at the same time, enhance social cohesion.' Or: 'Knowledge about religions and beliefs has the valuable potential of reducing conflicts that are based on lack of understanding for others' beliefs and of encouraging respect for their rights' (OSCE, 2007: 14).

Based on these premises, (12) key 'Guiding Principles' were proposed for OSCE states for promoting the teaching of religions and beliefs in their schools:

(1) Whenever teaching about religions and beliefs in public schools is provided in OSCE participating states, the following guiding principles should be considered:

(2) Teaching about religions and beliefs must be provided in ways that are fair, accurate and based on sound scholarship. Students should learn about religions and beliefs in an environment respectful of human rights, fundamental freedoms and civic values.

(3) Those who teach about religions and beliefs should have a commitment to religious freedom that contributes to a school environment and practices that foster protection of the rights of others in a spirit of mutual respect and understanding among members of the school community.

(4) Teaching about religions and beliefs is a major responsibility of schools, but the manner in which this teaching takes place should not undermine or ignore the role of families and religious or belief organizations in transmitting values to successive generations.

(5) Efforts should be made to establish advisory bodies at different levels that take an inclusive approach to involving different stakeholders in the preparation and implementation of curricula and in the training of teachers.

(6) Where a compulsory programme involving teaching about religions and beliefs is not sufficiently objective, efforts should be made to revise it to make it more balanced and impartial, but where this is not possible, or cannot be accomplished immediately, recognizing opt-out rights may be a satisfactory solution for parents and pupils, provided that the opt-out arrangements are structured in a sensitive and non-discriminatory way.

(7) Those who teach about religions and beliefs should be adequately educated to do so. Such teachers need to have the knowledge, attitude and skills to teach about religions and beliefs in a fair and balanced way.

(8) Teachers need not only subject-matter competence but also pedagogical skills so that they can interact with students and help students interact with each other in sensitive and respectful ways.

(9) Preparation of curricula, textbooks and educational materials for teaching about religions and beliefs should take into account religious and non-religious views in a way that is inclusive, fair and respectful. Care should be taken to avoid inaccurate or prejudicial material, particularly when this reinforces negative stereotypes.

(10) Curricula should be developed in accordance with recognized professional standards in order to ensure a balanced approach to study about religions and beliefs. Development and implementation of curricula should also include open and fair procedures that give all interested parties appropriate opportunities to offer comments and advice.

(11) Quality curricula in the area of teaching about religions and beliefs can only contribute effectively to the educational aims of the *Toledo Guiding Principles* if teachers are professionally trained to use the curricula and receive ongoing training to further develop their knowledge and competences regarding this subject matter. Any basic teacher preparation should be framed and developed according to democratic and human rights principles and include insight into cultural and religious diversity in society.

(12) Curricula focusing on teaching about religions and beliefs should give attention to key historical and contemporary developments pertaining to religion and belief, and reflect global and local issues. They should be sensitive to different local manifestations of religious and secular plurality found in schools and the communities they serve. Such sensitivities will help address the concerns of students, parents and other stakeholders in education (OSCE, 2007: 16–7).

It is this educational and *legal* consensus which means that the *Toledo Guiding Principles* '*should* be taken into consideration *by all OSCE participating States when devising schemes for teaching about religions and beliefs*' (OSCE, 2007, emphasis added).

The United Nations

Formed in the early 1990s, in the aftermath of the Cold War, the Special Rapporteur on freedom of religion or belief is an independent expert appointed by the UN Human Rights Council and has, since then, played an important role in monitoring infringement of religious freedom around the world. The mandate holder is to 'identify existing and emerging obstacles to the enjoyment of the right to freedom of religion or belief and present recommendations on ways and means to overcome such obstacles' (UN, 2012). In 2000, the Commission on Human Rights changed and widened the original mandate related to freedom of religion to 'freedom of religion or belief'. This reflects the earlier 1981 Declaration on the Elimination of All Forms of Intolerance and of Discrimination Based on Religion *or Belief* (emphasis added). This allowed the protection for and formal recognition of atheistic 'belief', an issue prevalent during the Cold War when the Declaration was made.

The Special Rapporteur has been mandated through Human Rights Council:

- to promote the adoption of measures at the national, regional and international levels to ensure the promotion and protection of the right to freedom of religion or belief.
- to identify existing and emerging obstacles to the enjoyment of the right to freedom of religion or belief and present recommendations on ways and means to overcome such obstacles.
- to continue her/his efforts to examine incidents and governmental actions that are incompatible with the provisions of the Declaration on the Elimination of All Forms of Intolerance and of Discrimination Based on Religion or Belief and to recommend remedial measures as appropriate.
- to continue to apply a gender perspective, inter alia, through the identification of gender-specific abuses, in the reporting process, including in information collection and in recommendations (UN, 2012).

The practical tasks for the discharge of the mandate include making 'urgent appeals' and writing 'letters of allegation to States with regard to cases that represent infringements of or impediments to the exercise of the right to freedom of religion and belief'. The Rapporteur also 'undertakes fact-finding country visits, and submits annual reports to the Human Rights Council, and General Assembly, on the activities, trends and methods of work' (UN, 2012).

In the post-9/11 decade, issues around freedom of religion or belief have, for the promotion of such freedom, attended to religion in *education*. A matter of months after 9/11, Amor (2001), then Special Rapporteur on Freedom of Religion or Belief, presented 'The Role of Religious Education in the Pursuit of Tolerance and Non-Discrimination' to the International Consultative Conference on School Education in Relation with Freedom of Religion and Belief, Tolerance and Non-Discrimination, Madrid, November 2001 (Oslo Coalition, 2012).

Such educational initiatives remain within the legal framework of Article 18 of the International Covenant on Civil and Political Rights and the provisions on the 1981 Declaration. In the following decade, school education continued to receive high priority within the Office of the Special Rapporteur on Freedom of Religion of Belief. At the sixteenth session of the Human Rights Council, Agenda item 3 was the 'Promotion and protection of all human rights, civil, political, economic, social and cultural rights, including the right to development'. Heiner Bielefeldt, now Special Rapporteur, remarked:

The school constitutes by far the most important formal institution for the implementation of the right to education as it has been enshrined in international human rights documents, such as the Universal Declaration of Human Rights (art. 26), the International Covenant on Economic, Social and Cultural Rights (art. 13), the Convention on the Rights of the Child (art. 28) and the Convention on the Rights of Persons with Disabilities (art. 24). The right to education is also anchored in basic documents of regional human rights protection systems (art. 12). There seems to be worldwide consensus that the right to education is of strategic importance for the effective enjoyment of human rights in general. Not least for this reason, article 28 of the Convention on the Rights of the Child demands that primary education be made compulsory and available free to all, whereas secondary education should be made available and accessible to every child. (UN, 2010, Paragraph 20)

In Paragraph 21, he states:

Besides providing students with the necessary knowledge and information in different disciplines, school education can facilitate a daily exchange between people from different ethnic, economic, social, cultural and religious backgrounds. The possibility of having face-to-face interaction of students on a regular basis is not less important than the development of intellectual skills, because such regular interaction can promote a sense of communality that goes hand in hand with the appreciation of diversity, including diversity in questions of religion or belief. Experiencing the combination of communality and diversity is also a main purpose of interreligious and intercultural dialogue projects. Thus the school provides unique possibilities for such a dialogue to take place on a daily basis, at a grass-roots level and during the formative years of a young person's development. (UN, 2010)

Concluding, the Special Rapporteur notes that 'freedom of religion or belief and school education is a multifaceted issue that entails significant opportunities as well as far-reaching challenges'. He recommends, 'States should favourably consider a number of principles in this regard and explicitly refers to the final document adopted at the International Consultative Conference on School Education in relation to Freedom of Religion or Belief, Tolerance and Non-discrimination [see above] and *to the Toledo Guiding Principles on Teaching about Religions and Beliefs in Public Schools*' (UN, 2010, emphasis added).

We see here then, through the office of the Rapporteur, an explicit and progressively consolidated link between religion and education.

The Alliance of Civilizations

The 2004 Madrid train bombings, with wars in Afghanistan and Iraq, led to a concerted effort to counter a seemingly accelerating clash of cultures, if not civilizations. From Spain emerged an intergovernmental group of senior politicians to form, under the UN's aegis, the Alliance of Civilizations (AoC). Soon after its formation, the AoC High Level Group (HLG) submitted to the UN secretary-general a report, underscoring the importance of education in 'preparing young people for an interdependent world' and called for education systems to 'provide students with an understanding and respect for the diverse religious beliefs, practices and cultures in the world' (AoC, 2009). Highlighting a shared mission between intergovernmental organizations and a body which would now include former world leaders, the AoC stressed, as others had before it, the need for intercultural education and 'the necessity to learn about and across differences', as in policy documents that include: the UNESCO (2006) *Guidelines on Intercultural Education*; the Commonwealth (2007) *Civil Paths to Peace: Report of the Commonwealth Commission on Respect and Understanding*; the Council of Europe (2008) *White Paper on Intercultural Dialogue 'Living Together as Equals'* (COE, 2008). Increasingly, the bridge was made between such policies and religion in education, such as in John Keast's (2007) *Religious Diversity and Intercultural Education: A Reference Book for Schools* and, as we have noted, the OSCE's (2007) *Toledo Guiding Principles on Teaching about Religions and Beliefs*. We might note also that so powerful has been Huntington's notional clash that *Toledo Guiding Principles* too consciously elaborates a nonconflictual confluence rather than a clash of civilizations.

The AoC formulated a practical measure to disseminate such political and educational policy thinking through a 'clearinghouse' on 'Education about Religion and Beliefs' (ERB). Again, we see the instrumentalist use of religion framed through democratic principles: *'Intrinsic to the goal of educating students about religions and beliefs are the instruments of civic and peace education, tolerance and ethics education, as well as global and cross-cultural education'* (AoC, 2012,emphasis added).

In defining 'religion' and 'belief', the ERB initiative follows the UN's (1981) and the OSCE's (2007) broad view of 'religion' and 'belief', encompassing not only 'traditional and long-established religions' but 'less well known and less well understood systems of belief'. It also includes 'non-religious systems of belief'. The clearinghouse '*focuses primarily on school education* for the following reasons' (emphasis added):

a) It is the stage that is the most important in forming educated opinions.
b) It is the stage where public policy can have the most influence, because in many states public funding of education offers the opportunity to have concomitant curricular influence.
c) It is probably the area where resources are available but scattered across different regions and therefore the AoC mechanism can be particularly useful (AoC, 2012).

The political rationale is one which is now so common and pervasive that it has become a pedagogical commonplace:

> Education about different religions and beliefs, and critically thinking about the nature of beliefs, enables populations to deal sensitively and tolerantly with the reality of today's globalized multi-cultural world where one will encounter people who believe in many different religions, or people who may not believe in any religion at all. (AoC, 2012)

As with the UN, the AoC clearinghouse shares the prioritization of, and thus focuses on, 'primary and secondary education about religions and beliefs'. The links between the latter and political education in the form of citizenship and human rights education is unambiguous: 'Material on civic education, tolerance education, ethics education, and other forms of education aimed at enabling us to learn to live together will also be featured.' The links between religion, politics and education have thus been progressively strengthened. The difficult-to-measure social and political efficacy of these initiatives is, naturally, problematic.

The Commonwealth

As the British Empire gradually came to an end, their former colonies and dominions formed the Commonwealth. The UK Foreign Office is formally called the Foreign and Commonwealth Office. The Commonwealth contains a range of non-aligned nations in Africa, Asia, Australasia and Canadian North America. Populous but politically less influential than Europe or the United States, the Commonwealth contains many countries where religious diversity has historically been and continues to be a source of political division and, very often, violent conflict. Commonwealth countries where Christianity and Islam vie for a balance of power include Nigeria. In India and Pakistan, Hindu–Muslim violence was an integral part of the communal violence that marked the Partition in 1948, tensions which have resurfaced in many ways since. As part of a wider global trend recognizing religion's renewed role in many aspects of global governance, the Commonwealth too has seen a new role for religion in education.

A 2009 Faith and Education Seminar at the Commonwealth's headquarters at Marlborough House, London, met to forward the mandate of the Commonwealth heads of government 'to promote tolerance, respect, enlightened moderation and friendship among people of different races, faiths and cultures as well as explore initiatives to promote mutual understanding and respect in the Commonwealth'. Beginning with Islam as a case study, the seminar, organized by the Commonwealth Foundation – which 'helps civil society organizations promote democracy, development and cultural understanding' – and the Aga Khan University Institute for the Study of Muslim Civilisations (AKU-ISMC) addressed faith, culture and education across the Commonwealth. Given the predominance of a wide range of Christian denominations in the Commonwealth, the seminar also drew on limited Christian perspective, namely, the 'Christian experience presented by the Church of England'.

On education, Jyotsna Jha, education adviser at the Commonwealth Secretariat, suggested, 'It is the responsibility of schools, faith based or otherwise, to inculcate values of respect and understanding for all religious groups while at the same time develop capacities for critical thinking to promote continuous social change without being divisive.' Given that 'religion matters hugely to the identity of Commonwealth's citizens', the Faith and Education seminar explored how the organization could 'engage with people have to acknowledge and harness these beliefs'. Not least through education, since 'the reality is that for millions of young people in developing countries, faith structures are major and critical providers of education' (Commonwealth, 2009).

The question of 'how people and communities with different identities can respect and understand each other and work together to advance development and social cohesion' was addressed in *Civil Paths to Peace* (Commonwealth, 2007), as part of the report of the Commonwealth Commission on Respect and Understanding, chaired by Nobel Laureate Amartya Sen. The Faith and Education Seminar heightened the importance of religion in education as part of this wide political process. The Commonwealth too thus adds further evidence of the growing interrelationships between religion, politics and education.

Religion, politics and education: ancient disputes

These contemporary political developments are complex variations of ancient disputes. What is new about the modern-day context is the dramatic shift of power from religious authority to secular power, one of the marks of modernity itself.

In Christian tradition, the relations between politics and religion were an acute problem for the early church. It is more complex than some educational commentators assume and more than a matter of citing Jesus's famous declaration to 'Render unto Caesar what is Caesar's and render unto God what is God's.' A clearly authentic statement of Jesus', which appears in all three synoptic Gospels, this seemingly clear distinction between the authority of God and Caesar has itself been open to a wealth of scholarly interpretation. Pilgrim (2000) thus identifies three in the New Testament responses to issues of church and political authority: (a) a partial but ambivalent *accommodation* (the surface meaning of 'Render unto Caesar'), evident through the Gospels of Matthew, Mark and Luke; (b) *acceptance*, a call for Christians to be subservient to political authority (Romans 13 and 1 Peter); and (c) a radical *rejection* of the world and its political authority which can be associated with the Gospel of John, but most especially with the Book of Revelation (see also Bryan, 2005).

In Western theological tradition, the conundrum – how to marry political power with religious authority – was shaped most notably by Constantine's conversion, marking a turning point of the Church and of Europe. Two Edicts of Toleration, 311 and 313, respectively, by Galerius and Constantine (Cross and Livingstone, 1997; Fordham, 2012), marked an accommodation to religious pluralism in Roman law, formally signifying the end of three centuries of sporadic Christian persecution (Rahner, 1992). It meant, however, more than simply an end to persecution: 'The sovereign autocrat was inevitably and immediately involved in the development of the church, and conversely the Church became more and more implicated in high political decisions' (Chadwick, 1990: 125). Constantine's presence at the church's first ecumenical (worldwide) council at Nicea in ad 325, for example, marked an even closer formal alignment between the Roman Empire and Christianity. There were some unfortunate developments for the church: 'It was the misfortune of the fourth-century church that it became engrossed in a theological controversy [Arianism] at the same time as it was working out its institutional organization. Doctrinal disagreements quickly became inextricably associated with matters of order, discipline and authority' (Chadwick, 1990: 133).

But the *extent* of political and religious authority, and the relations between the two, soon became an acute theological as well as political problem. St Augustine (1983b) in the late fourth and early fifth century elaborated this most powerfully in the *City of God*. Augustine delineated two spheres of influence, the domains of the earthly city and the city of God, with the former always ultimately subject to the latter. It was this which marked the relations between Christian nations and Christian Church, the close relations between the two which defined the era of Christendom.

Even in the fourth and fifth centuries, this political-theological issue was also a *pedagogical* problem. In the early years of his conversion, as we read in his *Confessions*, Augustine was eager to distance himself from and largely reject his own classical education. Many of the books (*Confessions* contains 13) give incidental insight into its nature, from elementary schooling (Books One and Two), the home education his mother Monica received (Book Nine), to his higher studies and life within the secular academy (Books Four through to Eight). Even post-Constantine, it was not all of a matter of choice. Book Eight, which marks Augustine's decisive conversion, also includes insights into the restrictions placed on Christian teachers, notably during 'the days of the Emperor Julian [when] Christians were forbidden to teach literature and rhetoric' (Augustine, 1983a: 191; also Augustine, 1998). Book Four gives the greatest sense that Augustine felt that his years in the study and teaching of Greek and Roman texts were wasted years.

Later, Augustine was more accommodating. Augustine's (1999) *On Christian Teaching* is a good illustration. Augustine addresses here the acceptable usage of classical works in Christian teaching and learning. Less interested in content than method, the issue is the how pre-Christian texts could be incorporated into Christian teaching. Augustine suggests that rhetoric could be put to good use in conveying the Christian message. The substantive issues (the use of Greek philosophy, Aristotle and others) were a dominant theme from the Renaissance onwards. It was marked in medieval Scholasticism with its synthesis of Greek philosophy and Catholic theology, preeminently by Aquinas. Christian humanism, thinkers like Erasmus, and even the younger Thomas More would embrace classical thought. By the Enlightenment, shifts to secular political power would be mirrored in a secular reorientation of education, supplanting revelation for reason. This is evident from Locke's *Some Thoughts Concerning Education* through Rousseau's *Emile* to Kant's *Lectures on Pedagogy* (see Cahn, 2009). An acute pedagogical problem of early Christianity would thus become a chronic one, helping shape if not Western civilization in entirety then much of its educational provision.

Summary

There is much modern-day international political interest in the *uses* of religion in education. This is often perceived as a *means* of establishing understanding between cultures and religions. Interest in religion in education extends even to those countries where religion is not part of the school curriculum in state schools. There are however dangers in too close an alignment of religion in education to political purposes, however benign and well intentioned. There is an obvious political antecedence to this view. Overly close relationships between religion and politics was at the root of separations of the church and state from the Reformation onwards. In the long history of church–state relations, some frame the present era as a not unwelcome post-Christendom (Murray, 2004).

England is a particularly interesting case, in that the Reformation established here the head of state as head of the church. With England in mind, T. S. Eliot pointed out the risks of too close an alignment of political and religious ideals. In *The Idea of a Christian Society*, after his conversion to Anglican Christianity (and even writing as an Anglican), Eliot argued that to 'identify any particular form of government with Christianity is a dangerous error; for it confounds the permanent with the transitory, the absolute with the contingent':

> Forms of government, and of social organisation, are in constant process of change, and their operation maybe be very different from the theory which they are supposed to exemplify. A theory of the State may be, explicitly or implicitly, anti-Christian; it may arrogate rights which only the Church is entitled to claim, or pretend to decide moral questions on which only the Church is qualified to pronounce. On the other hand, a regime may in practice claim either more or less than it professes, and we have to examine its working as well as its constitution. We have no assurance that a democratic regime might not be inimical to Christianity in practice, as another might be in theory . . . Those who consider that a discussion of the nature of a Christian society should conclude by supporting a particular form of political organisation, should ask themselves whether they really believe our form of government to be more important than our Christianity; and those who are convinced that the present forms of government of Britain is the one most suitable for any Christian people, should ask themselves whether they are confusing a Christian society with a society in which individual Christianity is tolerated. (Eliot, 1938: 37–38)

Though nominally theocratic states exist today, where theological principle dominates political governance, religious–political relations are rarely conceived of now in Eliot's terms. In global governance, however, we have noted emergent programmes for religion in education to achieve political goals. We might even say that there are international currents (e.g. the OSCE) encouraging approaches to the teaching of religion in education which contribute to what are ultimately political *goals* through political *directive*. What is also *new* in these modern uses of religion in education is the *transnational* collaborative effort. The idea that there could be 'rules for the world', to take Bennett and Finnemore's (2004) conception of the UN, is a very new political idea. It seems such 'rules for the world' could be applied to the political principles for religion in education.

Seemingly perennial, such matters are unlikely to find any immediate political, theological or even pedagogical resolution. As Swaine (2006: 1) puts it, 'Despite their steps forward with respect to toleration, stability and legitimacy, the liberal democracies of the new millennium have inherited unresolved and what appear to be ultimately irresolvable differences.' In the next chapter we examine how researchers of religion in education have sought to show how it might be possible.

Before we proceed, however, it a worthy reminder that at the late eighteenth-century source of the Enlightenment itself, Friedrich Schleiermacher's (1799) *On Religion: Speeches to Its Cultured Despisers* already derided the idea of religion reduced to utilitarian principles, least of all political ones:

> High renown it were for the heavenly to conduct so wretchedly the earthly concerns of man! Great honour for the free and unconcerned to make the conscience of man a little sharper and more alert! For such a purpose religion does not descend from heaven. What is loved and honoured only on account of some extraneous advantage may be needful, but it is not in itself necessary, and a sensible person simply values it according to the end for which it is desired. By this standard, religion would be valueless enough. I, at least, would offer little, for I must confess that I do not believe much in the unjust dealings it would hinder, nor the moral dealings it would produce. If that is all it could do to gain respect, I would have no more to do with its case. To recommend it merely as an accessory is too unimportant. An imaginary praise that vanishes on closer contemplation, cannot avail anything going about with higher pretensions. I maintain that in all better souls piety springs necessarily by itself; that a province of its own in the mind belongs to it, in which it has unlimited sway; that it is worthy to animate most profoundly the noblest and best and to be fully accepted and known by them. That is my contention, and it now behoves you to decide whether it is worth your while to hear me, before you still further strengthen yourselves in your contempt. (Schleiermacher, 1799)

Reflecting on the political successes and failures of the Enlightenment, only four decades after Schleiermacher's famous discourse, it was the young Frenchman Alexis de Tocqueville in *Democracy in America* [1836] who predicted precisely Schleiermacher's fears of a future political utilitarianism for religion: 'If the unbeliever does not admit religion to be true, he still considers it to be useful' (Tocqueville, 2003: 123).

Religion in Education: Contemporary UK, European and US Research Perspectives

2

Introduction

As religion in education has become an international political priority, this chapter analyses leading UK, European and North American initiatives to show the research correlative: the predominance of politics in the *research agendas* of religion in education as well. The first initiative examined is the 'Religion in Education: A contribution to Dialogue or a factor of Conflict in transforming societies of European Countries' (REDCo) project. This is the largest initiative of its kind funded by the European Commission and has been significant in scale and impact beyond the eight participating countries (REDCo, 2012). The second emerges from the work of the American Academy of Religion (AAR) Task Force on the role of religion in American public schools, resulting in the *American Academy of Religion Guidelines for Teaching about Religion in K-12 Public Schools in the United States* (AAR, 2012). These initiatives closely mirror the political direction of religion in education as outlined in Chapter 1. If the studies selected are European and American, they reflect *political* and *politicizing* global trends in religious education research and the direction of wider policies of religion in education worldwide.

Other chapters examine how state religious education has been shaped by research agendas configured by other disciplines. Chapters 3, 4 and 5 analyse a range of phenomenological, philosophical, psychological and sociological influences, and their interdisciplinary variants. Chapter 5 in this regard specifically examines how different research disciplines have shaped modern religious education pedagogy. The studies in this present chapter are intended therefore as illustrative not exhaustive, focusing for the most part on the political determination of research agendas, or what Willaime (2007) calls a 'double constraint' of sociological circumstance and legal requirement on religious education.

The studies are, *though selective*, indicative of a newly dominant international research agenda, one which reflects the political concerns and orientations of religion in education. In terminology, 'religion in education' is used here to intimate the broadening of concerns (the wide political interest of religion in education) beyond the traditional confines of the curriculum subject of 'religious education'.

Researching religion in education

The United Kingdom and Europe

There have been increases in funding for research examining religion in a range of disciplinary contexts in the United Kingdom and across Europe (Woodhead, 2011), the major Arts and Humanities (AHRC) and Economic and Social Research Council (ESRC) Religion and Society initiative being a paramount exemplar, including a range of research initiatives around religion in education (AHRC/ESRC, 2012; Conroy, 2011a). In specifically educational terms, while there are special interest groups (SIGs) in the British Educational Research Association and other parallel national research bodies across Europe, research on religion in education across Europe remains arguably the interest of specialists with long-standing interests in the subject. A search, for example, of the word 'religion' in the umbrella organization for educational researchers in Europe, the European Educational Research Association, will elicit very little substantive let alone sustained interest around religion in education (EERA, 2012). While this might not surprise us in the heartland of the Enlightenment, it is perhaps curious for a continent where many and diverse national educational systems provide for what in England is referred to as the 'dual system', allowing state funding for schools of a religious character and schools of a more secular nature, and where there are few restrictions (except in France) on the teaching of religion in either. This is more curious when by comparison we note the American context where the teaching of religion is absent or restricted in public schools, but in which continental context, in contrast to Europe, we do see mainstream educational research interest. This is clearly demonstrated by James Nelson's (2010) 'The Evolving Place of Research on Religion in the American Educational Research Association' which provides a map of a burgeoning if, for constitutional reasons, still contentious field.

The REDCo research project is an example of one specialist religion in education interest group making significant impact across and beyond Europe. REDCo was funded by the European Commission and involved universities from eight European countries (University of Warwick, England; Universities of Hamburg and Muenster, Germany; VU University, The Netherlands; University of Stavanger, Norway; Russian Christian Academy for Humanities, St Petersburg, Russia; Tartu University, Estonia; The Sorbonne, Paris, France; and University of Granada, Spain). The project aimed 'to establish whether studies of religions in schools can help to promote dialogue and reduce conflict in school and society'. Its main research focus was young people, aged 14–16, but included studies of teachers in the wider role of religion in different state educational systems.

The REDCo project has produced a significant number of research outputs, in its own words, determined by its funders, a leading political agency in Europe, as 'a necessary approach to address the core question laid out by the European Commission, how religions and values can contribute to dialogue or tension in Europe'. Drawing together researchers in the humanities and social sciences, the intention was 'to gain better insight into how European citizens of different religious, cultural and political backgrounds can live together and enter into dialogue of mutual respect and understanding, developing their respective evolving positions . . . in the context of educational institutions'. A core aim 'was to look at the challenges facing religious education in the context of the current change in European societies and its importance for dialogue and mutual understanding without disregarding potential problems': 'Taking account of confrontational as well as dialogue potential, this allowed us to develop impulses for the future peaceful coexistence of people of different religions'. The REDCo Project represents then in its own terms a 'necessary approach to address the question, how religions and values can contribute to dialogue or tension in Europe' and 'to gain better insight into how European citizens of different religious, cultural and political backgrounds can live together and enter into dialogue of mutual respect and understanding' (REDCO, 2012).

A key political-pedagogical driver was to support the recommendations of the Council of Europe and the OSCE *Toledo Guiding Principles on Teaching about Religions and Beliefs in Public Schools* (OSCE, 2007). We noted in Chapter 1 that the latter *Toledo Guiding Principles* originate from a NATO-aligned Cold War security organization. This sharpening further of the political focus of religion in education to *security* concerns seems to leave the REDCo team unperturbed. Indeed, the status of the OSCE has itself been lauded as a new and seemingly positive development for religion in education. This can be demonstrated by the opening lines from one of the subject's leading international journals, dedicated to a special issue of the REDCo project:

> Especially in the years following the events of 9/11, 2001 in the USA, religion has become a major topic of public debate globally. In academic literature, there has been a growth in writing about the place of religion in the public sphere . . . and in policy development, at European and wider

> international levels, there has been close attention to education about religions and beliefs in schools. The Council of Europe completed its first ever project on the religious dimension of inter-cultural education, which includes a Recommendation by the Committee of Ministers – the Foreign Ministers of the 47 member states – that all young Europeans should learn about religious diversity (Council of Europe 2008). The Organisation for Security and Cooperation in Europe, the largest security organisation in the world, published the *Toledo guiding principles on teaching about religions and beliefs in public schools*, again arguing that education about the diversity of religions and beliefs in society should be a part of everyone's general education . . . The United Nations Alliance of Civilisations programme makes a similar recommendation through its education about religions and beliefs [programme]. (Jackson, 2011a: 105)

Politically, the remit of REDCo is indeed impressively wide, its recommendations were addressed to: EU institutions (Parliament, Commission, Council of Ministers), Council of Europe, United Nations (UNESCO, General Assembly, Alliance of Civilizations), national educational bodies of EU-member states, educational research associations, non-governmental organizations, religious organizations, universities and schools within the European Union. The qualitative and quantitative research was carried out across eight countries: Germany, England, France, the Netherlands, Norway, Estonia, Russia and Spain (REDCo, 2012; also Jackson et al., 2007; Jackson, 2011a). The project's main aim was 'to establish and compare the potentials and limitations of religion in the educational systems of selected European countries. Approaches and constellations that can contribute to making religion in education a factor promoting dialogue in the context of European development have been addressed through historical and contemporary studies' (Weisse, 2009a: 14–5; also Jackson et al., 2007). Weisse contextualizes the transnational religious-political setting for the educational programme:

> The wide religious and societal spectrum covered by our REDCo countries and the challenges of social transition they face can be briefly summarised as follows: Germany, with two established churches (Catholics and Protestants) and Norway with one (Lutheran) are moving towards religious pluralism. The Netherlands and England/Wales both have established churches (Anglican and Reformed, respectively), but can also look back on a long (though not unchallenged) tradition of religious pluralism. Traditionally majority-Catholic France has a laicist system facing a rising number of challenges through the increasing relevance of religion in public discourse. Spain as a predominantly Catholic country is experiencing an increasing religious and interreligious opening with a lively public discourse on new approaches towards Catholic RE and on the introduction of Islamic RE. Russia and Estonia both have strong religious traditions (Lutheran in Estonia, Orthodox in Russia) which have long been marginalised by Communism. In recent years, both societies have become increasingly open towards religious influences. (Weisse, 2009a: 14–5)

'In spite of a wide range of societal and pedagogical backgrounds', Weisse suggests, researchers held 'a common conviction', that 'religion must be included in schools, as religion is too important a factor in the social life and the coexistence of people with different cultural and religious backgrounds throughout Europe to be excluded there' (Weisse, 2009a: 14–15).

Jackson (2009) relates this to other educational contributions from the Council of Europe and the establishment of the new European Wergeland Centre for Education for Democratic Citizenship and Human Rights, including the dimension of religion, to be based in Oslo. The European Wergeland Centre (EWC), a European Resource Centre on Education for Intercultural Understanding, Human Rights and Democratic Citizenship, is now established. The EWC's mission is to build bridges between policy, research and practice. EWC collaborates with a wide range of transnational bodies, particularly the Council of Europe and in Norway with the Norwegian Ministry of Education and Research and the Norwegian Ministry of Foreign Affairs (www.theewc.org/). Jackson highlights two other European initiatives: Education for Democratic Citizenship and the Council of Europe *White Paper on Intercultural Dialogue* (CoE, 2008) Jackson identifies education for democratic citizenship (EDC) as a priority for the Council of Europe in strengthening 'pluralistic democracy, human rights and the rule of law in Europe'. EDC is 'seen *broadly*, as inclusive of many aspects of human rights education, civic education, peace education, global education and intercultural education', evident in the 2005 European Year of Citizenship through Education. It is acknowledged that EDC has not tended to deal explicitly with religion in citizenship education in part because religion's place within intercultural education, 'intercultural education being considered to be a sub-set of EDC' (Jackson, 2009: 32–6; again, CoE, 2008; on religion in intercultural understanding, see also UNESCO, 2006, 2011).

The Organisation for Security and Co-operation in Europe/ODIHR is then noted. The main contribution of the OSCE/ODIHR has been the development of '*a standard setting document*' (emphasis added), the *Toledo Guiding Principles on Teaching about Religions and Beliefs in Public Schools*, the OSCE *Toledo Guiding Principles* are then noted here as '*a standard setting document*' (emphasis added). Willaime directly demonstrates the increasingly close correlation between the political and pedagogic through the document's authorship by an 'inter-disciplinary team including international human rights lawyers, educators and academics from a cross section of religious and philosophical backgrounds' and its intent, to give 'close attention to legal issues in relation to freedom of religion or belief and education'. The argument for the inclusion of the study of religions and beliefs in public education has a 'human rights emphasis' which is different from the Council of Europe's 'cultural' argument 'although *all* of the Council of Europe's work is grounded ultimately on human rights principles':

> The first premise is that freedom of religion or belief predicates plurality: if freedom of religion or belief is a given for society, then society inevitably will be plural. The next premise is that, if society is to be cohesive, plurality requires tolerance of difference. The conclusion is that tolerance of difference requires *at least* knowledge and understanding of the beliefs and values of others. This would be so whatever the approach specifically taken to religious education in particular countries. In other words, the document supports the inclusion of a just and fair approach to religious difference, whatever the system of religious education or education about religion in particular states (Jackson, 2009: 32–6).

The *Toledo Guiding Principles*, Willaime suggests, merit worthy of 'close attention within and beyond Europe'. International attention has indeed been gained for this initiative, notably, as observed in the last chapter, through the UN's Special Rapporteur on Freedom of Religion or Belief.

Core REDCo research findings present a seemingly comprehensive picture of student endorsement for the political goals of teaching religion in education:

- Irrespective of their religious positions a majority of students are interested in learning about religions in school.
- Students desire peaceful coexistence across religious differences, and believe that this is possible.
- Students believe that the main preconditions for peaceful coexistence between people of different religions are knowledge about each other's religions and worldviews, shared interests, and joint activities.
- Most students would like to see school dedicated more to teaching about different religions than to guiding them towards a particular religious belief or worldview.

Although there is evidence of the effectiveness of religion in education programmes advancing a measured tolerance – those 'who learn about religious diversity in school are more willing to enter into conversations about religions and worldviews with students from other backgrounds than those who do not have this opportunity for learning' – the finding suggests a disparity between attitudes in the school and classroom and the wider society: 'The majority of students appreciated the religious heterogeneity in their societies, although a range of prejudices were expressed.' This places some question marks over the actual effectiveness of the teaching of religion as a means to achieve said political goals. Thus: 'Students are generally open towards peers of different religious backgrounds. At the same time they tend to socialise with peers from the same background as themselves, even when they live in areas characterised by religious diversity.' Or: 'Students often express a tolerant attitude more at an abstract than a practical level. The tolerance expressed in classroom discussion is not always replicated in their daily life world.' It is students 'for whom religion is important in their [own] lives are more likely to respect the religious background of others and value the role of religion in the world'. Based on such broad student support, and though recognition is given to 'different national traditions, norms, legal systems and pedagogical approaches in dealing with religion in education', REDCo policy recommendations 'support the policy recommendations of the Council of Europe and the *Toledo Guiding Principles*' (Weisse, 2009a: 1–4).

Willaime (2007) makes four general observations about religious education in Europe: (1) 'School instruction about religious faith is a strong indicator of the way church–state and school–religion relations are constructed inside a given national framework' (examples cited are Greece, Italy, the United Kingdom, Germany, Ireland); (2) 'However great the diversity of state–church and school–religion relations to the various European countries may be, and however many national approaches to the treatment of religion in education they may have, they are all confronted with similar challenges', including 'secularization', the 'lack of religious acculturation amongst school students and their loss of contact with religious life' and 'an overall religious pluralisation'; (3) 'There is also the need to strengthen the role of religious knowledge in public school education' mirroring 'in spite of a high degree of difference which shows no sign of disappearing, a broad consensus in Europe of the need for instruction on religion in public schools'; (4) With the exception of France, 'in practically all those countries, including those which joined the EU in 2004, there exist courses dedicated to the study of a religion or religious matters in general' (Willaime, 2007: 57–9).

Willaime, in sum, identifies three models of religious education in Europe: (1) 'no religious instruction in schools'; (2) 'confessional religious instruction'; (3) 'non-confessional religious education' (Willaime, 2007: 60). There are three developments identified which are shared with the REDCo project as a whole: (1) 'A growing integration of religious education, be it confessional or not, with the overall educational goals of the school'; (2) 'an increased openness, in different degrees, to the religious and philosophical plurality of European societies'; (3) that the latter developments 'raise tensions and engender conflicts' (Willaime, 2007: 60 ff.).

Willaime and the REDCo Project here identify a pedagogical–political convergence: the *pedagogical* imperative of multifaith teaching to address Europe's religious pluralism is also a *political* imperative to address the needs of peaceful democratic coexistence amidst religious pluralism, a problem long familiar to political liberalism (see Rawls, 2005). Willaime usefully frames this as a 'double constraint': 'a *sociological* one, in that the religious and philosophical pluralization of European societies obliges them to include ever more alternative religions and non-religious positions into their curricula, and a *legal* one, through the importance of the principle of non-discrimination on religious or philosophical grounds (as well as others such as gender or race) in international law, especially in the European Convention on Human Rights' (Willaime, 2007: 65, emphasis in original). The pattern is not as one would expect homogenous. Each country of the study reflects not only the autonomy of each nation over its national education but also a variety of responses addressing religious pluralism: in France (Willaime, 2007: 87–102); Spain (Willaime, 2007: 103–22); Russia (Kozyrev and Federov, 2007: 133–58); Estonia (Valk, 2007: 159–80); England (Jackson and O'Grady, 2007: 181–202); The Netherlands (Avest et al., 2007: 203–20); Norway (Skeie, 2007: 221–42); Germany (Knauth, 2007: 243–65).

A critical issue is whether of all this political interest in religion in education means that, counter to classical secularization theory, religion has not been marginalized. REDCo researchers hold that it is evidence of counter-secularization:

In most European countries, we have assumed for a long time that increasing secularisation would lead to a gradual retreat of religion from public space. *This tendency has reversed itself in the course of the past decade as religion has returned to public attention.* (Weisse, 2011: 112, emphasis added)

A counter-argument here would be that the involvement of religion in education within such explicitly political contexts, rather than *countering* secularization, actually presents *confirmatory* evidence of a key expectation of classical secularization theory, that is, the loss of influence in public and political life. Religion in education shows a new prominence, but its terms are political.

Whether we accept these accounts as evidence of counter-secularization or not, we can accept that there has been increased attention to teaching world religions in schools. Thus, within two generations, Europe has transformed close to two millennia of Christian orientation in education – even in its incipient medieval forms – into a plural, multifaith orientation, facilitated through religious education. What the REDCo researchers mean by counter-secularization in Europe at times then reads more like a decline in Christian influence. Take Knauth's summary of the German context:

> Up to the 1960s, religious education in public schools was taught in close cooperation with established churches. It was based on dogmatic and systematic theology and familiarized students with the Bible, the hymnbook, and central parts of church history. Its stated aim was to introduce the Gospel to the (mainly baptized) pupils as the liberating Word of God. Today, nearly 50 years later, religious education has opened itself to religious and cultural plurality It defines its purpose from its standing as a school subject, and therefore in pedagogical as well as theological terms. Every religious community which carries a share of responsibility for religious education in schools thus faces the challenge of interpreting its own religious tradition in a context of religious diversity and cultural heterogeneity. (Knauth, 2007: 244)

Religious education has become, then, increasingly enmeshed with influential political agencies across a wide spectrum of geopolitical contexts. Such close and integral involvement with such political agencies may almost inevitably change the subject and at least potentially mould its interests to those political forces. REDCo as an initiative has, in this regard, *itself* become politically significant. We simply need to note its influence in a range of European and international political agencies. There are of course unexplored questions here about how sound the findings are of the research itself. This is not in any sense to question the academic integrity of the research, but the close congruence of funding by political institutions committed to 'diversity management' and research findings, which provide ready-made pedagogical strategies to achieve these political goals, raises issues of independence between funding and findings.

The United States

The idea that the US government would be inclined to 'diversity management' would almost certainly be deemed unconstitutional by the First Amendment of the United States Constitution, that 'Congress shall make no law respecting an establishment of religion, or prohibiting the free exercise thereof' (Yale, 2012). The First Amendment is usually sufficient to account for why religion does not appear in the curriculum of American public schools.

It can be noted that today its absence as a distinctive subject is just as pronounced as its absence is in France. Given what we have noted about the revolutionary contexts in both countries, and the nature of these revolutions, this should not surprise us. Yet the matter is not so clear-cut.

Certainly, Alexis de Tocqueville, in his 1830s visit from France to America, noted that, in contrast to his European homeland: 'By the side of every religion is to be a found a political opinion' (Tocqueville, 2003: 118). The value of the Enlightenment separation of church and state, he makes clear, is to the advantage of both: 'The church cannot share the temporal power of the state without being the object of a portion of that animosity which the latter excites' (Tocqueville, 2003: 122–3). He is therefore dismissive of the Enlightenment animosity to religion and expectations of its demise: 'The philosophers of the eighteenth century explained in a very simple manner the gradual decay of religious faith. Religious zeal, said they, must necessarily fail the more generally liberty is established and knowledge diffused.' 'Unfortunately', he remarks, 'the facts by no means accord with their theory'. In France, Tocqueville 'had almost always seen the spirit of religion and the spirit of freedom marking in opposite directions'. In America, Tocqueville notes that 'the religious aspect of the country was the first thing that struck my attention; and the longer I stayed there the more I perceived great political consequences resulting from this' (Tocqueville, 2003: 121). This confirms what he had earlier stated: 'Religion in America takes no direct part in the government of society, but it must be regarded as the first of their political institutions' (Tocqueville, 2003: 120). And in America, 'education and liberty are the daughters of morality and religion' (Tocqueville, 2003: 84).

A century later, in 1925, the trial of a science teacher, John Scopes, in Dayton, Tennessee, would show a terser, more divided relationship between religion, politics and education. The Scopes or 'Monkey Trial' centred on whether Darwinian evolutionary theory could be taught in public schools. A school textbook had been introduced a decade before the Scopes trial, in 1914. It was George William Hunter's extensively used *A Civic Biology*, which gave an account of Darwinian evolutionary theory. William Jennings Bryan, a former Congressman, launched a religiously motivated anti-evolutionary challenge which would become a legal one. The Tennessee House of Representatives successfully introduced, with near unanimity, a bill prohibiting the teaching of 'any theory that denies the story of the Divine Creation of man as taught in the Bible, and to teach instead that man has descended from a lower order of animals'. With Tennessee Senate approval, the Butler Bill came into law, the first law in the United States banning the teaching of evolution, and within a matter of weeks the American Civil Liberties Union sought teachers to test the law in court. Authorities in Dayton, seeing in this an opportunity to generate publicity and regenerate the local economy, found a willing volunteer in sports coach and part-time teacher of biology, John Scopes. Scopes was duly indicted, tried and, within a 5-day trial which attracted massive media attention, found guilty.

National Public Radio, formerly National Educational Radio Network, provides an outline of the account. This is indicative not only of the continued contemporary media interest in the Scopes's trial but because, in media history, the live radio broadcast of the trial was the first of its kind. Media attention was focused on the lead prosecutor, a conservative evangelical statesman, William Jennings Bryan, and, for the defence, the renowned liberal attorney Clarence Darrow. That Judge John Raulston instructed the Reverend Lemuel M. Cartright to open the proceedings with a prayer was perhaps an indication that a guilty verdict was not unpredictable.

The NPR presents a sketch of the trial:

> 13 July 1925 – In an effort to have the Butler law declared unconstitutional, defense attorney Clarence Darrow delivers a long, fiery speech arguing that the law violates freedom of religion. Darrow argues that 'we find today as brazen and as bold an attempt to destroy learning as was ever made in the Middle Ages'.

> 14 July 1925 – In the third day of the trial, Darrow objects to the practice of opening the trial with a prayer. Judge Raulston overrules the objection, noting that he has instructed the ministers who offer the prayer to 'make no reference to the issues involved in this case'.

> 15 July 15 1925 – Judge Raulston overrules the defense's motion to have the Butler law declared unconstitutional. Raulston says in his ruling that the law 'gives no preference to any particular religion or mode of worship. Our public schools are not maintained as places of worship, but, on the contrary, were designed, instituted, and are maintained for the purpose of mental and moral development and discipline'.

> In an afternoon session that day, a not guilty plea is entered on Scopes's behalf. Each side presents its opening statements. The prosecution questions the superintendent of schools and two of Scopes's students, who testify that Scopes taught his class about evolution. The defense questions zoologist Maynard Metcalf, who testifies that evolution is a widely embraced theory in the scientific community.

> 17 July 1925 – Judge Raulston rules in favor of a motion by prosecutors to bar expert testimony by scientists. Raulston argues that the experts' opinions on evolutionary theory would 'shed no light' on the issue at hand in the trial – whether Scopes violated the state's anti-evolution laws. Many reporters leave town, believing that the trial is effectively over. Scopes is recruited to write news stories on the trial for some of the delinquent journalists.

> 20 July 1925 – With the proceedings taking place outdoors due to the heat, the defense . . . calls Bryan to testify as a biblical expert. Clarence Darrow asks Bryan a series of questions about whether the Bible should be interpreted literally. As the questioning continues, Bryan accuses Darrow of making a 'slur at the Bible', while Darrow mocks Bryan for 'fool ideas that no intelligent Christian on earth believes'. (NPR, 2012)

The guilty verdict was returned on 21 July 1925. Five days later, Bryan dies in his sleep in Dayton. Buried in Arlington National Cemetery, Bryan's tombstone is inscribed with the words, 'He kept the Faith.' In January of the following year, the Tennessee Supreme Court ruled that the Butler law was constitutional but on a technicality overturned the guilty verdict on Scopes. In the mid-1950s, *Inherit the Wind*, a play based on the trial, opens on Broadway, and in 1960 is made into a film which is loosely based on the Scopes trial, and which also opens on Broadway, with Scopes returning to the Dayton movie theatre for the premiere. In 1967 the Butler Act is repealed, and the same year John Scopes publishes his memoir of the trial, *Center of the Storm* (see Larson, 2008; NPR, 2012).

Debates over evolution would continue, and on both sides of the Atlantic. In England, in 2008 what Melanie Phillips defined as the 'secular inquisition' and 'totalitarian atheism' focused on another high-profile case when Professor Michael Reiss, then Royal Society's director of Education, addressed the British Association for the Advancement of Science suggesting, in Philips' words, 'that teachers should accept that they were unlikely to change the minds of pupils with creationist beliefs – i.e., that the world was created literally in six days. Instead of dismissing creationism as a misconception, teachers should try to explain why it had no scientific basis' (Phillips, 2008). Reiss was later forced to resign from his post as Director of Education at the Royal Society.

Mary Midgley's (2007) short monograph *Intelligent Design Theory and Other Ideological Problems* commissioned by the Philosophy of Education Society of Great Britain details the issues of teaching 'creationist' alternatives to Darwinian evolutionary theory within the science curriculum. We note that the issue here, as with the Scopes trial, is the teaching of such views not within religious education, but Midgley argues, 'The challenges of fundamentalism should be rigorously confronted and proposes radical changes in the training and practice of science and religious studies teachers to enable them to deal with the specific challenge of Intelligent Design Theory,' Her aim is conciliatory, aiming to prevent students leaving school 'as either bigoted fundamentalists or bigoted atheistical pseudo-Darwinists'.

More than vestigial traces of the issues which the Scopes trial raised are apparent today in what are called 'American culture wars', a term of now immense and potent currency in all aspects of American life, as Chapman's (2010) literally encyclopaedic treatment indicates. The term was coined by James Davison Hunter (1991), as a variant of conservative-liberal divides in US politics; Hunter used the term to show how such divisions brought radically different and divisive attitudes over family, art, education, law as well as politics. The culture wars divide over the recognition of the Bible's importance and, fundamentally, its inerrant truth. In this regard it is a replaying of the origins of fundamentalism, a term of self-designation arising from Protestant evangelical Christianity to determine its resistance to liberalism and modernity at least insofar as it retains a view of the inerrancy of the Bible (Ruthven, 2007). The role and influence of fundamentalism continues to be a live one in American politics of education (see Laats, 2012), and particularly as focused on issues of evolutionary theory and creationism (Witham, 2005).

The term fundamentalism itself can be traced to a 12-volume collection called *The Fundamentals* (Dixon and Torrey, 1910–15), preceding but setting a framework for understanding the intensity of feeling which the Scopes trial generated, and can be identified by a regeneration of evangelical Protestant theology from the late nineteenth century and early twentieth (Dorian , 1998). The intemperate contemporary language about the

fundamentalist alliance with 'far right' politics is apparent in Hedges's (2008) *American Fascists: The Christian Right and the War on America*; though there are many balanced and theologically informed accounts, paramount among them is the work of James Barr, whose 1991 Gifford Lectures analyse the relationship between 'fundamentalist' beliefs in the inerrancy of the Bible, wider issues of biblical criticism and natural theology (Barr, 1995).

Like any such dichotomy risking oversimplification, the term 'culture wars' – seen as impacting on the arts, media and education as much as politics – resonates through religion in American public school debates, and a disparate literature reflects this: from religion as a part in the history of American education (Dierenfield, 2007; Nord, 1995; Urban and Wagoner Jr., 2008; Waskey, 2006), through accounts of US education as a 'civil religion' which defines America (Bankston III and Caldas, 2009) to practical guidelines on constitutional law related to religion in public schools (Lofaso, 2009). But the Scopes trial remains seminal. It should be borne in mind, however, that two decades before the trial, academic and professional associations had already formed around issues of scholarship and pedagogical practice in religion and education.

Early strands of professional and professorial interest in religion are illustrated by the formation of two associations in the United States dedicated, respectively, to religious education and the study of biblical studies, theology and religion more generally: the Religious Education Association (REA), founded in 1903 by William Raney Harper, the first president of the University of Chicago; and the American Academy of Religion (AAR), founded in 1909. If we note these organizations' accounts of their own history, we see however that school education and university research have been influential in both organizations. For the REA, its founding roots were obviously in religious education. It first convention centred around not only the predominant Christian and biblical emphasis of turn of the twentieth-century America but also the new philosophical and psychological approaches to pedagogy. John Dewey and George Albert Coe were among the speakers, the first of an illustrious line of such speakers and a widening membership over its now over a century of existence. *Religious Education*, its journal, was established in 1906. In 2003, the REA merged with the Association of Professors and Researchers in Religious Education (APRRE). APRRE was itself formed from a section of the National Council of Churches. The REA and APRRE merged in 2003 to form REA: APRRE. With a religiously diverse membership, both organizations have long standing interests researching religion in education.

The AAR was conceived originally from an idea in 1909 by Professor Ismar J. Peritz of Syracuse University to stimulate scholarship and teaching in religion through an association of biblical scholars. Peritz was joined by three colleagues – Irving Wood (Smith College), Raymond C. Knox (Columbia University) and Olive Dutcher (Mount Holyoke College) – and together they founded the Association of Biblical Instructors in American Colleges and Secondary Schools. We note its originating focus on biblical scholarship, and its bridging of higher and secondary education.

The biblical emphasis was accentuated when, in 1922, the group became the National Association of Biblical Instructors. According to the AAR the acronym of NABI, for 'prophet' in Hebrew, arguably underlined some missionary zeal underpinning scholarly endeavours. *Journal of the NABI* followed but only 4 years later, and being perhaps aware that the acronym might have other associations, became the *Journal of Bible and Religion*. NABI was retained however as the name of the organization until 1963, 'when the association, sparked by dramatic changes in the study of religion' became the American Academy of Religion and subsequently their journal becoming the *Journal of the American Academy of Religion* (JAAR). A collaboration of the Society of Biblical Literature (SBL) and the AAR formed in 1969 the Council for the Study of Religion. The AAR is still closely associated but administratively separate from the SBL.

The world's largest association of university teaching and researchers in religious studies and theology, from a founding membership of four, the AAR, has a specialist sectional interest in religious education which has long debated matters. As framed by Greenawalt (2007), the question 'Does God belong in public schools?' reflects a debate polarized between those who favour the status quo and those who seek limited revision (Moore, 2007). The AAR Task Force, headed by Diane L. Moore of Harvard's Divinity School addressed this. The investigation was based on a premise that teaching of religion (in history or literature for example) already inevitably exists, but needs more fully now to be recognized, or as Moore (2010) has it, as a programme which is 'Constitutionally Sound, Educationally Innovative'.

Religion, the AAR Task Force points out, is 'actually deeply embedded in state curricular standards across the disciplines and is especially prominent in the areas of history, social studies, and English'. In spite of this, she comments, 'few teachers have had the opportunity to learn about religion from the religious studies lens appropriate for public schools'. Furthermore '(unlike other disciplines), until now there were no content and skill guidelines for educators about religion itself that were constructed by religious studies scholars'. To address this gap, the American Academy of Religion (AAR, 2010) published the *American Academy of Religion Guidelines for Teaching About Religion in K-12 Public Schools in the United States* as a resource for teachers and citizens.

Two Supreme Court rulings in the 1960s defined religion's role in public education: *Engel v. Vitale* (1962), concerning prayers in public schools, the ruling suggesting government could not constitutionally support this; and *Abington v. Schempp* (1963), concerning devotional reading of the Bible, or the saying of the Lord's Prayer, the ruling being government could not constitutionally support this either. While these judgements were seen by some as upholding the then separation of church and state, the foundational First Amendment of the US Constitution, 'others felt that they signalled the demise of a common moral foundation that served to unite all Americans amidst our diversity'. As lead author of the document, Moore suggests that these 'same tensions persist today, and many trace the roots of contemporary conflicts regarding religion in the public sphere to these rulings' (AAR, 2010: 3).

Though the heart of these decisions addressed what was not permissible in public education, Moore comments, there was an important affirmation in *Abington v. Schempp* regarding what *was* allowed of religion in schools: 'It might well be said that one's education is not complete without a study of comparative religion or the history of religion and its relationship to the advancement of civilization. It certainly may be said that the Bible is worthy of study for its literary and historic qualities' (AAR, 2010: 3). The AAR Task Force argues that this perspective has often been overlooked, that these and similar rulings 'meant that religion in all forms was banned' (AAR, 2010: 3; again, for overviews of religion in American education, see, for example, Greenawalt, 2007; Lofaso, 2009; Nord, 1995; Urban and Wagoner Jr., 2008).

The *Guidelines* were drafted by the AAR task force in cooperation with public school educators, teacher educators and the broad membership of the AAR. Three fundamental premises inform the project: 'First, there exists a widespread illiteracy about religion in the U.S.; second, there are several consequences that stem from this illiteracy, including the ways that it fuels prejudice and antagonism, thereby hindering efforts aimed at promoting respect for diversity, peaceful coexistence, and cooperative endeavours in local, national, and global arenas; and third, it is possible to diminish religious illiteracy by teaching about religion from an academic, non-devotional perspective in primary, middle, and secondary schools' (AAR, 2010: 4).

Since teachers are expected to teach about religion in a variety of ways in their classrooms, it is these which form the framework and pedagogical model of the AAR Task Force about teaching religion in American schools. The three most common occasions arise when: (1) the curriculum demands coverage of the historical origins of religious traditions or their contemporary relevance; (2) the novels or stories they teach have explicit religious themes or allusions; and (3) their students raise questions based on their own experiences and knowledge. How teachers respond to these expectations 'differs greatly, and the choice of approaches used by teachers is influenced by their subject area, their training, and their own personal views'. Three approaches are identified: the historical, the literary, tradition-based methods and a cultural studies approach. The latter, Moore argues, 'incorporates dimensions of all these approaches and is promoted by religious studies and education scholars' (AAR, 2010: 9–10).

The historical is 'commonly used in social studies classes where religion occurs within courses or lessons focused on history':

> The strengths of the historical approach are clear: the origins of a religion and its development are presented in historical context with the political and cultural influences represented as central to understanding how that religion emerged, gained followers, and spread . . . in practice teachers report that they lack the knowledge base in religious studies required to address the historical complexities of religion adequately. Furthermore, religions are often only explored in their pre-modern contexts in ways that can leave students with the impression that 1) religion became (and continues to be) obsolete in the modern era; or 2) that religious beliefs formed and then solidified into unchanging systems. Students rarely learn how religions continually evolve and change

beyond the eighteenth century, nor are they given the necessary tools to knowledgeably consider and evaluate the roles religions play in modern cultures. (AAR, 2010: 9–10)

The literary approach is common 'in English language arts classes in which students read religious texts themselves or novels, stories, and poetry with religious themes and/or imagery'. Using this approach, 'teachers help students gain an appreciation of the way that religion infuses all aspects of culture by seeing how religious allusion and metaphor can become a common language that is shared by a people':

> When the focus is on religious texts themselves, students learn to appreciate their literary value and how religious texts influence literary styles . . . The challenge is that most educators lack the training in religious studies that is required to provide the appropriate information about religion relevant to the texts that are studied. In the absence of such training, teachers often rely on their own devotional experiences of a tradition or reference other devotional interpretations as adequate sources of information. This often leads to partial or otherwise problematic interpretations as well as a limitation on the types of texts assigned. Teachers will understandably shy away from texts representing or informed by traditions or expressions that are unfamiliar. (AAR, 2010: 9–10)

The traditions-based approach she notes is often represented in history textbooks, the focus 'often on certain categories that apply to many religious traditions, such as beliefs, texts, rituals, origins, and holidays, or on essential questions that religions address related to the purpose of life, how one should live, and various interpretations of identity':

> This approach can help students see common themes in religious traditions and can provide a useful framework for understanding the varieties of religious expression. In looking at religious art or rituals, students can gain an appreciation for the ways all religions shape and are shaped by the culture around them. The main weaknesses of this approach are that 1) it often fails to adequately represent the internal diversity of religious traditions, and 2) it can exaggerate the commonalities among traditions. Additionally, the categories for comparison are themselves often shaped by particular religious assumptions (e.g. by including categories such as 'founder' and 'sacred text') that are not universally relevant and which therefore promote a biased and limited framework for analysis. (AAR, 2010: 9–10)

The cultural studies approach is used 'by those trained in religious studies programs and is well suited for area studies classes or classes that incorporate a multicultural lens of analysis':

> The strengths of the cultural studies approach are that 1) it helps students recognize that religion is a part of the fabric of human experience and that in order to understand it one must consider religious beliefs and practices as they shape and are shaped by all elements of culture; 2) it provides tools to understand how some religious beliefs and expressions become culturally and politically prominent, while others become culturally and politically marginalized; and 3) it provides tools to recognize and analyze the interpretive dimensions of all knowledge claims. The main challenges related to this approach are that 1) it requires training in religious studies; and 2) it requires teachers to slow down and cover less content with more depth. (AAR, 2010: 9–10)

Articulating this further, Moore suggests, 'The distinction between religious studies and a devotional approach to religion at the outset of a lesson or unit will clarify educational goals and minimize confusion and anxiety.'

In America (and the natural European parallel would be France) clearly, then, teaching about religion in public schools brings with it particular challenges that teachers seldom face when addressing other subject areas. Students in a physics course rarely come to class with a sense that they have particular insights that will be relevant and helpful to a class discussion of vectors, but when the subject is religion, students can feel that their own personal experiences give them special knowledge and authority. Often students will have strongly held ideas about the positive or negative role of religion in the world, ideas about religious and non-religious people and ideas about particular faiths. Teachers also may feel that their own background in a particular religious tradition prepares them sufficiently to teach that tradition, or may have views about religion and its relevance in their classroom that shape how they teach religious topics. Thus, one of the first challenges for teachers and students alike is to examine what assumptions they harbour about religion generally and religious traditions in particular.

The effectiveness of the *AAR Guidelines for Teaching About Religion in K-12 Public Schools in the United States* 'will be measured by its usefulness for teachers and the implementation of its suggestions in public schools and schools of education'. The AAR is 'eager to share the document more broadly and to solicit feedback from teachers nationwide'. As part of her own research, Moore is presently (2012) seeking teacher and teacher educator volunteers to participate in a pilot study trial of the AAR guidelines in classrooms. Study results will inform future revisions.

What is noteworthy, however, is the political framing of the concluding justification for religion in education: *'Given that one of the primary purposes of mandatory schooling in the United States is to provide students with the skills necessary to function as active and informed citizens of our multicultural democracy, understanding the religious dimensions of our multiculturalism is a vital yet underdeveloped component of that important purpose'* (Moore, 2010, emphasis added). 'Those of us,' she writes, 'who were centrally involved in drafting and vetting these guidelines realize that their publication is only a beginning, but we hope they will provide a meaningful resource for teachers and other citizens who wish to strengthen literacy about religion in our nation.' The US constitutional separation of religion and the state has not shown it immune to Willaime's 'double constraint'.

The AAR's position is but one of a growing interest around religion in education. The First Amendment Center and the Biblical Literacy Programme are other leading examples of organizations and programmes committed to furthering some form of teaching of religion in public schools. I have concentrated on developments in the AAR because this is where the force of influence of such developments has been most pronounced and likely to be most impactful. However, the American Educational Research Association also merits close attention as the interests of its members, largely related to public institutions, also begin to attend to questions of religion in education. Again, James Nelson's (2010) 'The Evolving Place of Research on Religion in the American Educational Research Association' provides presently the most up-to-date review of such developments. A belated interest in such subjects by the American Educational Research Association will not surprise organizations like the AAR or the Religious Education Association where such interest has been flourishing for a century.

Summary

The projects examined in this chapter have a dual emphasis on research and pedagogy at the interface of religion, politics and education. They are important because they are influential in determining, or at least in forming the thinking that would hope to determine, the role of religion in education, a rationale dominated by political directive. This is currently more apparent in the European than the American context. This should not be a surprise when the funders for the research are themselves the very political agencies and their policies on religion and education which are being examined. The impact of such thinking on the international stage is however becoming increasingly apparent.

A key problem in political theory since the Enlightenment – that is, since the organizing principle of politics ceased to be religious – has been that of how to incorporate plural religious and cultural standpoints/views/lifestyles, and, given these, the respective limits of tolerance. A key political problem has also been and remains an educational one.

...

Religious Education and the Religious Life: Theology and Faith Schools

3

Chapter Outline

Introduction

For as long as religious traditions have been concerned with education, religious education has been integral to the religious life. The separation of religious education and the religious life emerged only with the modern-day provision of education itself, and became acutely apparent with secular state provision for religious education.

It is thus we see a discernible shift, in such secular religious education contexts, to the use of the term 'religion in education' rather than, or at least alongside, religious education (see Chapters 1 and 2). Chapter 4 will analyse the specific and reciprocal relationship here of religious education and secularity, a twin influence on religious education itself and citizenship. Chapter 5 will examine the wider impact of religious education pedagogy in a secular context, and show how religious educators here have sought ways to ground the principles of teaching, learning and assessment without the foundational link between religious education and the religious life.

This chapter examines such historical-contemporary relationships. In the section headed 'Religious Education and the Religious Life', I treat the *historical* relationship, specifically within Western Christian context. In the section headed 'Theology and Faith Schools', I outline what I mean by theology, and provide exemplars of faith schools which demonstrate the *contemporary* relationship between religious education and the religious life.

Religious education and the religious life

The connections, broken but still retained, between religious education and the religious life, are reflected in definitional changes in the term 'religious education' itself.

Astley (1994) provides an overview of the term 'religious education' which highlights the disagreements about the term: the religiously plural definition, also accepted by secular religious educators; Protestant and Catholic uses of the term; and the different Protestant uses of the term on the two sides of the Atlantic. Thus,

> in the United States Christian education has historically been a Protestant term. It is often claimed that it now has some rather negative connotations, carrying overtones of indoctrination or circumscribed and triumphalistic interpretations. Primarily, however, it denotes the formative (usually including the evangelistic) activities of the church in developing Christian beliefs, attitudes and over behaviours. As such its denotation is the same as that of the phrases Christian education and Christian nurture as used in Britain. Catholic, and more recently some others, prefer to describe this activity as 'catechesis', but the more popular and ecumenical term for it (which is in principle usable by members of other religions also) is 'religious education'. Religious education in the US therefore in its Christian redaction is usually seen as church sponsored and church oriented activity leading to the development of a wide range of Christian outcomes in its learners. (Astley, 1994: 35)

When Astley says that religious education is 'in principle usable by members of other religions also', he is certainly correct about Britain. Astley's *Christian Religious Education*, from which these definitions are drawn, was published in the early 1990s when religious traditions from Buddhism, Christianity, Judaism, Islam, Hinduism and Sikhism were drawn together by the government agency responsible for religious education and, essentially, asked what content would adequately reflect their respective traditions. This shows primarily the interesting contemporary move within state religious education to use religious traditions to define the secular subject even though the latter has separated religious education from the religious life. However, it also shows that despite this separation, the faith communities themselves recognize a subject in secular context called religious education, and, if their cooperation is a mark of approval, some at least see value in it.

These latter comments also justify Astley's description of understandings of religious education on the other side of the Atlantic:

> In British debate the activities outlined [as above] are often described as 'nonconfessional'. This does not imply a limited denominational objective, but merely formation in religion – the (intentional) nurturing of a particular religious commitment. The current British usage is broadly as follows: religious education . . . specifies a general educational activity, usually treated as part of schooling, that educates children about religion. Currently this is usually taken to involve an emphatic but nonevangelistic and nonformative (often described as nonconfessional) educating activity focused on a variety of religions. Religious education is also regarded as having the additional functions of developing the learners' own religious or quasi-religious sensitivities, and their search for meaning and truth. (Astley, 1994: 36)

Christian education, on the other hand, he says is 'used in Britain for confessional activity of teaching the Christian religion', though

> many prefer the terms 'Christian nurture' for this activity; some (especially Catholics) retain the hallowed, but somewhat archaic term 'catchesis'; others describe it as 'confessional religious education'. The situation is complicated by the fact that in Britain many 'church schools . . . see their work as 'Christian nurture' rather than, or at least alongside 'religious education'. (Astley, 1994: 36–7)

This 'terminological problem' leads Astley to the definition of Christian religious education. He is not primarily talking about religious education in secular schools 'but rather about a confessional churchly activity of evangelism, instruction and nurture': 'Christian religious education' is thus 'the process whereby Christian learning takes place'. It 'often involves', he states, 'teaching', that is, 'the intentional (promotional, enabling, aiding) of Christian learning' (Astley, 1994: 37). That it 'often involves' teaching shows the difficulty of linking intentionality with context. It could be a church group. It could be any other informal activity; but how informal before it loses its intentionality? This problem is compounded when we read that Christian religious education is 'a person's learning to be Christian'. This sort of learning might not be formal or intentional at all. Dramatic conversion or profound life experience might enable a person to learn to be a Christian. But would this be religious education?

Indeed, what Astley derides as the 'somewhat archaic term' of 'catechesis' points to an early church context in which informal instruction in the faith and formal faith formation were difficult to separate. It would be more correct to see catechesis then as ancient rather than archaic. Catechesis (from the Greek meaning 'instruction') refers to and has its origins within the New Testament. In the early church it was the (often oral) means of instruction among persecuted associations of Christians when public schooling would have been unthinkable. There was therefore some necessity in secrecy. The Christian home would also be the setting for instruction. Catechesis provided then the early (formal and informal) structural foundations on which all subsequent Christian education would be based, in Christian homes and in catechumenal (often secret) places of instruction, later developing into the formal structures of catechumenal schools. It is from this Greek word for instruction that is derived the instructional guides on Christian teaching known as the catechism. The earliest instructional guide outside of the New Testament itself was the Didache.

Astley's work is thus a useful starting point for seeing the problems of defining religious education. The problems, as Astley highlights, are apparent in differences in approach between Christian traditions; they become acute when religious education becomes separate from religious life. The definitional problem is not simply idle theorizing. In no other subject do the aims and intentions that underpin the subject vary so greatly. There are those with a commitment for example to religious education (in Britain) being concerned primarily with Christianity, and even to an extent Christian nurture (Thompson, 2004), and if not Christian nurture then at least as an inspiration for faith (Felderhof et al., 2007), or those who at least lament the passing of Christian religious education within state schools but are resolved to face a different future (Copley, 2007). Even a commitment to religious education without religious commitment (so to speak) is no resolution. The range of philosophies and pedagogies of secular religious education testifies to a lack of consensus over the aims and purposes of the subject.

Legislation in Britain early separated religious education from the religious life. From its origins in the 1870 Education Act, it was not expected to be distinctive of any Christian denomination. In the 1944 Education Act, it was also distinguished from the 'secular' curriculum; the subject however was still called religious instruction and was closely associated with worship within the school. The changing of the subject's name from religious *instruction* to *education* in subsequent decades would shift the subject more towards integration as a part of the secular curriculum. This would give force to Ninian Smart's (1969a) argument that religious instruction, even called education, was closely associated with religious tradition as *instructional*, handing down knowledge (*telling* what is the case, 'teaching that'). For Smart, non-instructional *education* in religion 'teaches how', not what, to think. Religious education, as the subject came to be called, was for Smart still insufficient: to Smart the subject change of name implied openness but belied confessionalism. Smart thus encouraged the use of 'religious studies'. He had used the term to define the Department of Religious Studies he founded at Lancaster University. In schools, the curriculum subject is still divided between religious education and (when examined) religious studies.

We note in passing too, a no less dramatic separation of the study of religion from the religious life in the universities. Where the subject was most often called 'theology', it is now as often called religious studies. Even where it is called theology there are efforts to underline the fact that no religious belief is necessary. Take this notion back one hundred years, in schools and/or universities, and the notion would have been conceivable, the study of 'natural religion' and an emergent 'science of religion'. Take the notion back a further hundred years, to the beginning, say, of the nineteenth century, and the argument that a university theologian or a schoolteacher of religion was not concerned with the religious life would have been regarded as puzzling, or more likely cause for censure. As Eliade (1959: 216) comments in an early chronology of the academic study of religion: 'The science of religions, as an autonomous discipline devoted to analysing the common elements of the different religions and seeking to deduce the laws of their evolution, and especially to discover and define the origin and first form of religion, is a very recent addition to the sciences' (see also Pals, 2008).

There are those who wish to ensure as much epistemological distance as possible between religious education and not only its former Christian forms but also any religious life, except that which involves its academic study. Cush's (1999) paper distinguishing between religious education, religious studies and theology remains a useful discussion, challenging 'the assumption that religious education is a second order activity of lesser status':

> Whilst recognising the closer relationship that Religious Education has with Religious Studies, it examines the contribution Theology can make to non-confessional RE, and suggests that academic Religious Studies and Theology should put an end to their historic quarrel. The use of the word 'Theology' to describe the activity engaged in by pupils when exploring their own beliefs and values is examined and rejected. It concludes that the three disciplines should view themselves as equal partners with distinct, but complementary roles. (Cush, 1999: 137)

The very need for a discussion shows a fundamental educational movement. It is as new as the history of the study of religion as a 'science'.

Through Christian history, then, religious education has been indissolubly linked to the religious life (see Anthony and Benson, 2003; references throughout Cross and Livingstone, 1997; Knight, 2012). Scant as the attention to Christian education has been by mainstream modern theology (Ford, 2000, 2011), any notion that religious education could be dissociated with the religious life would for most of Christian history be regarded as meaningless. A notable problem presents itself however when we search the New Testament for the word 'religious' or 'education'. The word 'religious', like 'religion', of Latin origin, was not current within the New Testament except by particular reference to, for example, the Jews, Greeks, Romans, often characterized as the collective 'pagan' or 'barbarians', by those outside the civilization of Greece or Rome. Concordances using a multiplicity of biblical translations show this (e.g. Bible Gateway, 2012). Nor will we find the term 'education', also of Latin etymology, in the New Testament. Once more, search of any biblical concordance will show this. There are nevertheless many references in the New Testament, as there are in the Old Testament, to terms such as 'teaching', 'taught' and 'learning', and all ultimately derive and find sustenance, meaning and purpose in the holy. In terms of such teaching and learning, the notion that it would be directed to anything other than the religious life again would be meaningless.

The primary purpose of religious life remains directed to salvation. Ethical guidance, advice on attitudes to political authorities, and so forth, are all subject and subsumed within the eschatological and salvific context. In the Gospels, Jesus, who 'taught with authority', presented ethical and moral teaching which is familiar even to the non-Christian: for instance, the Sermon on the Mount or the practical wisdom of parables. However, even the political implications of these teachings, in the early church and subsequently, must all be regarded as subservient to salvation, classically expressed in Matthew: 'Seek ye first the kingdom of God' (Mt. 6.33). St Augustine thus later delineated the earthly city (of temporal, civic concern) and the city of God (eternal, and the destiny of the elect). The eschatological context is apparent too in the 'Great Commission': "Go therefore, teach ye all nations.' But it too is set in the context of the last days: 'Behold I am with you all days, even to the consummation of the world' (Mt. 27.19–20). The Acts of the Apostles tell precisely of the spreading of this message through the teaching of the apostles; the epistles of Paul, John, James and so forth, provide insight into the spread of the message in written form. These words, as one commentator suggests, 'are the charter of the Christian Church as a teaching institution' (Pace, 1909).

In the post-apostolic age, the earliest formal education was for catechumens, a catechumen meaning someone in preparation for baptism. Entirely with the truths of salvation according to the Gospels, as well as other Christian teaching, this catechumenal learning was almost exclusively based either in secret locations or in the homes of Christians. In a persecuted church there was no possibility of any institutional structure the like of schools. With Christian expectation that they were living in the last days, the end times, the most intense periods of persecution drove Christian education underground.

However, the catechumenal model became in later times, when Christians were freer to practice and propagate the faith, the model for catechumenal schools. The early schools served a wide constituency, both lay (that is non-clerical) Christians and those preparing for the priesthood or other roles such as the deaconate within the church. Courses of study however included not simply Christian teaching, philosophy and theology, but, and depending on the nature of the school, classical (that is Greek and Roman) learning as well. The early church itself was greatly divided on the role of the latter in the former. One of the oldest catechumenal schools was, perhaps unsurprisingly, in the Lateran, Rome; among the most well-known schools outside of Rome was at Alexandria. These schools took on the role of defending the Christian faith against the pagans. This characterization of pagan was the assumed collective name for all outside the Christian faith, except Judaism, with which Christianity retained in its first decades an antagonistic relationship. After the destruction of the Temple in Jerusalem, the pagan world would become the chief opponents of Christianity, and the catechumenal schools a defence against pagan learning and persecution.

Given the reciprocal hostility between the Christianity and the pagan or classical world, it is unsurprising that attitudes differed among Christian theologians in attitudes to Greek and Roman learning. Such teachers at the catechumenal schools had often been formed by classical Roman education. They differed (even those who shared similar Roman education) on whether it was profitable for Christians to know of such a heritage or not. Justin Martyr (AD 100–AD 165), whose school at Ephesus sought to unite Greek and Christian learning, wrote his *Apology* for a dual purpose: as a pedagogical synthesis of pagan and Christian learning; and as a task for communication, by the synthesis conveying that Rome had nothing to fear from Christianity. Clement of Alexandria (AD 150–AD 215) also attempted a synthesis of Greek philosophy and Christian theology. Origen (AD 185–AD 254), Clement's successor at Alexandria was so keen to unify pagan and Christian traditions that he was thought to be heretical.

Tertullian (AD 150–AD 230) took a diametrically opposite view, and had little patience with the synthesizers, especially in the light of persecution by this same learned civilization, which he addresses in *Of Schoolmasters and Their Difficulties*. In another work, he takes a more offensive line and delights in envisaging the future for the learned but unrepentant pagan:

> But what a spectacle is already at hand – the return of the Lord, now no object of doubt, now exalted, now triumphant! What exultation will that be of the angels, what glory that of saints as they rise again! What the reign of the righteousness thereafter! What a city, the New Jerusalem! Yes, and are still to come other spectacles – that last, that eternal Day of Judgement, that day they laughed at, when this old world and all its generations shall be consumed in one fire. How vast the spectacle that day, and how wide! What sight shall wake my wonder, what laughter, my joy and exultation? As I see those kings, those great kings, welcomed (we are told) in heaven, along with Jove, along with those who told of their ascent, groaning in the depths of darkness! And the magistrates who persecuted the name of Jesus, liquefying in fiercer flames than they kindled in their rage against Christians! Those sages, too, the philosophers blushing before their disciples whom they taught that God was concerned with nothing, that men have no souls at all, or that what souls they have shall never return to their former bodies! And, the poets trembling before the judgement-seat not of Minos, but of Christ whom they never looked to see! (Fordham, 2012)

This is part of a wider address in which Tertullian is asking whether it is permissible for Christians to partake also in the then common entertainments: arena, circus and theatre. And so the matter of cultural synthesis extends theological concern to practical Christian living.

Cyril of Jerusalem (AD 315–AD 386), conscious of the need for purity of faith, wrote 24 catechetical lectures for this purpose: 18 instructions or lessons, often delivered, as much symbolically, during Lent, for catechumens, that is, those preparing for baptism; and 4 or 5 'mystical' treatises, to be delivered to those same who have passed after baptism at Easter to become full members of the Christian Church.

Basil the Great (AD 331–AD 396), classically educated in Constantinople and Athens, founder of Christian monasticism in the East, was convinced of the ultimate superiority of the scriptures over Greek philosophy. Writing to his Sophist philosopher friend Libanius, in a letter more genial than the following terms indicate, Basil writes: 'I . . . am now spending my time with Moses and Elias, and saints like them . . . If ever I learned anything from you, I have forgotten it' (Fordham, 2012).

Jerome (AD 340–AD 399), who studied and for a time was deeply enamoured of Cicero Horace and Virgil after study at Antioch, could find no ultimate reconciliation between pagan literature and Christian scriptures, asking, 'What communion does light have with darkness?' In part of a longer letter written to a woman friend, Eustochium, he writes (around AD 383–AD 384):

> Suddenly I was caught up in the spirit and dragged before the Judge's judgment seat: and here the light was so dazzling, and the brightness shining from those who stood around so radiant, that I flung myself upon the ground and did not dare to look up. I was asked to state my condition and replied that I was a Christian. But He who pre-sided said: 'Thou liest; thou art a Ciceronian,

not a Christian. "For where thy treasure is there will thy heart be also." ' . . . I began to cry out and to bewail myself, saying: 'Have mercy upon me, O Lord, have mercy upon me' . . . At last the bystanders fell at the knees of Him who presided, and prayed Him to pardon my youth and give me opportunity to repent of my error, on the understanding that the extreme of torture should be inflicted on me if ever I read again the works of Gentile authors. In the stress of that dread hour I should have been willing to make even larger promises, and taking oath I called upon His name: 'O Lord, if ever again I possess worldly books or read them, I have denied thee.' (Fordham, 2012)

He adopted an ascetic life in the Chalcis desert, and became renowned for the translation of the Bible into Latin, a translation which came to be known as the Vulgate.

John Chrysostom (AD 345–AD 407), who studied in Antioch under Libanius, was among the first Christian theologians to write specifically with concern not only for combating heresy but also for the formation of the young, in *Concerning the Education of Children*. As with so much of this period, it was Augustine (AD 354–AD 430) who was to have the most significant and lasting influence. Despite his indebtedness to the Greek and Roman traditions of education, *Confessions*, of all Augustine's works, makes plain his rejection of pagan learning. In a later work, *On Christian Teaching*, he shows a more moderate approach to the techniques if not the content of pagan learning, suggesting ways in which the Christian message might even benefit from learning something of the skills of the rhetorician.

These schools and their theologians would form a critical challenge not only to pagan literature and philosophy but also to Christian heresies, including Gnosticism, Docetism, Manichaeism, Neo-Platonism, Marcionism and Arianism. Arianism, for instance, later pre-occupied the Council of Nicea. But Nicea (AD 325) incidentally would mark the end of the period in which the catechumenal schools served to form the faithful and defend the Faith against its opponents.

The Council of Nicea, headed symbolically by the emperor Constantine himself, marked that time in ecclesiastical history when Christianity itself became politically permissible. The fall of Rome found the church adapting its teaching mission to the conversion of barbarian tribes, those who invaded Rome itself and those who belonged to former territories of the Empire. It was in this period that monasticism would take on many of the educational tasks of the catechumenal institutions, and have wider educational roles. With the fall of Rome, the classical system of Roman and pagan education would collapse. Church-led educational institutions would emerge from this, particularly through monasticism from the early sixth century onwards, and for which St Benedict is rightly credited with a founding role. The church's contribution to education after the fall of Rome clearly did not begin here (we have noted the forms of early catechesis), but monasticism would greatly enhance the spread of a more general education across Europe thereafter.

St Benedict was born in Nursia in AD 480, and died in Monte Cassino, AD 543, and between those dates fashioned a European model of monasticism that would significantly would significantly shape medieval European life, including the world of Bede with which this book opened. The account of Benedict's life on which all subsequent others inevitably draw is the *Dialogues* of St Gregory (540–604), based in large part on accounts by disciples who knew Benedict. We know with some certainty he was of noble parentage and was educated in elite public schools in Rome. Benedict's experience of the worldliness of these schools in the late 400s (Augustine had noted the same in the late 300s) led him to abandon his education for a life of seclusion in what then were deserted mountains outside Rome. The stage of his education he abandoned is disputed. Some accounts have Benedict leaving as a boy of 14, others as he had entered into the stage of higher learning. Though his age at this time is disputed, the rejection of his former life is not. The core point is not the stage of his learning but his renunciation of it. St Gregory puts it, 'giving over his books, and forsaking his father's house and wealth, with a mind only to serve God, he sought for some place where he might attain to the desire of his holy purpose; and in this sort he departed, instructed with learned ignorance and furnished with unlearned wisdom' (Fordham, 2012). This narrative provides insight into the existence of a system of education following the fall of Rome and the Christian dissatisfaction with it. The *Rule* of St Benedict became the main organizing principle for the network of monasteries that spread to all countries of Western Europe (the East had an organized monasticism of its own) over the next thousand years.

Though it was the intention of Benedict to form monasteries not schools, such were the needs of society that the monasteries began to provide welfare of many sorts, including health and education, as well as the scholarly preservation of texts of Greek, Latin and Christian through the 'Dark Ages'. In England, this is roughly the period of Anglo-Saxon history. Bede's *History* arises from a monasticism which both preserved and shaped the time. Monastic schools here served initially the needs of those seeking the religious life. Later a distinction was made within the schools concerning the education of children of the laity. Thus the distinction arose between 'internal' and 'external' schools within the monastery:

> It was part of the purpose of monasticism to meet this need and to supply not only to the members of the religious orders but also to children committed to the care of the cloister the moral religious, and intellectual culture which could not be obtained elsewhere without lowering the Christian standard of life. There were parochial schools also, which, while they aimed at fostering vocations to the priesthood, contributed to the education of the laity, the chief portion of the burden of lay education in the early Middle Ages was borne by the monasteries. The earliest monastic legislation does not clearly define the organization of the 'internal' and 'external' schools. Nevertheless, it recognizes the existence in the monastery of children who were to be educated, not for the cloister, but for the world. (Pace, 1909)

Besides the study of scripture, and the monastic liturgical life, the monastic curriculum included the seven liberal arts (deriving from Greek and Roman educational models), the *trivium* and *quadrivium*: grammar, rhetoric, dialectic, arithmetic, geometry, astronomy and music. A not dissimilar curriculum is found in Plato's *Republic*. The monastic curriculum, however, also included architecture and building with visual and decorative arts, above all evident in the scriptorium. In the monasteries there was 'academic' and as well as 'practical' learning.

From the monasteries, other schools arose responsive to a similar diversity of needs: the parochial schools (concerned with the education of priests, and education in parishes), cathedral schools and chantry schools (associated with charitable foundations). All were concerned with education centred on the needs of the church, in the broadest sense of clergy and laity. Often written into the later foundations was a commitment to the education of the poor. From around the thirteenth century, guild schools, hospital schools and city schools caused some tensions, and perhaps competition, with the older forms of ecclesiastical schooling. Hospital schools and city schools might be said to be the tacit beginnings of the secularizing of this education.

The twelfth and thirteenth centuries were also times of a wider European Renaissance, a revival of that learning admired and reviled in the early church. The new learning provided the foundations of the medieval synthesis of such learning, particularly philosophy with theology, known as scholasticism. But a far wider enterprise, structural and institutional, would help provide too the foundations of the modern, present-day 'knowledge economy':

> Medieval universities – such as Paris, Bologna, and Oxford – generally had four faculties: arts, medicine, law, theology. The faculty of arts was seen as entry level, qualifying students to go on to more advanced studies in the three 'higher faculties'. The result of this development was that theology became established as a significant component of advanced study at European universities. As more and more universities were established in Western Europe so the academic study of theology became more widespread. (McGrath, 2007a: 103–4)

McGrath here describes the establishment of medieval universities as 'perhaps the most important moment in the history of theology as an academic discipline'.

Profound as the Renaissance was in transforming the environment of medieval scholarship, no movement in the history of Christendom was more radical in the restructuring this broad educational provision than the Reformation. As one commentator argues:

> The destruction of this vast and varied system of ecclesiastical legislation is a fact of general history. The schools, as a rule, disappeared with the institutions to which they were attached. The confiscation of the monasteries, the suppression of the benefices on which the chantries were founded, the removal of the guilds from the control of ecclesiastical authority, the suppression of cathedral and canonical chapters and the sequestration of their possessions by the State, were the immediate cause of the cessation of this kind of educational activity on the part of the Church at the time of the Reformation and afterwards. (Pace, 1909)

The monasteries destroyed in sixteenth-century Europe, fine examples as they were of medieval art and architecture, were only secondarily concerned with aesthetics or education. Yet these were integrally related to the devotional life of the church, the unravelling of which met with a disorientation of the faithful, narrated in Eamon Duffy's (1994) *The Stripping of the Altars*. In England, the dissolution of a thousand-year Catholic monastic heritage was in part only the beginning of a process of educational change wrought by Protestantism.

Chantry schools, cathedral schools, city, guild and hospital schools would be affected; and so too would the two mediaeval universities of Oxford and Cambridge, no faculty in either being more profoundly affected than those in theology.

As even secular political theorists credit (Rawls, 1995; Taylor, 2007), the Reformation fracture of Christianity would lead inexorably to Enlightenment. The decline of theology's influence was the basis of new secular *intellectual* foundations. As MacCulloch (2009: 769 ff.) has convincingly argued, the elements of the eighteenth-century Enlightenment were in place by the end of the seventeenth. In England, notable figures in political science were Thomas Hobbes and John Locke, in science Francis Bacon and Isaac Newton. Though varying in religiosity, all these thinkers (even Hobbes, even Newton) retained a biblical worldview. But this new intellectual openness also paved the way for an eighteenth-century Enlightenment more unambiguously critical of Christianity.

Science and political philosophy would exert the greatest influence. In England, the founding of the Royal Society was the pinnacle, Isaac Newton its most illustrious member, and one-time president. Newton's early classical, mathematical and scientific knowledge gained at Grantham grammar school show the broad currents of seventeenth-century education. Newton's schooling would have included the Bible, retaining a lifelong fascination for the prophetic texts of Daniel, and the Apocalypse (Ackroyd, 2007: 15–24).

The non-conformist, particularly 'Puritan' case for freedom of religion, would in this seventeenth-century context have wide political implications. John Milton's *Areopagitica* defines to a large extent still the liberal democratic foundation of wider political freedoms, particular the freedom of expression. It was originally a parliamentary response to the Licensing Order of 1643, at the time of a Civil War politically restrictive of publication. The *Areopagitica*, as became the title of Milton's famous 1644 text, derives from Paul's address to the Athenians in Acts 17.18–34. In the mid-seventeenth century, then, we note that Milton's *Areopagitica* would still find an audience in parliament that would see nothing inappropriate in combining the authority of scripture to justify freedom of publication. Such liberality centred on political rights and freedoms would permeate seventeenth-century political life, provide the foundations for such thinking in the Enlightenment in the following century and in many regards still guide political as well as pedagogical thinking today (Luxon, 2012).

If the *Areopagitica* was a fulcrum point of modern political liberality, its use of biblical and wider Christian justifications would after this point decline, politically and educationally. Profoundly affected by Milton, the other seventeenth-century figure who exerted the greatest subsequent influence on Enlightenment and a growing social and political secularity was John Locke. Educated at Westminster School, John Locke towers as the political philosopher of his age. Locke wrote his *Letter Concerning Toleration* in 1693, in the aftermath of the English Bill of Rights (1689). The letter contained his 'thoughts about the mutual toleration of Christians in their different professions of religion' in which he esteems 'toleration to be the chief characteristic mark of the true Church'. As with Milton, what is striking is that the age's leading political thinker uses the Bible to sustain philosophical argument (Axtell, 1969; Locke, 2009).

Locke, renowned for *Two Treatises of Government*, also wrote *Some Thoughts Concerning Education*, encapsulating liberal political philosophy in pedagogical terms. Mindful that education should be responsive to 'the child's natural genius and constitution' which 'God has stamped', Locke outlines a curriculum: 'arithmetic' (paragraph 180); 'acquaintance with globes' (paragraph 181; and, with geography, 'chronology ought to go hand in hand' (paragraph 182); further, it 'would be strange if the English gentleman should be ignorant of the law of his country' (paragraph 183); 'rhetoric and logic, being the arts that in the ordinary method follow immediately after grammar' (paragraph 186); 'physics' and other sciences, with reverence here for 'the incomparable Mr Newton' (paragraph 194). Scripture studies are given no great prominence, though as with political works, they a bedrock for his pedagogy (Locke, 2009: 179–99). As Morgan (2004: 682) points out, such works represent 'real political debate and concrete events'. Locke responds to the emergent 'Enlightenment' and looks forward to a politically and pedagogically progressive world, but also harks back, retaining the biblical view of the world at a time when its direct influence in political and wider intellectual spheres was waning, as Gay (2009) comments: 'Like many other revolutionary, John Locke was also a conservative, at once transmitting and transforming traditional ideas' (Gay, 2009: 200). Tradition in the late seventeenth century was still holding its own, but its grip was being loosened.

However, after Locke's *Thoughts Concerning Education*, the wider national and international missionary imperative of Bible teaching is shown in the 1698 formation of the Society for Promoting of Christian Knowledge (SPCK) with aims to 'counteract the growth of vice and immorality' and the 'gross ignorance of the principles of the Christian religion' (SPCK, 2012).

Just over a century after the formation of the SPCK, in 1811, the SPCK established the National Society for the Promotion of the Education of the Poor in the Principles of the Established Church to establish primary schools in England and Wales. Today, the National Society is the Church of England's main body for the promotion of religious education, and wider links between the Church of England and education (National Society, 2012). The non-conformist British and Foreign School Society (BFSS) was founded in 1808, and today offers support to 'organizations that reach out to children and young people in remote or impoverished areas, improving inclusivity in education and providing much-needed facilities'. The BFSS archive is a world-leading archive on elementary education in the nineteenth century (BFSS, 2012).

The Roman Catholic Relief Act in 1829 (or Act of Emancipation) returned freedoms back to the Catholic Church lost since the Reformation, including the right of Catholics to sit as members of Parliament. The Catholic Church also began to establish schools, as with the aforementioned Anglican and other Protestant denominations for the socially and economically deprived of England, often in the cities which were expanding rapidly as a result of the Industrial Revolution, against a wider political backdrop of Irish independence. Today the CES (Catholic Education Service of England and Wales) directs Catholic education, particularly religious education (CES, 2012).

In post-Reformation context, initiatives by such religious societies made provision for religious education long before legal or statutory provision, as the Catholic Church had in a diverse numbers of organizational contexts (monastic, cathedral, chantry, etc.) in pre-Reformation times. Formal state provision of religious education in England would have to wait until the 1870 Education Act, though such provision was evident much earlier across continental Europe. The claim that religious education 'in any society exists in relation to the whole process of education and the life and traditions of the society in which it operates' (Copley, 2007: 2) may seem uncontentious, but, at least in Western Europe, it is fallacious. Analysis of pre-Reformation educational provision shows that institutional structures may have taken particular national form but the educative principle was derived from Christian biblical and theological foundations, by their nature unrestricted by national borders. To the extent that Protestant and Catholic Christian traditions still influence such educational provision, the same idea of transnational biblical and theological foundations forming the educative principles in church schools still holds today, as much as it did in medieval context. The difference in all national contexts today is that societies are religiously plural. It is one reason why faith schools themselves are seen as potentially divisive of national life in that their sources of authority are beyond national borders.

This Christian Catholic heritage, and especially the ancient, historic link between religious education and the religious life, is nowhere more apparent than in the origins of the word 'religious' itself. Deriving from the Latin 'to bind', or as a noun 'obligation, bond, reverence', the original use of the word 'religious', in Middle English, is from monastic life, referring to the manner in which an individual was 'bound', in general terms of course to Christian faith, but more particularly to monastic vows. In Benedictine context, the order obliged monks and nuns, as in all religious orders, to vows of chastity, obedience and poverty, but the Benedictine order added also the requirement of 'stability', that is, a commitment to a particular monastery, modelled in many ways to a commitment to a monastic's new 'home'. For this reason the Latin derivation of 'religious' meaning 'to bind' had a specific meaning, one originating in a freely chosen commitment to the religious life. This is why members of monastic orders of monks and nuns are still referred to as 'religious', meaning members of a religious order.

All this said, in England, during the 1944 reading of the Education Bill, cross-party and cross-denominational support was evident. There was no perceptible objection when R. A. Butler commented:

> Let us hope that our children – to use words found in one agreed syllabus – may gain knowledge of the common Christian faith held by their fathers for nearly 2,000 years; may seek for themselves in Christianity principles which give a purpose to life and a guide to all its problems. In so vital, personal and individual a matter as the teaching of religion, the State cannot claim to possess absolute authority, or to speak the final and decisive word. The churches should never forget their own responsibility for the out-of-school period. The responsibilities – and the burdens – must be shared. (Hansard, 1944)

There was recognition that religion was as divisive a factor in British politics, though it is difficult to imagine religious education being a matter for heated discussion as a member of Parliament comments:

> I speak as a member of the Church of England. We must all be thankful that religious education controversies are no longer the current coin of party politics. The time has far gone now when that story was told of the voter who asked a candidate, 'Do you believe in religious education?' and the candidate, who was an unusually honest man, said, 'No, as a matter of fact I do not,' to which the voter replied, 'Well, I do, so you can go to hell.' (Hansard, 1944)

The same member of Parliament reaffirmed 'two great principles': 'that a full and equal opportunity of education is the right of every child, and that a Christian foundation is the only and essential basis of real education'.

Theology and faith schools

In England, as elsewhere in Europe, the story of religious education *today* is integrally related to the development of state education. Even here, though, we might add the caveat that international political factors (see Chapters 1 and 2) now shape the role of religion in education. Vestiges of Christian heritage were nevertheless long apparent for many decades after the 1870 Education Act made elementary education compulsory, not least in the form of its compulsory provision for religious education (or 'instruction', as then called). The 1870 Elementary Education Act, drafted by Liberal MP William Forster, provided for elementary education up to age 13, administered through 'board schools'. Christianity is far from integral to the 1870 Act. Section 7 allows parents to withdraw children from 'religious instruction'. Section 14 (the 'Cowper-Temple clause', after Liberal MP William Cowper-Temple) states, 'No religious catechism or religious formulary which is distinctive of any particular denomination shall be taught in the school'.

The Christian churches in the form of the *Voluntary Schools Association* lobbied to gain the same financial advantages as the board schools, a matter which in 1888 was investigated by the Cross Commission, and for which the 1902 Education Act enshrined 'public funding for the secular curriculum in church schools' (Gillard, 2011; Wilson, 2011). However, in addition to the sociological pressures – the Industrial Revolution, the need for a basic, that is, elementary education for an urbanized workforce – that necessitated the legal framework of the 1870 Act, the latter was also promulgated against a backdrop of widespread intellectual (i.e. epistemological) assaults on Christianity. Against challenges both political and epistemological that arose from the eighteenth-century Enlightenment, in the nineteenth century, in the political context which allowed unprecedented intellectual freedoms, new fundamental challenges to religion emerged: from the natural sciences, the most notable was from the 1859 publication of Darwin's *Origin of Species* (Desmond, 1997; Desmond and Moore, 1992);

but there were also new and widespread assaults on religion itself, not least from emergent social and psychological sciences (Pals, 2008). However, the *range* if not the intensity (and social acceptability) of scepticism towards Christianity was a significant, post-Enlightenment backdrop against which the 1870 Education Act made religious education compulsory.

It is through these influences – growing intellectual scepticism of religion and the impact of this upon religious education itself – that the separation of religious education from the religious life would occur most profoundly. It is particularly marked in the third of Willaime's (2007) three models of religious education in Europe: (1) 'no religious instruction in schools'; (2) 'confessional religious instruction'; and (3) 'non-confessional religious education' (Willaime, 2007: 60).

However, in England and many countries, a 'dual system' allowed for the continued existence of what were then firmly called 'church schools'. In England such schools were funded by the state. As the prospect 1944 Education Act was discussed in Parliament, Butler stated: 'Throughout the history of the church schools – and when I mention "church schools" I am using a general term and not referring to schools of any particular denomination – two interweaving strands are discernible, namely, an ever-changing adjustment of the measure of public assistance to enable them to meet the ever-growing costs of education, accompanied by a steadily increasing measure of public control.' The matter however is not simply economic: 'We have been asked why the dual system cannot be done away with and all schools placed under a uniform control with the expenses found from public funds. I will explain the difficulty in which one is placed in attempting to reform the dual system by saying that this proposition is advanced by two sets of people who propound exactly the opposite ways of giving effect to it. To some, it would be an essential part of such an arrangement that doctrinal teaching should be available in all schools according to the wishes of the parents. Others, on the other hand, consider that religious education is the responsibility of the churches and not of the schools, and on that account favour the secular solution' (Education Bill, 1944). Even in those countries where such funding was not available (for instance, in France and America) private faith schools continued to exist, those which retain the link between religious education and the religious life.

We have already noted, too, Willaime's double 'legal' and 'sociological' constraints on the religious education curriculum, and this in varying degrees across all three contexts or forms of religious education in Europe. The same pressures continue to have marked institutional and structural effects: in terms of *sociological constraint or pressures*, religious plurality has meant an increased demand from diverse religious communities for their own schools; in terms of *legal constraint or pressures*, if state funding is available for Christian (Catholic and Protestant) schools, by the terms of legislative equality (especially through human rights legislation), it could not be denied, though it was long resisted, for schools of other religious traditions.

In these faith school contexts, theology continues to ground not only religious education but the life of the school, in other words, the link is retained between religious education and the religious life. In definitional terms, the use of theology here adds yet further complications to the task of religious education. Theology is generally accepted as a discipline proper to higher level, college, seminary or university study. We have noted, for example, McGrath's point about the significance of theology in the foundation of the medieval universities themselves, though the place of theology in universities today, three centuries after the Enlightenment, cannot be said to resemble anything like its original importance. Alasdair MacIntyre (2009), in *God, Philosophy, Universities* makes plain a lament for the loss of the integrative role in university research once provided by theology.

But I want to take here a broader and much more commonplace, simpler, notion of theology, less technical than its literal meaning of 'the science of God' or one deriving from medieval times when it was regarded as 'the queen of sciences'. A modern-day statement for those beginning in academic theology is provided by McGrath (2007a), as the 'systematic study of the ideas of a religion, including the foundations, historical development, mutual relationship, and application to life of these ideas'. In foundations, this 'relates to identifying the sources on which these ideas are based, and how they relate to each other'. In Christian theological terms, these sources include the Christian Bible, tradition, reason and experience. As McGrath says, 'some of the most important debates within Christian theology have concerned the priority that ought to be given to each of these elements' (McGrath provides a useful discussion of each of these four sources; McGrath 2007a: 121–51). 'Development', or 'historical theology' as it is often referred to, 'concerns the ways in which these ideas have emerged over time'. 'Relationships' as McGrath says, 'considers the way in which Christian ideas relate to each other'. 'Applications' in Christian theological settings, is concerned 'with the difference that the ideas of Christian theology make to the way in which Christians relate to each other, pray, worship, and exist in the world. Christian theology is not just a set of ideas: it is about making possible a new way of seeing ourselves, others and the world.' McGrath's overview also provides a more technical introduction to the 'architecture of theology', which he delineates as including the branches or specialist disciplines within theology: biblical studies; systematic theology; philosophical theology; historical theology; pastoral theology; and spirituality, or mystical theology. As McGrath (2010) has detailed in a more personally reflective work, theology is more than about its academic contexts. If this was the case the reasoning of Christianity would have not have flourished. Theological perspective is not simply, as McGrath suggests, a matter of doctrinal statement, but an attitude, a 'discipleship of the mind'. Faith, trust and experience in Christian experience provide firmer foundations than matters of argument.

It is this sense of theology which I have in mind in using the term. It pervaded early Christian teaching which was vouchsafed by experience, sustained in the catechumenal schools of the early church, as a support for, not a source of, faith. We rarely if ever read of accounts in the New Testament of conversions through argument, though St Paul, notably when in Athens, the ancient home of philosophy, often appeals to reason. His road to Damascus experience, related in the Acts, is certainly not a result of philosophical reasoning. The principle of the priority of faith is well articulated in the twelfth century by the aphorism of St Anselm explaining the relationship between Christian belief in relation to theology and reason, as faith reasoning through the principles of belief, as 'faith seeking understanding'. The order of Anselm's axiom is important: faith comes before understanding or reason.

Nevertheless, there is a wider debate about the extent to which theological frameworks – say, for example, in Christian education (as defined earlier by Astley) – are or should be influenced by other, epistemological c onstraints or pressures. For example, how far should Christian religious education draw on insights from secular learning, for instance, the social and psychological sciences? Jack Seymour (1996) outlines the implications for religious education. James Michael Lee (1996) in 'Religious Education and Theology' argues trenchantly that religious education has been highly influenced by the social sciences, reflecting a more general debate reviewed by John Milbank (2004) in *Theology and Social Theory*. We can see this questioning of how far secular knowledge should inform religious understanding as a modern reframing of debates that had taken place in the early church from Tertullian and Origen to Cyril of Jerusalem, Jerome and Augustine.

To whatever extent Christian or other forms of faith-informed or faith-directed religious education is impacted by secular thinking, it retains a foundational theological orientation. Meant in this simple way, I use the word 'theology'. Whether this is 'theology' in a technical sense might be contested. However, we need to recall that the specialist language of the university theologian is itself derived from these simpler early church origins. It was an argument after all of Protestant reformers that Catholic scholastic theology had precisely lost that connection. To put things even more simply, the relationship between theology and faith schools evidences a bond retained between religious education and the religious life, whereas in secular religious education it is lost. Theology is not simply a way of arguing but a way of being in and seeing the world. C. S. Lewis, the English author and popular theologian, put it thus: 'I believe in Christianity as I believe that the sun has risen, not only because I see it, but because by it I see everything else.'

In contemporary Western societies, greatly diversified in terms of religious plurality, the range of examples of such relations between religious education and the religious life is itself diverse and plural. Thus, in 2010, I commissioned a number of contributions to the *Religious Education Handbook* (Gearon, 2011), one major section of which provided an opportunity for senior representatives from faith communities to reflect on faith education provision within their respective traditions; including the Roman Catholic, Church of England, Jewish, Hindu and Muslim schools.

Roman Catholicism

As we have noted in the early part of this chapter, the history of Christian education has been characterized by differing degrees of accommodation and tension between secular influences (in the early church it was Roman and Greek) which arose in relation to Christian faith and its message of and primary function to proclaim salvation. Many of the questions of Christian education through the centuries also focused on establishing orthodox teaching in the light of what were considered misleading or heretical doctrine. Beginning with Nicea, the ecumenical councils of the church were established in the post-Constantinian period to deal with especially acute questions of doctrine and Catholic teaching. For the most part, these were theological. In the Reformation, the Council of Trent (1545–63) was the chief source of authoritative Catholic teaching which formed part of what became known as the Counter-Reformation. By the nature of the widespread challenges to Roman Catholic authority in matters of doctrine, it was also in large part a systematic reassertion of said Catholic authority in relation to all matters pertaining to and understood in the widest sense of Christian teaching.

There would not be another ecumenical council for another 300 years. The First Vatican Council (1870–1) was held further to reassert this authority, not simply in the light of the now established Protestant churches but the growing – political, intellectual – secularism which had emerged across Europe from the late eighteenth century onwards. Vatican I's affirmation of papal infallibility – or more properly the authority of the teaching authority of the church in matters of faith and morals through the Magisterium – can be seen as an assertion of ecclesiastical authority in a post-Enlightenment world in which the church faced challenges to its authority which were now more pronounced from secular sources. For the next century, the church was seen as largely and explicitly in opposition to the developments which had emerged from the Enlightenment. Two important documents suffice to illustrate this: the statement known as the *Syllabus of Errors* (1864) by Pope Pius IX which condemned the principles of liberalism, including those perpetuated through new forms of state education; and the Encyclical of Pope Pius X on the Doctrines of the Modernists (1907).

The Second Vatican Council (1962–5) was announced by Pope John XXIII not as a response to any particular doctrinal crisis but as a way of redressing an impression that the church has become perceived entirely separate from the concerns which faced the modern world. It was thus known as a pastoral council and met to consider the contributions of the church in the modern world. There is no compromise on doctrine but its tone was more outreaching and conciliatory. It thus included a *Decree on Ecumenism* (Vatican II, 1975: 452–69) and a *Declaration on the Relations on the Church to Non-Christian Religions* (Vatican II, 1975: 738–41).

Vatican II's *Declaration on Christian Education* (1965) presents in this context 'some fundamental principles concerning Christian education, especially in regard to schools'. The first of these was 'an inalienable right to education'. In this regard: 'Due weight being given to the advances in psychological and intellectual sciences, children and young people should be helped to develop their physical, moral and intellectual qualities' (Vatican II, 1975: 726–7). This is inseparable from a right to a specifically Christian education, so that 'they are gradually introduced to a knowledge of the mystery of salvation' and 'become daily more appreciative of the gift of faith which they have received'. Recognizing that the 'task of imparting education belongs primarily to the family', there are too 'duties and rights vested in civil society inasmuch as it is its function to provide for the common good in temporal matters'. Education is however 'in a very special way the concern of the Church, not only because the Church must be recognized as a human society capable of providing education, but especially as it has the duty of proclaiming the way of salvation' (Vatican II, 1975: 728–9). In universities and institutions of higher learning, including teacher education, 'the Church endeavours systematically to ensure that the treatment of the individual disciplines is consonant with their own principles, their own methods, and with a liberty of scientific enquiry': 'Its object is that a progressively deeper understanding of them may be achieved, and by a careful attention to the current problems of these changing times and to the researching being undertaken, the convergence of faith and reason in the one truth may be seen more clearly'. This follows the tradition 'of the doctors of the Church and especially St. Thomas Aquinas': 'Thus the Christian outlook should acquire . . . a public, stable and universal influence in the whole process of the development of higher culture.' Those so educated should both be 'ready to undertake the more responsible duties of society' and also 'to be witnesses in the world to the true faith' (Vatican II, 1975: 735). Vatican II's is accommodating to developments in the secular sciences, conscious of the role of Christian education to wider society and yet uncompromising on the principles of faith.

In the closing years of the twentieth century, the Catholic Church reiterated these principles in the *Religious Dimension of Education in a Catholic School* (Vatican, 1997) and *The Catholic School on the Threshold of the Third Millennium* (Vatican, 1998). While none of the recognition of the contributions of the secular sciences or the wider contribution of the church in and through education is disregarded, the latter document arguably introduces a tone pertinent to a more acute sense of the dominance of said secular influences, one which recalls the perceived dangers made explicit in particular by the influences of the 1864 *Syllabus of Errors*:

> The threshold of the third millennium education faces new challenges which are the result of a new socio-political and cultural context. First and foremost, we have a crisis of values which, in highly developed societies in particular, assumes the form, often exalted by the media, of subjectivism, moral relativism and nihilism. The extreme pluralism pervading contemporary society leads to behaviour patterns which are at times so opposed to one another as to undermine any idea of community identity . . . The phenomena of multiculturalism and an increasingly multi-ethnic and multi-religious society is at the same time an enrichment and a source of further problems. To this we must add, in countries of long-standing evangelization, a growing marginalization of the Christian faith as a reference point and a source of light for an effective and convincing interpretation of existence. (Vatican, 1998: paragraph 1)

In education, the document recognizes the broadened scope of educational institutions and those secular disciplines (vis-a-vis our consideration of the early church):

> The sciences of education, which concentrated in the past on the study of the child and teacher-training, have been widened to include the various stages of life, and the different spheres and situations beyond the school. New requirements have given force to the demand for new contents, new capabilities and new educational models besides those followed traditionally. Thus education and schooling become particularly difficult today. (Vatican, 1998: paragraph 2)

This pressingly secular context calls, it argues, 'for courageous renewal on the part of the Catholic school':

> The precious heritage of the experience gained over the centuries reveals its vitality precisely in the capacity for prudent innovation. And so, now as in the past, the Catholic school must be able to speak for itself effectively and convincingly. It is not merely a question of adaptation, but of missionary thrust, the fundamental duty to evangelize, to go towards men and women wherever they are, so that they may receive the gift of salvation. (Vatican, 1998: paragraph 3)

Here is outlined the relationship between the school, religious education and religious life, the school 'cannot be considered separately from other educational institutions and administered as an entity apart, but must be related to the world of politics, economy, culture and society as a whole' (Vatican, 1998: paragraph 17).

Different national contexts will manifest greatly different challenges for Catholic education so framed. Historically, these challenges have included fundamental legal obstacles to any Catholic education (in England, for instance, it was only after the 1829 'Act of Emancipation' that such schools were permissible). In a political current of anti-Catholicism, McAfee's (1998) treatment, for instance, of religion and race in 1870s American public education shows a vastly different context from England in the decade of the 1870 Education Act, and a contrast to the progressively more positive if nuanced acknowledgement by successive US administrations of non-public state education, especially the contributions of religious agencies (McAndrews, 2006). In contemporary context, where international human rights legislation provides a theoretically universal legitimacy for schools of a religious character, Catholic schools still face the particular policy and related institutional challenges of different national contexts (Hayes and Gearon, 2002; McLaughlin et al., 1996). Ward (2011) provides a recent overview of Catholic educational provision in England and Wales, including support by the Catholic Education Service of England and Wales, as well as detailing how these national school contexts are underpinned by the universal principles of Vatican teaching which I detailed earlier. This relationship between national institutional frameworks and universally applicable guidance on Catholic education is a principle known as subsidiarity, where the church essentially delegates to local and national context the day-to-day working authority of ministry, here of education.

In all, critical tensions in both historical and contemporary context are generally discernible. We can say these relate in complex ways to tensions between religious and secular authority, in matters political as well as educational and intellectual. These we have seen can be traced not to antiquity. Perhaps another pertinent and more generalizable feature of education according to religious principles – and one not simply relevant to subsidiarity in Catholic education – is the manner in which the sources of religious authority in education often transcend or originate beyond national boundaries.

The Church of England

This notion that sources of religious authority in education transcend or originate beyond national boundaries is less easy to assert, of course, in relation to national church contexts such as the Church of England, but its principles of course do not originate within the state, and through the worldwide Anglican Communion extend beyond it.

Education and especially religious education remains at the heart of the very mission of the Church of England. The Durham Report (Ramsey, 1970) thereby explicitly focused on the 'fourth R', namely religion (playing on the preeminence of traditional English education of the three 'Rs' of 'reading, writing and arithmetic'). In institutional terms, *The Way Ahead: Church of England Schools in the New Millennium*, published in 2001, clearly articulated such principles (Dearing, 2001); or rather rearticulated those tenets of principle which had been central to the Church of England since its foundation. The need for the institutional structures of schools for the faith of the nation was recognized long before the 1870 Education Act which made elementary education compulsory in England. The Dearing Report, much in the way Willaime has outlined for wider European context, recognized the need to be both 'inclusive' of growing religious diversity, and also the need to maintain a 'distinctive' Christian ethos, curriculum and outlook through mission.

A decade later, *The Church School of the Future* (Chadwick et al., 2012), the Church of England thus 'reaffirms that Church schools stand at the centre of its mission'. In this regard, the report recognized that the Anglican Church as a major provider of schools needs to strengthen and clarify the assertion of this role at governmental, synodical, diocesan and local levels', that this 'approach is essential if the Church's mission and ministry to education through its school system is to thrive'. A time of rapidly changing institutional school forms, in any form of partnership, the report stresses that these need to be always based on 'strongly held core values and the essential Christian ethos'. Relationships with state authority at the local and national level must be underpinned and strengthened by partnerships between parishes and their local schools and local community, including the relationship between school managers and clergy. As Dearing had mentioned a decade earlier, the Chadwick Report deals to a great degree with such institutional matters and how the Church of England can maintain its system of schools and the considerable task of educating over a million young people in primary and secondary contexts.

In both of the latter, the Chadwick Report stresses distinctiveness 'is about more than organisational arrangements and designation as a school of religious character': 'It must include a wholehearted commitment to putting faith and spiritual development at the heart of the curriculum and ensuring that a Christian ethos permeates the whole educational experience.' And here the role of religious education is seen as paramount: 'High-quality religious education (RE) and collective worship should continue to make major contributions to the Church school's Christian ethos, to allow pupils to engage seriously with and develop an understanding of the person and teachings of Jesus Christ' (Chadwick, 2012: 4).

Janina Ainsworth, director of the National Society indicated something of the scale of provision within the Church of England. In addition to around 1,000 independent schools (among a total of 1,300 in England), over 4,800 schools in England are Church of England schools. Each school is located within one of the 43 Church of England dioceses, each with its own Diocesan Board of Education. The terms of the Diocesan Boards of Education charge these schools to 'promote or assist in the promotion of religious education and religious worship in schools in the diocese and in the promotion of church schools in the diocese'.

Diocesan directors of Education and their staff support all the church schools in relation to buildings, funding, inspection and curriculum. Support for church schools comes in the form of guidance, advice and support from local and national bodies including local authorities, Diocesan Boards of Education and The National Society. The National Society, founded as we noted in 1811, 'exists to inform and encourage Church schools throughout England and Wales and to promote Christian education with national and local government and other national organisations'. Strategic activities include:

- the development and management of Section 48 inspections – the Statutory Inspection of Anglican Schools (SIAS),
- providing a national church vision on education,
- promoting the development of standards in and provision of schools and
- providing professional support for school advisers and officers working for Diocesan Boards of Education (Ainsworth, 2011).

The curriculum aims of a Church of England school 'aims to be distinctively Christian and inclusive to all children, young people and their families. Church schools follow the national statutory curriculum', their distinctiveness residing 'in putting spiritual development at the heart of the curriculum, within a community rooted in Christian values' (Ainsworth, 2011; see also www.christianvalues4schools.co.uk/).

In this context, the Church of England accepts the broad terms of *Religious Education in English Schools* (QCA, 2010):

> Religion and beliefs inform our values and are reflected in what we say and how we behave. RE is an important subject in itself, developing an individual's knowledge and understanding of the religions and beliefs which form part of contemporary society. Religious education provokes challenging questions about the ultimate meaning and purpose of life, beliefs about God, the self and the nature of reality, issues of right and wrong, and what it means to be 'human.' In this it accedes to the notion that religious education develops pupils' knowledge and understanding of Christianity, of other principal religions, other religious traditions and worldviews that offer answers to questions such as these. (Ainsworth, 2011)

But the Church of England endorses this framework with the qualification that religious education 'is not just an academic subject, but, lying at the very heart of the curriculum, has an important role in reflecting and conveying the distinctively Christian character of the school'.

Religious education in church schools is expected to help pupils to:

- think theologically and explore the great questions of life and death, meaning and purpose;
- reflect critically on the truth claims of Christian belief;
- see how the truth of Christianity is relevant today and face the challenge of Jesus's teaching in a pluralist and postmodern society;
- develop the skills to handle the Bible text;
- recognize that faith is not based on a positive balance of probabilities but on commitment to a particular way of understanding God and the world;
- respond in terms of beliefs, commitments and ways of living;
- develop a sense of themselves as significant, unique and precious;
- experience the breadth and variety of the Christian community;
- engage in thoughtful dialogue with other faiths and traditions;
- become active citizens, serving their neighbour;
- find a reason for hope in a troubled world; and
- understand how religious faith can sustain them in difficult circumstances and in the face of opposition (Ainsworth, 2011).

In terms of inspection, the religious life of such schools, including its ethos and its religious education, is governed by the special provisions of Section 48 of the Education Act 2005 which 'evaluates the distinctiveness and effectiveness of the school as a church school'. The Statutory Inspection of Anglican Schools (SIAS) framework focuses on four questions:

1. How well does the school, through its distinctive Christian character, meet the needs of all learners?
2. What is the impact of collective worship on the school community?
3. How effective is the religious education? (This only applies to voluntary aided (VA) schools.)
4. How effective are the leadership and management of the school as a church school? (Ainsworth, 2011).

The National Society assists in providing guidance on fulfilling these requirements for both inspectors and schools themselves. Teachers 'of all religious beliefs and none are welcomed to work in any church school provided they will work within the school's Christian ethos and distinctive church school character'.

Judaism

After Christian schools, Jewish schools have the oldest tradition as part of education in Britain. Jewish schools, though, as with all the religious traditions, schooling within Judaism is of considerable antiquity:

The first Jewish school in the UK, established in 1732, still exists to this day. The Jews Free School (JFS) has moved across several sites over the centuries but today is in Kenton in North West London and is the largest Jewish schools in the country with over 2000 pupils. But not all Jewish schools are this large. At present there are around 100 Jewish schools in England, of which about 40 are voluntary aided and the remainder are independent. (NB – there are no voluntary controlled or foundation Jewish schools or Academies with a Jewish character). These schools range in size from small (1 form entry or less) to very large (over 2000 pupils) and they are diverse in terms of the particular denominations within Judaism that they serve. The majority of Jewish schools are in London but there are also schools in Manchester, Leeds, Liverpool, Birmingham and Glasgow. (Lawton, 2011)

As these schools 'represent different denominations within Judaism, the religious authority overseeing schools also varies':

The Chief Rabbi is the religious authority for the largest grouping of Jewish VA schools (www.chiefrabbi.org) and in the maintained sector, the two significant Jewish educational bodies which could be likened to diocesan authorities are the United Synagogue (www.theus.org.uk), which takes the Chief Rabbi as its religious authority and therefore represents the mainstream orthodox Jewish community, and the Jewish Community Day School Advisory Board, part of the Leo Baeck College (www.lbc.ac.uk), which represents the progressive Jewish community. (Lawton, 2011)

Today, according to Lawton, 'approximately 60 per cent of Jewish children of school age attend Jewish schools compared to around 25 per cent 30 years ago' and there now 'more than 26,000 Jewish pupils attending Jewish schools compared to less than 13,000 some 30 years ago and as of January 2009, there were 15,500 children in maintained Jewish schools and 12,000 in independent Jewish schools'. Indeed, about 'sixty per cent of school age Jews now attend Jewish schools' which are in the majority voluntary aided.

Other forms include of Jewish education include:

In modern times, Charedi education [which] is characterised by a very deep commitment to learning the classic texts of Judaism, particularly the Talmud for boys and the Torah and its midrashic commentaries for girls, so that Charedi schools – almost all private and usually fairly small – will devote most of a long school day to this study, reserving only perhaps a couple of hours a day for secular studies. (Lawton, 2011)

Lawton emphasizes how deeply ingrained and central education is within the Jewish community:

In Charedi communities learning is the norm and many men will restrict their earning capacity to spend more time learning. For example, a shop keeper might open his shop for fairly restricted hours so that he can attend classes and seminars. Luckily, other Charedim in the area who probably frequent his shop will be happy to shop with him in his restricted hours since they too will want to get along to the classes! Thus learning in these communities is something to be done by adults and prepared for by children. A young Charedi man walking along the road with earphones plugged in is much more likely to be listening to a Talmudic discourse than any kind of music. Women learn too but usually their learning will be more generalised and discursive, rather than text based, but that is changing especially amongst the Modern Orthodox and women's seminaries are growing up which provide at least an intensive learning programme for a gap year or more after school. The rise of learning for women is starting to challenge traditional understandings of how far women can take leadership roles in the religious dimensions of Jewish communities. (Lawton, 2011)

According to Lawton, only around 20 per cent of Jews in the United Kingdom do not receive some formal Jewish education, but such children will nevertheless 'attend part-time classes, usually on a Sunday morning and usually only up to the age of Bat or Bar Mitzvah (12 or 13 years old)'. Though Lawton considers this 'a far less satisfactory arrangement for Jewish education', he suggests 'parents might make this choice because they do not live near a Jewish school or because they feel it is more important for their children to integrate into non-Jewish society as early as possible' (Lawton, 2011).

Hinduism

There are at present (2012) two Hindu schools in the United Kingdom: Swaminarayan School (www.swaminarayan.brent.sch.uk/); and the Krishna Avanti Primary School (www.krishna-avanti.org.uk/). The Hindu Academy, according to Jay Lakhani 'has been promoting education in Hinduism through mainstream schools and colleges' (visit www.hindu-academy.org). Formerly known as the Vivekananda Centre, the Hindu Academy has been open for over 20 years. It is 'a non-sectarian body and aims to present a broad and comprehensive vision of Hinduism', the aims of the academy are:

- To promote a structured study of Hinduism leading to GCSE, AS and A2 qualifications in Hinduism.
- The academy operates nationally and runs classes in Hinduism at many cities and locations in London.
- It interacts with schools in both the private and public sectors and helps with assemblies, seminars and discussions for sixth forms.
- It also offers Hindu input towards PGCE courses at several British universities.
- The academy offers a pluralistic vision of religion which sits well with a science-oriented (secular and humanist) worldview.
- The academy continues to offer a rational contribution in the media on many contemporary issues relating to Hinduism (like Shambo the bull or open air cremations) (Lakhani, 2011).

Islam

The move for Muslim communities to provide children within them a Muslim education dates to the early 1980s. As Trevathan says, 'just exactly what this is has precipitated much debate' but '[w]hatever the case may be, there is little doubt that it has been instigated by the fear of an encroaching secular outlook provided by British education':

> The anxiety is that Muslim values are dissipated within the young as a result of undergoing such an education. On the other hand there is a significant number of Muslims who, wishing their children to succeed within British society, actively encourage their children's attendance within state provided schools. The result is a mixed bag of initiatives. (Trevathan, 2011)

By far the most common form of such Muslim education is 'the after school or weekend madrasahs or schools' which 'usually centre around the local mosque for the purpose of getting children to read and memorize the Quran'. Even those 'who look favourably at state provided education may well require their children's attendance at these madrasahs'. Travathan highlights 'a growing criticism of these initiatives based on dissatisfaction with rote learning, ill educated imam and a propensity for corporal punishment' (Trevathan, 2011).

Other Muslim schools are 'the *Dar al Ulooms* (Place of Knowledge)' which are also known as also madrasahs: 'Many of these tend to exist in the Midlands and northern areas of England and cater primarily though not exclusively to children of Pakistani and Bengali youth. One renowned school of this nature is the Dewsbury Markaz with a school population of 600 boarding and day pupils.' These schools 'are usually private boarding schools and the curriculum is devoted almost entirely to what is termed the Muslim Sciences (or Disciplines). The aim here is to produce Imams (Mosque prayer leaders), Ulama (theologians/scholars) or Hufuz (those who have memorized the Qur'an)' (Trevathan, 2011). With classes held mainly in Urdu and Arabic, Trevathan stresses that 'such madrasahs should not be immediately equated with extremism given the notoriety that the word has gained through media coverage':

> The word madrasah simply means school but usually equated with a full Muslim curriculum. Many of these institutions provide what would be considered, on an unbiased and closer inspection, a classical liberal education insofar that they are thoroughly grounded in things like Greek logic and rhetoric and complex theological and philosophical arguments. Should one replace the Ancient Greek or Latin with the Arabic language the picture is further complemented. It may come as a surprise that many of those who graduate from such institutions are well equipped to take on Higher Education Degrees within British universities as a result. (Trevathan, 2011)

Other schools have an ostensibly Western and secular curriculum. These are often 'private and cater mainly for the middle professional classes' but 'established and maintained by Muslims for Muslims', though in principle open to children of all faiths or none. The King Fahd Academy in London is cited by Trevathan as an example. Founded by the Saudi embassy, diplomats' children are among those served along with a diverse London Muslim community, though mainly Arab in terms of cultural background.

In addition to these, there are Muslim VA schools 'that are to be equated with Anglican, Catholic or Jewish schools', supported in part by funding from local education authorities, such schools being required to teach the National Curriculum and subject to the same inspection framework as other schools receiving similar financial support. The rationale for such schools is also similar to the arguments offered by other religious traditions that Muslims as taxpayers, like Anglicans and Catholics have a right to have their religion represented in the British education system. During the Thatcher years a mounted struggle took place for such ventures by segments of the community headed by Yusuf Islam (formerly Cat Stevens). Resistance from governmental authorities were perceived as being composed of fears of educating a 'fifth column' of Muslims at the expense of the state. In 1998 with the advent of the Labour government coming to power, the first Muslim Voluntary School, the Islamia Primary was allowed. Several other ventures followed and there are presently nine schools of this nature now established. Currently, there are approximately nineteen of such schools in various stages of the application process. (Trevathan, 2011)

It is with regard to the establishment of Muslim education within the British system that Trevathan argues that this 'has precipitated a wider debate on faith schools generally'. There have always been secular objections to schools of a religious character. These secular arguments have now broadened as well as intensified.

For and against faith schools

The literature for and against educational – curricular and institutional – provision centred on faith is wide and often polemical. Debate generally centres on whether it is the role of the state to provide financial support for schools of a religious character or whether such schools, especially in the religious ethos and education they provide, is a social good or, in the most extreme forms of the counter-argument, a positive harm not only for society as a whole but for the well-being and development of children.

Halstead (2011) outlines seven arguments for and against faith schools. The arguments supporting them state:

- minorities have the right to maintain their social, cultural and religious identity;
- the more general right, enshrined in human rights law (notably Article 2 of the European Convention on Human Rights; see also the foundational Article 26 of the UN Universal Declaration of Human Rights);
- faith schools offer an environment for the development of students' identity;
- plural societies respect and have a commitment to 'group rights' and faith schools are an important aspect of this;
- faith schools provide a coherent moral framework within students' religious tradition;
- faith schools have higher than average levels of academic attainment (see the websites of the National Society or Catholic Education Service of England and Wales for evidence that this argument is often used by religious traditions themselves); and
- faith schools provide 'an environment where the spiritual side of life is valued and taken seriously', including 'the links between religion and other areas of human achievement'.

Arguments against them state:

- faith schools make it 'more difficult for children to grow into autonomous adults (a central aim of liberal education)';

- covertly or overtly, faith schools indoctrinate children;
- faith schools may 'encourage children to develop certain fundamentalist or extremist views';
- faith schools are socially divisive;
- faith schools do not contribute as much as state schools to civic values and or social and community cohesion;
- faith schools enshrine social and economic equality by covert admissions criteria and selection; and
- the 'public funding of faith schools is an unjustifiable violation of conscience for taxpayers who are non-believers' (adapted from Halstead, 2012: 103–7; see also Jackson, 2003).

Halstead provides of the more balanced treatments a debate often framed in more polemical terms, and whose origins date in England to the Swann Report (DfES, 1985).

The Swann Report examined wide political and educational issues for an increasingly 'multicultural' Britain. The teaching of religion in schools soon became bound up with (what are now still heated) debates around multiculturalism, racism and British identity. Hull's (1990) editorial for the *British Journal of Religious Education* argued that the promotion of the superior truth of one faith was 'religionism', equating 'religionism' with racism. Hull's argument is as much about theology and epistemology as legality. He argues that, religions, though plural, essentially, are different manifestations of the same ultimate truth. It is an educational version of the pluralist argument from philosophical theology (e.g. as espoused by Hick, 1989). Swann was published only 3 years before the 1988 Education Reform Act and this would enshrine similar attitudes towards the nature of religion in legislation. Though religious education should, stated the act, be in the main Christian, there was now a legal requirement to teach 'the principal religions represented in Britain' (see Hull, 1989). This enshrined in law a recognition of Christianity which was in classroom practice receding even as the law came into effect (see Thompson, 2004). Despite the inelegant language and theology of Hull's phrase 'religionism' for teachers and school children, this notion has become a default position through a carte blanche legal and educational equality of status for all religions.

In England, the National Secular Society and the British Humanist Association, with high-profile support, provide less than decorous attacks on religion and faith schools. But there is something more fundamental usually in operation. As Halstead points out, some people 'find religious schools unacceptable simply because they find religion unacceptable' (Halstead, 2012: 107).

Summary

A growing and increasingly systematic scepticism of Christianity and religion in general marked the intellectual milieu of the 1870 Education Act. This would, as we shall see, directly impact upon the purposes and pedagogies of religious education.

However, in England and many countries, a 'dual system' allowed for the continued existence of schools of a religious character. In England such schools were funded by the state. Even in countries where such funding was not available (for instance, in France and America) private faith schools continued to exist, which did and do retain the link between religious education and the religious life. In countries such as England, though, the dual system has been directly impacted in distinctive ways by the logic of Willaime's double constraint of legal framework and sociological conditions. In sociological terms, religious plurality has meant demands from diverse religious communities for their own schools. In law, state funding available for Catholic and Protestant schools has been extended to other religious traditions.

In *Rethinking Religious Education and Plurality*, Jackson (2004) concludes that religious education faces two requirements for its future success: teachers knowledgeable in world religions and pedagogical consensus over the subject's aims and purposes. Cush's (2007) paper 'Should Religious Studies Be Part of the Compulsory State School Curriculum?' declares in relation to these two requirements: 'I believe that we are not far from the first, and already working towards the second': 'At a number of international conferences, I have been impressed that in spite of areas of disagreement, particularly between those working in confessional religious education and those working in non-confessional contexts, there has been surprising agreement as to the aims of religious education, especially among practising teachers.' At such conferences, she suggests, 'teachers from many different contexts basically agreed that the aim of religious education is threefold – putting it very simply':

> To understand, respect and get on with others who may hold different beliefs, values and traditions from our own; to develop tools for critical and reflexive thinking about our own beliefs and values and those of others, and using the insights gained from studying religious and non-religious beliefs, values and traditions to address some of the crucial issues facing humanity such as peace and conflict, human rights, wealth and poverty and the natural environment. This approach to religious education can be employed in contexts that are either 'confessional' or 'nonconfessional' in overall emphasis. (Cush, 2007: 225)

I have attended over the same period many of the same international conferences and it can be admitted that there is some degree of consensus amongst delegates – from organizations such as AULRE (the Association for University Lecturers in Religion and Education); EFTRE (the European Forum for Teachers of Religious Education) and ISREV (the International Seminar in Religious Education and Values).

But representative as these aims of religious education may be, in secular religious education teaching there remains (as Chapter 5 demonstrates) continued disagreement about these aims and their accompanying pedagogies. Cush's suggestion, however, that consensus of stated religious education aims extends to faith traditions is simply not supportable. Though faith traditions have made some accommodation to the aims of religious education in secular contexts, such aims are not and never could be sufficient in these faith contexts where religious education remains an integral part of the religious life.

As we might expect, justification for secular religious education finds support from those quarters which question the educational validity of religious education in faith contexts, often described as and denigrated by the label 'confessional'. But even from secular quarters, the support for secular religious education is not unqualified. If the arguments for and against faith schools are different from those for and against religious education, they are now often conflated.

The next chapter examines how religious education fares and is formed by the secularity which frames such debate. The alliance between religious education and secularity, it can be shown, is not always an easy one.

Religious Education and Secularity: Issues of Cohesion, Diversity, Pluralism

4

Chapter Outline

Introduction

The first chapter identified how the contemporary interface of religion, politics and education reflects modern-world variations on ancient disputes. The second chapter outlined how political agendas around these issues have come to dominate research agendas for religion in education. The proximity of developments in the second is directly related to developments in the first. Religious education and the wider contexts of religion in education have come then to be closely associated with, in widest sense, the political. The political is arguably the leading rationale for religious education today, that is, religious education makes a recognizable contribution in the coherence of societies which are culturally diverse and religiously plural. We have seen that a problem of political liberalism has taken on pedagogic form. The contemporary role of religion in public and political life is the most commonly used justification for religious education's inclusion in the curriculum. While all religious traditions have a natural interest in cultural, social and political life, the risk is that this political-pedagogical move reduces religion to its public and broadly conceived political dimensions. This is to limit religion to its social usefulness, that is, principally to issues of cohesion, diversity and plurality.

This occurs most markedly where religious education in secular state provision has been separated from the religious life. The third chapter showed the far wider scope of religious education within the faith school context. Here there is resistance to the breakage between religious education and the religious life. This is not to say that religious traditions reject involvement in social and political involvement. Histories of religion show that social and political involvement is an integral part of at least the moral commitment of religions.

The story of the Anglo-Saxon king from Bede's *Ecclesiastical History* remains paradigmatic: the story of the king's conversion does not mean the setting aside of politics but the recognition of its temporal limitations.

This profound shift has occurred due to the involvement of political agencies, the state primarily, in religious education itself. State involvement in religious education then not unnaturally leads inevitably to state-directed aims for the subject as for any other subject. In effect, this means or has meant an historical separation in such contexts of religious education from the religious life. So the problem for state religious education is historical and deeply intractable. In its separation from the religious life, it has needed to seek foundations in secular alternatives. I am using the notion of secularity in as neutral a way as possible, simply to mean that which is not determined by religion. Historically, for example, even at the height of medieval Christendom, the ecclesiastical authority of the pope vested in the political authority of kings the right to reign in their own temporal domains. Augustine's definition of the two cities, the earthly city and the city of God, would mean, however, that the former would always be answerable to the latter.

The history of modernity from Reformation to the present has been the story of a shifting of this ecclesiastical authority into the realm of secular political power. Thus it needs to be noted that in its most commonly used current forms, the secular has in recent centuries taken on a meaning associated with a lessening of religious influence, and from the Enlightenment onwards, a series of radical alternatives to religion. These have been ideological and political as well as epistemological, marked across the natural sciences, the social and psychological sciences, as well as philosophy.

In secular *epistemological* terms, the natural, social and psychological sciences, as well as philosophy have maintained their ascendant position in secular institutions, from schools to universities. These secular epistemological frameworks have, as we shall see in Chapter 5, dramatically shaped religious education. Still, these secular epistemological alternatives to religion have hardly seen religious life replaced by them.

In secular *political* terms, however, religion remains in a strong position, and worldwide continues to hold a prominent role in public and political life. In these same secular political terms, the persistence of religion has been a marked problem in political liberalism. In educational terms, Willaime has shown that the double constraint of legal and sociological factors have shaped and influenced the religious education curriculum. In the last chapter, in England at least, we have seen how these same legal and sociological factors have shaped and influenced too the institutional diversity of religiously plural faith schools. In terms of a political secularity, religion remains a problem for secular politics *and* education: How can social and community cohesion be achieved amidst cultural diversity and religious pluralism? The curricula impact on this problem has been twofold, not only on religious education, as we have noted, but also on citizenship education. While some citizenship education is explicitly engaged with historical perspective (Heater, 2004), much current work in this field seems to have accepted the political principles with limited historical perspective (reviews of contemporary citizenship education research include: Arthur and Davies, 2008; Arthur et al., 2008; Osler and Starkey, 2006). In work I previously undertook on human rights education (Gearon, 2004), it was in this context, as in others (Gearon, 2008), where I emphasized not only the need for but the necessity of constantly reinterrogating historical perspective, a view endorsed by Forest (2004) in the Fall 2004 issue of the *Harvard Educational Research*.

Issues of cohesion, diversity, pluralism

Citizenship education

The late Sir Bernard Crick was a pivotal figure in the introduction of citizenship, a national curriculum subject in England, as the lead author of *Education for Citizenship and the Teaching of Democracy in Schools: The Final Report of the Advisory Group on Citizenship* (Crick, 1998). In his introduction to Derek Heater's (2004) *History of Citizenship Education*, Crick provides a fourfold definition of citizenship:

> Firstly, it can refer simply to a subject's rights and duties to be recognised as a legally permanent inhabitant of a state – irrespective of the system of government of that state; but the principles behind such recognition can vary greatly, especially in relation to migrants. Secondly, it can refer to the more specific belief (often called 'civic republicanism' . . .) that countries that enjoy constitutional government, representative government or democracy depend upon a high degree of active participation by inhabitants who themselves as active citizens, not simply good subjects. Thirdly, it can refer to an ideal (once held by the Stoics of antiquity, now often called 'global citizenship') that we should all act as citizens of one world: that for the sake of peace, justice and human rights there must be limitations of international law on the sovereignty and power of individual states' powers. And fourthly, 'citizenship' can refer to an educational process; learning and teaching in schools and colleges show how to improve or achieve the aims inherent in the second and third meanings. (Crick, 2004: 2)

In November 1997, following proposals in the education White Paper, *Excellence in Schools*, the secretary of state for Education and Employment pledged 'to strengthen education for citizenship and the teaching of democracy in schools', and to that end set up this advisory group with the following terms of reference: 'To provide advice on effective education for citizenship in schools – to include the nature and practices of participation in democracy; the duties, responsibilities and rights of individuals as citizens; and the value to individuals and society of community

activity.' The framework document setting out the group's terms of reference explained that it would cover: 'the teaching of civics, participative democracy and citizenship, and may be taken to include some understanding of democratic practices and institutions, including parties, pressure groups and voluntary bodies, and the relationship of formal political activity with civic society in the context of the UK, Europe and the wider world [and] an element of the way in which expenditure and taxation work, together with a grasp of the underlying economic realities of adult life.' The framework document also made clear that the secretary of state expected the main outcomes of the group's work to be: 'a statement of the aims and purposes of citizenship education in schools; a broad framework for what good citizenship education in schools might look like, and how it can be successfully delivered – covering opportunities for teaching about citizenship. Within and outside the formal curriculum and the development of personal and social skills through projects linking schools and the community, volunteering and the involvement of pupils in the development of school rules and policies.'

A political scientist, and incidentally the first official biographer of George Orwell, Crick clearly envisaged a secular political framework for citizenship as a subject, seeing its origins in pre-Christian classical tradition: 'In the political tradition stemming from the Greek city states and the Roman republic, citizenship has meant involvement in public affairs by those who had the rights of citizens: to take part in public debate and, directly or indirectly, in shaping the laws and decisions of a state. In modern times, however, democratic ideas led to constant demands to broaden the franchise from a narrow citizen class of the educated and the property owners, to achieve female emancipation, to lower the voting age, to achieve freedom of the press and to open up the processes of government.' This, for Crick, provided the opportunity for a more informed 'citizen democracy', one which could be facilitated through citizenship as a distinct subject in the curriculum.

The national curriculum framework which emerged drew directly from the definition of the component elements of citizenship from Marshall (1950), a threefold framework:

- *Social and moral responsibility.* Children learning from the beginning, self-confidence and socially and morally responsible behaviour both in and beyond the classroom, both towards those in authority and towards each other.
- *Community involvement.* Pupils learning about and becoming helpfully involved in the life and concerns of their communities, including learning through community involvement and service to the community.
- *Political literacy.* Pupils learning about and how to make themselves effective in public life through knowledge, skills and values (Crick, 1998).

In national curriculum terms this would be translated as:

- knowledge and understanding about becoming informed citizens;
- developing skills of enquiry and communication; and
- developing skills of participation and responsible action (DfEE, 1999).

Citizenship was conceived as part of an historically determined secular framework. There was no reference to religion, and even cultural diversity played little part in its formulation.

The events of 9/11 in America, the riots in northern English cities in November of that year, the 2004 Madrid bombings and in England the four coordinated '7/7' attacks in London in 2005 all provided a political backdrop to a perceived urgency that citizenship education should contribute more to matters of social and community cohesion. The largely inter-ethnic disturbances of 2001 in Bradford, Burnley and Oldham led the Home Office to publish the Cantle Report on Community Cohesion (Home Office, 2002). The Cantle Report argued for greater regard to school ethos which reflected cultural diversity within school themselves and the wider community. The Cantle Report also recommended that citizenship education should do more to address these issues. The need for increased emphasis to be placed upon community and social cohesion across education found a new urgency after the 7/7 bombings. A Commission on Integration and Cohesion (CIC) followed. A key finding of their final report, *Our Shared Future*, saw the matter not as local or national but worldwide: 'Major international events, such as 11 September 2001 and the London bombings in July 2005, have contributed to the debate on community cohesion and shared values, particularly because the latter were perpetrated by British-born Muslims.' It urged that in 'the wake of these events, community cohesion is a key focus for the Government' (CIC, 2007).

A former headteacher, Sir Keith Ajegbo was commissioned to examine what citizenship education could contribute to issues of diversity. The 'Ajegbo Report', the *Diversity and Citizenship Review* (DCSF, 2007) as well as its own deliberations on national and international events presented a series of findings and recommendations. Finding 14 shows the importance of historical perspective in education: 'In order for young people to explore how we live together in the United Kingdom today and to debate the values we share, it is important they consider issues that have shaped the development of UK society – and to understand them through the lens of history' (Ajegbo, 2007: 96). Of course, what history citizen educators have historically chosen as significant is critical. It is not the longer view of Christian influence but the more recent history which is seen as critical, and thus the report recommends attention to:

- contextualized understanding that the United Kingdom is a 'multinational' state, made up of England, Northern Ireland, Scotland and Wales;
- immigration;
- Commonwealth and the legacy of Empire;
- European Union; and
- extending the franchise (e.g. the legacy of slavery, universal suffrage, equal opportunities legislation) (Ajegbo, 2007: 12).

Like Enlightenment political advocates of citizenship, and their precursors democracy, rights and the social contract (from Hobbes and Locke through to Rousseau and Paine), the contemporary proponents of citizenship education (Dewey through to Crick) regarded religion, and particularly it must be said Christianity, as part of the political problem, an obstacle to those rights and models of democratic governance which the eighteenth century largely introduced in incipient form. Like Crick, Ajegbo was ideologically resistant then to a history earlier than those in which modern-day diversity was apparent. It is in this light that we must see the critical Recommendation 22, which underscored the necessity that citizenship education should include a new 'explicitly developed' stand, entitled 'Identity and Diversity: Living Together in the UK'. This strand, the report states, 'will bring together three conceptual components':

1. critical thinking about ethnicity, religion and 'race';
2. an explicit link to political issues and values; and
3. the use of contemporary history in teachers' pedagogy to illuminate thinking about contemporary issues relating to citizenship (Ajegbo, 2007: 6–12).

The revised National Curriculum (2007) did then subsequently include a new core strand of 'Identities and Diversity: Living Together in the UK'.

Besides encouraging developments emergent from the Cantle Report, including the latter developments in citizenship education, the Home Office developed a dual strategy which, along with education, indeed often in collaboration with education, launched the Prevent Agenda which, under Labour and Conservative-Liberal Coalition governments have sought ways of using education for facilitating not only the political goals of social and community cohesion but a more narrowly conceived security agenda (Home Office, 2005, 2011a–c). We see here a UK national agenda which mirrors in education the political and security concerns apparent in diverse agencies: from the CIA and USCIRF in America; the OSCE in Europe, internationally across UNESCO (especially UNESCO, 2006, 2011); and in the specific offices of the UN Special Rapporteur on Freedom of Religion or Belief. All of these agencies have, as previous chapters have demonstrated, shown an interest in religion, some offering practical interventions with regard to religion in education.

We can conclude then that there has been a heightened role for issues of social cohesion, especially around diversity and pluralism, providing in turn a heightened role for religion in citizenship education, which has historically tended to be defined in narrow secular terms. The main exemplars above are related to developments in England, but there is a burgeoning international policy and research literature now on the ways in which citizenship education can make a contribution to social cohesion through addressing cultural diversity and religious pluralism.

Religious education

If citizenship has been so affected by issues of cohesion, diversity and pluralism, we need barely note from foregoing chapters that religious education has been unarguably impacted. Manifest through European REDCo research and pedagogy and the AAR report on teaching religion in public schools, increasing political emphases – invariably again around issues of cohesion, diversity and pluralism – mean religious education's contribution here is doing much to define the subject. While it has given the subject renewed justification, such moves also risk limiting religious education to its public and political face.

Jackson's (2004) *Rethinking Religious Education and Plurality* is a critical text here; the interest it generated was arguably as notable in the United States as across Europe through REDCo. In America, *Rethinking Religious Education and Plurality* was the subject of a symposium of the American Academy of Religion.

Jackson outlines six responses to religious pluralism in and through religious education: (1) various defensive retreats from plurality and denials of its impact on 'social and personal identity', associated with linkages either to identity of British and Christian identity and 'Christian indoctrination'; (2) the retreat from religious pluralism to 'private or semi-private space', commitment to education within a faith tradition, a position which argues 'religious education should only take place in such schools, and is an anachronism in the common, secular school'; (3) a radical postmodern approach ('a normative postmodern pluralism') which fully embraces plurality, dispenses with 'oppressive' traditions and divisions between them, and in religious education encourages children and young people essentially to create and shape their own faith narratives; (4) a position which recognizes plurality but which 'attempts to retain the integrity of different religions as discrete systems of belief', closely associated with religious literacy, at root a phenomenological approach; (5) acknowledges plurality but seeks to keep the debates consciously open, engaging pupils in such debates, with a theoretical emphasis on the radical differences within and between traditions which emerges from the ethnographic study of microcommunity rather than macrotradition, with a pedagogical emphasis on dialogue with and between pupils about their own plural stances; (6) the citizenship position which sees that pluralism can be dealt with as a secular subject concern in the curriculum, the extreme view of which argues that religious education is in a secular context therefore redundant; and (7) which Jackson identifies (with position 5) as his own preferred strategy, which – much as I have argued in and as if to confirm my arguments in Chapters 1 and 2 – Jackson states 'that the most appropriate pedagogical responses to plurality in the common school provide a framework of democratic values which respect diversity within the law and allow pupils to clarify and refine their own positions on religion' (Jackson, 2004: 2–3).

A closer look at the nonstatutory guidance *Religious Education in English Schools* (DCSF, 2010) reflects and provides further evidence of a growing consensus over this approach. The *Guidance* states:

> The UK has a rich heritage of culture and diversity. This is continuing today in an era of globalisation and an increasingly interdependent world. Religion and belief for many people forms a crucial part of their culture and identity. Religion and beliefs have become more visible in public life locally, nationally and internationally. The impact of religion on society and public life is constantly brought to public attention through extensive media coverage. (DCSF, 2010: 6)

The *Guidance* acknowledges wider 'rapid pace of development in scientific and medical technologies and the environmental debate' that 'present new issues which raise religious, moral and social questions', and that new internet-based forums facilitate learning and encourage participation in public discussion of such issues 'in a new and revolutionary way'. It acknowledges, naturally, that 'religious education provokes challenging questions about the ultimate meaning and purpose of life, beliefs about God, the self and the nature of reality, issues of right and wrong, and what it means to be human' and develops 'pupils' knowledge and understanding of Christianity, of other principal religions, other religious traditions and worldviews that offer answers to questions such as these'. The *Guidance* contextualizes 'religion and beliefs' as informing our values 'in what we say and how we behave' and reiterates religious education as an 'important subject in itself'; it does so by stressing its contribution to 'developing an individual's knowledge and understanding of the religions and beliefs which form part of contemporary society'. In so doing it stresses the subject's contribution to 'pupils' personal development and well-being and to community cohesion by promoting mutual respect and tolerance in a diverse society'. Thus the subject 'can also make important contributions to other parts of the school curriculum such as citizenship, personal, social, health and economic education (PSHE education), the humanities, education for sustainable development and others' (DCSF, 2010: 6–7).

The *Guidance*, citing Section 78(1) of the 2002 Education Act, states that all pupils should follow a balanced and broadly based curriculum which 'promotes the spiritual, moral, cultural, social, mental and physical development of pupils and of society, and prepares pupils for the opportunities, responsibilities and experiences of later life'. This is a variant of the defining rubric which underpinned the major Education Acts of 1944 and 1988. These spiritual and other aspects of development are referred back to political context: 'Exploring the concepts of religion and belief and their roles in the spiritual, moral and cultural lives of people in a diverse society helps individuals develop moral awareness and social understanding.' Further, in terms of 'personal development and well-being', religious education, the guidelines suggest, 'plays an important role in preparing pupils for adult life, employment and lifelong learning. It helps children and young people become successful learners, confident individuals and responsible citizens.' Though the subject is said to provide children with 'the knowledge, skills and understanding to discern and value truth and goodness', it remarks that this is through 'strengthening their capacity for making moral judgements and for evaluating different types of commitment to make positive and healthy choices' (DCSF, 2010: 6–7).

On the socio-political dimension of the subject's stated contribution to community cohesion: 'RE makes an important contribution to a school's duty to promote community cohesion. It provides a key context to develop young people's understanding and appreciation of diversity, to promote shared values and to challenge racism and discrimination.' Effective religious education '*will* promote community cohesion' (emphasis added) in each of the four identified areas:

- The school community – RE provides a positive context within which the diversity of cultures, beliefs and values can be celebrated and explored.

- The community within which the school is located – RE provides opportunities to investigate patterns of diversity of religion and belief and forge links with different groups in the local area.
- The UK community – a major focus of RE is the study of diversity of religion and belief in the UK and how this influences national life.
- The global community – RE involves the study of matters of global significance recognizing the diversity of religion and belief and its impact on world issues (DCSF, 2010: 7–8).

Religious education subject matter 'gives particular opportunities to promote an ethos of respect for others, challenge stereotypes and build understanding of other cultures and beliefs'. This contributes to promoting a positive and inclusive school ethos *that champions democratic values and human rights'* (emphasis added). These aspects of the subject are yet further reiterated, and so religious education

- also builds resilience to antidemocratic or extremist narratives, enables pupils to build their sense of identity and belonging, which helps them flourish within their communities and as citizens in a diverse society;
- teaches pupils to develop respect for others, including people of different faiths and beliefs, and helps challenge prejudice;
- prompts pupils to consider their responsibilities to themselves and to others, and to explore how they might contribute to their communities and to the wider society (DCSF, 2010: 7–8).

These goals are not however simply secular impositions. One of the distinctive models of modern state religious education, in line with its democratic values, is the incorporation of religious communities themselves. The inclusion of faith communities in state religious education has been apparent since the introduction of the *Model Syllabuses for Religion Education* (QCA, 1998a; SCAA, 1994). A positive aspect of this was the *Faith Communities Working Group Reports* in which each of the six major world religions represented in Britain made important contributions to defining from their own faith tradition perspectives what content should be taught. That this has been in part a continued contribution of religious communities is noted by the *Guidance*. The rationale for their inclusion is this:

> Members of religions and belief organisations can make a real contribution to RE both locally and nationally. By working with people whose beliefs they may or may not share in an atmosphere of respect and mutual understanding, faith and belief representatives can act as models of community cohesion in action. (DCSF, 2010: 37)

The document *Religious Education: The Non-Statutory National Framework* (DfES, 2004) and the 2010 *Guidance* have extended both the range of these religious traditions (through the incorporation of 'religions and beliefs') and the inclusion of secular, especially humanist, perspectives.

Despite this range and depth of accommodation by religious education to secular, political agendas, there remain several levels of critique of religious education itself from vituperative secular sources. Many of those critical of faith schools are also critical of religious education. We noted earlier that some people 'find religious schools unacceptable simply because they find religion unacceptable' (Halstead, 2012: 107); in the same manner some people find religious education unacceptable too because they find religion unacceptable. I outline here two forms such arguments take: the argument of indoctrination and the argument against compulsion.

Religious education and secularity

The argument of indoctrination

The most extreme secular argument against religious education finds its origins in a wider antipathy to religion in the eighteenth-century Enlightenment. Religion limits, inhibits, controls the thinking of adults through the power it exerted in childhood. The Jesuit aphorism 'Give me a child at seven and I will show you the man' was meant constructively, but has frequently been misinterpreted. The notion – of controlling the adult by exerting such influence on the child – was challenged from the seventeenth century on by John Locke in *Some Thoughts Concerning Education*. A century later, more severe critiques of religion are evident in Jean-Jacques Rousseau's *Emile* and Immanuel Kant's posthumously published *Lectures on Pedagogy*. The tradition which came to be known as liberal education emerged from this. It is apparent in Dewey's *Democracy and Education*. In modern liberal education pedagogy is the mirror of political principle.

Seventeenth and eighteenth as well as later twentieth and twenty-first century versions of liberal education all hold the conjoint educational principles of (a) developing a child's freedom of thought, and thereby (b) enabling the autonomy of the individual. Where religion is seen to infringe on either principle, it is said in mild or extreme forms to be indoctrinatory. The argument always comes from secular sources but not all secular thinkers regard religious education as harmful; indeed, many like some members of the British Human Association regard it as positively useful. That said, some secular humanists are also equally wary of religious education, given the perceived historical and contemporary forms of it as an antiliberal, and at its extremes, an indoctrinatory force in a child's education.

Although forms of the indoctrinatory argument are found in current-day assaults on religious education, often secular humanism, the strongest forms of the argument emerged in two specific socio-political contexts of the Cold War era. Indoctrination thus appears in the sociology of religion literature of the 1960s and 1970s, preoccupied with emergent new religious movements, often defined as 'cults', and allegations of mind control and brainwashing against them. Then there are the wider explicit political contexts of the Cold War itself, particularly charges against political education in Maoist China and Soviet Russia as indoctrinatory. These religious and political extremes – the microlevel cultic group and macropolitics of the Cold War – account for a certain prevalence of this notion of indoctrination in an earlier religious education literature.

Thus one of the defences of religious education at the time comes from Barry Chazan's (1972) '"Indoctrination" and Religious Education'. The genealogy of indoctrination, he traces particularly to Kant: to indoctrinate is to limit the human capacity to think, to hamper autonomy; the converse of which limiting and hampering being the supposed aim of liberal education, is to encourage open minds through open enquiry, and enable individual autonomy. Chazan argues that 'religious education (along with moral and political education) is usually cited as the classic and paradigm case of indoctrinatory activity . . . this association has become a vehicle of an emotive polemic against the religious education enterprise'. Chazan addresses two questions. What is indoctrination? Is religious education indoctrination? Chazan suggests that the most 'immediate and striking' sense of 'indoctrination' is as a term of disapproval. That is, 'indoctrination' first and foremost refers to certain sorts of activities of the educational sphere which are disapproved of, regarded as undesirable or rejected. 'Indoctrination' is usually contrasted with such positive value terms as 'education', 'teaching' or 'instruction'. Here 'religious education is or is not' 'indoctrination' 'depending upon one's sympathy or disdain for the religious sphere and the religious way of life' (Chazan, 1972: 244).

While both convenient and popular, such an approach to the explication of 'indoctrination' is incomplete. He identifies three conceptions of indoctrination: the method argument, the content argument and the intention argument. In the method argument, indoctrination 'refers to the transmission of contents to the young via undesirable or distasteful methods', aimed at 'guaranteeing a student's acceptance of beliefs and/or ability to defend such beliefs', doing so 'by excluding alternative beliefs or by presenting them in such a way as to guarantee their rejection'. Pedagogically, this might include a range of methods which include 'incomplete, or one-sided arguments; deliberate falsification or suppression of evidence; charisma; repetition; management of facts; drilling'. In other words, these are methods 'which juggle facts and arguments so as to insure the acceptance of desired conclusions' (Chazan, 1972: 244). The flaw of this argument is that methods are not unique to those aspects of education usually charged with indoctrination. All forms of teaching and education could in some ways be regarded as indoctrination for all their apparent claims. Although Chazan does not cite Paola Freire's (1996) *Pedagogy of the Oppressed* or Ivan Ilyich's (1995) *De-schooling Society*, both present arguments which charge Western education as being contrary to their stated liberal claims: Freire sees education as upholding unequal economic power structures and as being fundamentally oppressive; Ilyich sees schooling as a means of social coercion and control. Variants of similar arguments about power of elites being maintained through the control of knowledge are used by Foucault.

The content argument regards indoctrination that Chazan defines as 'a question of what one teaches, rather than how': 'First, such contents are uncertain and/or speculative beliefs, in the sense that there is not enough evidence for their validity so that any sane and sensible person when presented with the relevant evidence would hold such beliefs.' That is, 'The contents of indoctrination are beliefs for which there is no convincing or publicly acceptable evidence: the salient characteristic of doctrines is the fact that they are not known to be true or false.' Second, 'is that they are integrated bodies or systems of beliefs about the most basic and ultimate issues of human existence': 'Indoctrination is not simply a question of inculcating the belief that Schweppes is tastier than Coca-Cola, but rather of inculcating beliefs in God, Socialism, the Good.' In short, the content argument focuses on the importance of what is being taught, fundamental beliefs, values and worldviews. Chazan rightly states it is not only religious forms of education that are susceptible to the content argument but also political (or read citizenship) and moral education, since each of these three spheres represent 'the prime examples of the transmission of comprehensive ideologies or belief systems which are not known to be true or false, and whose verification is speculative' (Chazan, 1972: 245). For this argument, Chazan highlights a key problem in its notion of verification:

> This school assumes that there exists one fixed set of rational and objective criteria for the verification of all phenomena. Such criteria are implied in the phrases: 'the sane and sensible person'; 'rational beliefs'; 'the rationality of the contents'. It is, however, simplistic to assume one set of fixed and certain rules of verification even within such specific spheres as science and mathematics, let alone for all spheres of human discourse and meaning. (Chazan, 1972: 247)

Philosophers of science from Karl Popper (1963, 2002) through Paul Feyerabend (1975) to Thomas Kuhn (1996) all identify the construction of scientific worldviews. That aspect of the content argument which suggests that religious (or political or moral) education is selective with the facts shows a naiveté about education itself, since all education is by necessity based upon some selection of materials considered useful for teaching and learning.

The intention argument is defined by the purposes underlying teaching and learning. Here indoctrination is 'the desire to implant unshakeably beliefs in others; that is, to the concern with having the young accept their beliefs from their elders in a non-questioning, non-critical manner'. In terms of liberal education, focusing as it is on encouraging individual autonomy, indoctrination 'begins when we are trying to stop the growth in our children of the capacity to think for themselves'. The indoctrinator in this scenario would be distinguished by illiberal and authoritarian intentions. If, however, intention is understood too simplistically, it manifests a naive liberalism, for 'it is obvious that there are certain aspects of education which are not aimed at, nor even open to, the child's rational or autonomous judgement', since many aspects of education are concerned with transmitting habits and behaviours none of which depend on inculcating a child's autonomy. In most countries education itself is a universal and compulsory aspect of a child's life, he or she does not have a choice to learn to read or write or become numerate:

> The crucial point in this discussion is the manner in which the question 'Is religious education the paradigm case of indoctrination?' is treated. If such a question is understood as referring to the history of religious education, or to the nature of contemporary religious educational practice, then the answer to such a question is clearly affirmative. However, if the question is taken in its purely logical sense ('is' meaning 'entails' or 'need entail') then the answer is clearly negative. (Chazan, 1972: 251–2)

An interesting development in this argument is a counter-attack that has come only in recent decades: religious educators have responded to such charges by arguing that what is going on in schools is a form of *secular* indoctrination. Terence Copley argues:

> Doctrines are the defined tenets, usually of a sect or religion. In its basic and non-pejorative sense, therefore, indoctrination is simply the communication of doctrine. The U.S. Navy used the term in this way as recently as the Second World War, to mean the basic rules and discipline for naval personnel. But like its sister word propaganda, which also had innocent beginnings, indoctrination came to be associated with the morally questionable activity of instilling particular beliefs and values into the unwilling or unaware. Historically it was assumed that the beliefs or doctrines to be 'indoctrinated' would be religious. But atheism has its own doctrines, for example, that there is no God, that this life is all that there is, and so on, which could equally be transmitted by indoctrination. (Copley, 2008: 24–5; also Copley, 2005)

Copley here usefully distinguishes between indoctrination and conditioning, the latter never as severe as the former, in which the will of the person is overridden in the process by a variety of sensory assaults and/or sensory deprivation. Copley 'indoctrination occurs when a person is given one view of the world in such a way that they cannot see any other':

> Their freewill is not destroyed, but they are fed partial information resulting in partial judgements. This deprives people of choice. We can therefore legitimately ask whether in some Western democracies . . . a secular indoctrination process is occurring. People who are products of a secular worldview have real difficulty understanding the claims of religions, which appear to them either as harmless private hobbies on the one hand, or dangerous fanaticism on the other. Their common question: 'What has religion done for me?' conceals an implicit answer, that religion is a therapy or package designed to enhance the Self. Religious fundamentalism, which is on the whole non-violent, and the visibly pre-modern stance adopted by particular religious groups, for example, Orthodox Christians in some eastern European countries, or particular Islamic groups in some northern European countries, appear equally inexplicable to a secular mindset. (Copley, 2008: 25)

Copley suggests indoctrination 'can occur in four major ways':

> The first is by planning and intention. The school curriculum of Nazi Germany and the media manipulation of North Korea provide examples. Most commentators have failed to note the second mode of operation for indoctrination, omission or exclusion, for example, of the religious dimension. Not presenting a set of beliefs can be as influential as presenting another set. If school curriculum omits religion altogether, what signal is sent to students?—that religion may be unimportant, or highly divisive, or both. Indoctrination can also occur by 'positioning', a process whereby a philosophy or idea or system is relegated to the periphery and thereby marginalized. In the high-school curriculum any subject that is taught for the minimum time on the minimum resources – perhaps by non-specialist teachers – and in the shabbiest part of the school campus may well be assumed by the students to be of minimal value. It may reflect the positioning allocated to that subject by the society in which the schooling is based. The fourth characteristic of indoctrination is to insist on asking one question rather than another, for example, 'Was Darwin *really* right?' compared to "Was Darwin right?" The nuance is entirely different and the question

contains a hidden answer. The tendency in some education programs to treat religions as if they are static belief systems may well illustrate another half-buried assumption. It is assumed that religions are optional sets of beliefs in the attic of the mind, rather than culturally influenced complex ways of life, with some constants (e.g., Torah) and some changing elements (e.g., attitudes to women). (Copley, 2008: 26)

The conflation of overly disparate exemplars seriously weakens Copley's case. Can we really compare the education of Nazi children and youth (for which see, e.g. Sunker and Otto, 2000) with classroom questioning of whether or not Darwin was 'right'?

Liberal educators are aware of these arguments' potential. The natural comparison is with education in totalitarian systems:

The sort of education attempted in totalitarian societies is seen as objectionable from a democratic perspective on precisely these grounds. In the pre-perestroika Soviet Union, for example, education attempted to shape a particular ideology in students based on a significantly controversial theory, of the good. This education was designed to bring about the sort of unified detailed, mental formation contained in the notion of vospitanie. In this process, individuality, criticism and variety were subordinated to Marxist–Leninist theory, which determined the aims and method of a monolithic and centralised system of schools. These schools, together with youth organisations and the media all conspired in a co-ordinated way to develop the ideal communist person, complete with the collectivist and atheistic beliefs [sic] qualities of character. (McLaughlin, 2011: 80–1)

However, although this is a strong case, such education was not always as successful in its stated intentions (on Fascist education, see Otto and Sunker, 2000; or in the early years of the Soviet Union, Kirkpatrick, 2002). The notion that liberal democracy can shift towards autocracy *has been* recognized (for instance, Popper, 1946; Talmon, 1961; Wolin, 2008) but as a theoretic possibility. If the counter-charge is that liberal education can risk veering to the particularist position, it cannot be said to withstand comparison with the totalitarian (as Copley attempts). McLaughlin takes up the charge of liberal democratic education adopting a particularist stance (in Wright's terms, this would be that a relativistic pluralism is being imbued under the guise of neutrality):

In contrast, education based on liberal democratic principles seeks to avoid such a particularistic formation. It might be argued, of course, that a liberal democratic form of education is itself based on a theory of the good which is 'particular' and 'significantly controversial'. Such an education, it might be claimed, also tries to shape a certain sort of person, and to impart a 'particular' individual identity. In reply, a proponent of 'liberal democratic' education will argue that, whilst there is some truth in these objections, education based on democratic principles seeks to reduce particularistic influences to a minimum. (McLaughlin, 2011: 81)

The case that secular religious education represents then a form of secular indoctrination is difficult to prove. On the other side of the charge, that religious education epitomizes indoctrination is especially weakened when secular religious education mirrors so closely liberal educational aims. In short, if the subject is now explicitly and systematically incorporating liberal goals of tolerance and understanding between cultures and religions, grounds for a critique on the basis of indoctrination become insubstantial.

We see, for example, even Richard Dawkins (2006, 2007), an advocate of secularism regarding religion per se as a pernicious, anti-intellectual and obscurantist force, recognizes the educative possibilities of liberal religious education in being able to debunk religion itself. In 2012, when the UK secretary of state for Education Religious distributed copies of the King James Bible to all schools in England, there was surprise when it was widely reported in the media that Richard Dawkins supported this initiative, but the news reports made plain he welcomed the move as it would enable children to see that the Bible 'is not a moral book and young people need to learn that important fact because they are very frequently told the opposite' (BBC, 2012). Religious education which does not do this is regarded as a 'wicked practice' (Dawkins Foundation, 2010). Thus, presently, despite much national guidance (for instance, DCSF, 2010) religious education in England is framed by 'locally agreed syllabuses' and state primary and secondary schools, and faith schools have greater freedom in this area of the curriculum than any other. The Dawkins Foundation (2012) thus announced: 'Richard Dawkins, the UK's most prominent atheist, will today call on Ofsted to force faith schools to bring religious education into the national curriculum.' Yet Dawkins's ire is retained for religious education which attempts to inculcate religious belief, and is in the context of religious education within faith schools where we see the conflation of his critique of both faith schools and the sort of religious education promoted there:

> Professor Dawkins said that the move [to introduce religious education into the National Curriculum] would be the first step in ending what he calls the 'wicked' practice of inculcating children with religious belief, as he steps up his campaign against religious education with a film that calls for the abolition of faith schools. (Dawkins Foundation, 2010)

The argument against compulsion

Many of those countries which have rigorously separated church from state did not permit, even prohibited, the teaching of religion in schools. We have seen, however, even in countries such as America where this is the case, religion can never be fully absent from any school curriculum insofar as religion will be encountered, particularly in history and literature. Those countries where religious education was not excluded have increasingly moved to political justifications for the subject often centring on cohesion, diversity and pluralism. England has been important here, modelling an influence which is now prevalent internationally. For some secular thinkers, even this – or perhaps we should say if religious education is simply this – provides still insufficient justification for including the subject as a compulsory part of the school curriculum. In fact, if religious education is concerned predominantly with issues of cohesion, diversity and pluralism – religious education's rationale is that we understand culture and religion in order to contribute to social and political order – then other subjects (such as citizenship) are at least equal to such a task.

John White (2005) thus asks: Should religious education be a compulsory school subject? Britain is an increasingly secular society, is his argument, and yet religious education remains a compulsory school subject. Is its *compulsory* status justifiable?

> Religious education was made compulsory in 1944 partly so as to support the moral values under-lying democracy. This civic justification faded after the war, but even today one official justification of religious education is in terms of moral education. Another has to do with understanding and respecting other religions and beliefs. (White, 2004: 151)

White concludes that 'neither is strong enough to support the continued existence of religious education as a separate, compulsory subject'. The same verdict, he argues, 'is passed on a third justification, based on a recommended switch in the content of religious education classes to the critical analysis of religious claims' (White, 2004: 151).

Britain is not only a secular society but becoming increasingly so: 'Its churches and chapels are increasingly preserved as historical monuments or turned to other uses – tyre warehouses, upmarket dwellings, rock-climbing centres'. 'The shopping centre of the London suburb where I live,' writes White, 'is called The Spire – after the only feature of the nonconformist church still remaining after the latter was pulled down to make way for commerce in the 1980s.' The Anglican church, he continues, 'around the corner from my house would also now be defunct, were it not for a deal cut ten years ago between the Bishop of St Albans and the leaders of the local Greek Orthodox community for the premises to be shared by both denominations'. These are sociologically as well as logically specious: one, sociological debate on secularization is far more nuanced; two, it is hardly the model of sociological sophistication for White to use the particularities of his neighbourhood, the particular, to generalize about Britain as a whole. A philosopher should know better. Yet, there are nevertheless sociological accounts which do support White's claim. While many secularization theorists have reversed their formerly held secularization theories (see Berger, 1999; Berger et al., 2007), White's account is supported by other sociologists, such as Steve Bruce (2002) in *God Is Dead*; or Callum Brown's (2001) lament for *The Death of Christian Britain*. The latter argument is distinctive in suggesting that secularization in Britain has not been a gradual process since the Enlightenment (as most secularization theory does) but has been marked and massive particularly since its cultural and moral erosion from 1960s onwards: post-1960 secularization has sent 'organised Christianity on a downward spiral to the margins of social significance' (Brown, 2001: 1).

White must therefore be allowed some justification for his view of secularization. Secularization for White counters the justification of religious education as a compulsory part of the curriculum in English state schools. He cites in particular the shift from the 1944 Education Act which made secondary religious education as the 1870 Act had made elementary religious education compulsory. This is what White calls the '1944 justification':

Part of the answer lies in the period just before and during the Second World War. In 1944 religious instruction (RI), as well as a daily act of corporate worship, was made compulsory in all state schools, subject to the right of withdrawal if parents desired this. It thus became the only compulsory subject, the former state control of the elementary curriculum having been abandoned in 1926 and state determination of the grammar school curriculum soon to be ended in 1945. Before 1944, there had been no bar to religious instruction in state schools, unlike some other countries. It was in fact still widespread. (White, 2004: 152)

He is only to some extent right when he claims that what 'made Britain decide to make it compulsory needs to be understood against the political background of the time'. Though this is a view taken by histories of religious education by religious educators themselves (Copley, 2007) White's political interpretation of religious education is far from the mark:

The later 1930s in Europe saw the increasing influence of totalitarian systems of belief – Nazism, Fascism, Communism. In 1938, the year of Munich, British official thinking was especially affected by the German experience: Germany had been revivified by an ideal: the Aryan religion had wrought a revolution in conduct; it had had, demonstrably and undeniably, 'a powerful effect on life and character'. Where was the counter-ideal to mobilize the energies and command the dedication of the British people? The Germans had, when they began their revival, nothing but belief: where was the belief behind the British way of life, which was now so sorely threatened? (White, 2004: 152)

White is thus simply factually incorrect in citing the significance of the *Spens Report* (1938) as underpinning the justification for religious education in political terms at the time. As we shall see in the next chapter, Spens presents a whole chapter on 'Scripture'. It rejects explicitly the cultural justification for the teaching of the Bible and Christianity, and there is no hint of any political justification for the subject.

For White, in the 1944 Education Act 'a firm association had been made between the Christian religion and the cause of democracy itself'. White reads present-day justifications of religious education as a means of social cohesion into a past debate: 'One of the reasons (in the explanatory sense) why RI became compulsory was its perceived importance as a foundation for civic unity.' In this case: 'The explanatory reason also functions as a seemingly plausible justificatory reason for the subject.' White claims too that 'on the other hand, the pressure to move towards interdenominational religious education, while certainly a causal factor, does not so obviously yield a justification for the subject'. For White still leaves unanswered this question: 'What arguments are there in favour of compulsory religious education based on agreement across the denominations?'

Setting aside these factual errors, White is on stronger ground in suggesting that in the post-War decades, 'the idea that religious education should encourage adherence to Christianity was replaced by a non-confessional approach, emphasizing an understanding of religion'. Its exclusively Christian emphasis was certainly removed and indeed enshrined in the 1988 Education Reform Act that the teaching of religious education should be in the main Christian, but also attend to the other principal religions represented in Britain; a largely Christian religious education was replaced by 'a multi-faith perspective, reflecting the plurality of religions now found in the society'.

White then makes an assault on justification of this new emphasis on the basis of morality: 'Children brought up within faith communities are inducted into moral rules and values embedded in their faith. There are issues here to do with the future autonomy of the child about the legitimacy of such induction.' What about 'the great majority of children, those who are brought up outside faith communities?' Other vehicles for this are most appropriate. There are now several possible candidates apart from religious education lessons, none of which face the particular problem which confronts religious education including school ethos, but in curriculum terms, 'If we want them to think clearly about ethical matters it would make better sense to rely on vehicles like school ethos, PSHE and citizenship rather than on religious education with its multiple potentialities for sowing confusion' (White, 2004: 157).

The argument 'that morality is logically independent of religion' he then puts to test: on grounds and motivation:

> Kantians look to the presuppositions of practical rationality itself; utilitarians to what promotes the greatest balance of happiness over distress; naturalists to what they take to be embedded in human nature. Other philosophers challenge the assumption in all these that morality needs *any* foundation. Lack of agreement among secular philosophers about the basis of morality should not be of much comfort, though, to those who believe morality is dependent on religion. In what way could it be dependent? What could replace the dots in 'We ought not to lie because . . .'? (White, 2004: 159)

A traditional view in Christianity, Judaism and other religions has been some variant of 'God has commanded us not to'. White simply challenges the morality of the Judaeo-Christian tradition: 'God's precepts, as revealed in the Bible, are often massively out of line with *our own* moral thinking' (emphasis added). Again, a philosopher should know better than to move from to this collective notion of a shared morality, what he means is the moral thinking of those such as himself who do not share the Judaeo-Christian worldview. Moving from the *grounds* for moral claims, he makes an even claim move to motivation: 'It is also sometimes argued that people will not be *motivated* to behave morally without religious reasons for doing so.' And from this premise he asks, 'Could religious education be justified on these lines?' White is correct in suggesting that this 'surely will not do', simply because it has never been an argument presented in religious education in any source I can detect where this form of moral argument has been presented. Indeed, as we noted in *Religious Education in English Schools: Non-Statutory Guidance 2010*, secular beliefs are now formally included in the subject. White is correct in asserting: 'Most people in the religious education world will agree that morality does not have to be based on religion, either motivationally or epistemologically.' But then in the modern history of the subject, they never had.

Moral education, White argues, 'is not the only aim of religious education in Britain today . . . Many religious educators would put the emphasis elsewhere . . . [on] about developing pupils' understanding of different religions'. White suggests that the study of religion should 'certainly feature in the school curriculum' but 'not as it features now'. Rather, it 'should be purged of the three blemishes which now mar it, as well as of its role in general moral education'. Whether this would leave religious education with a good case for remaining a separate curriculum subject is a further question': 'Does that mean it should be scrapped – that its legally privileged place in the curriculum as a compulsory subject from 5 to 16 should be abandoned?' He suggests possibly so – 'unless other reasons for it can do better than those officially provided'. The 'only valid justification for religious education depends on a radical change in its content'. Rather than 'teach children about different religions, it should engage them in the examination of religious claims – about the existence of God, for instance, or whether there is an afterlife. These involve epistemologically distinctive forms of argumentation, to which all pupils should be exposed'. But White argues that this is still insufficient justification for the subject:

> As far as I can see, there are *no* specifically religious questions – beyond those that already assume a religious framework, like 'Is God one person or three?' Questions like 'Is there an after-life?' may have religious *answers*, but they themselves are questions to which various considerations are relevant. There are scientific considerations which have a bearing on this as well as non-scientific ones. The same is true of 'Does God exist?' Despite appearances, this is not a religious question. If we take it that it means something like 'Is there a rational agent ultimately responsible for the existence of the physical universe?', this again is a question on which many perspectives bear, including those from science and from the history of the undermining of religious claims over the last three centuries. Religion has often been held to be an autonomous form of inquiry, but this is misguided. Its uniqueness comes only in its answers: the questions from which it starts generate inquiry in many different fields. (White, 2004: 161–3)

This 'new justification for religious education', White argues, 'is not powerful enough to keep it in the privileged position it is in now'. Further, although 'theological arguments for the existence of God and other matters have become enormously complex over the centuries', and this might justify religious education's place in the curriculum, for a sophisticated treatment of these topics more curriculum time than is available would be needed. And White implicitly questions whether such a philosophical approach is warranted: 'We are dealing with schoolchildren, not university specialists in theology. Labyrinthine arguments are no more in place here than in work on political or moral issues. In any case, given that discussion must be conducted fairly, involving children with recondite argumentation may lead them to believe, erroneously, that the weight of evidence falls on the pro-religious side.' He sees, therefore, 'no justification . . . for the status quo, where religious education is compulsory'. Indeed, since 'questions about the creation of the universe, life after death, etc. bring in scientific and philosophical as well as religious perspectives', there is 'no good reason for keeping the title religious education for work of this kind' (White, 2004: 163–4).

White's paper provoked a response from Andrew Wright (2006) and the latter's claim that religious education should be precisely about such philosophical material, religious education as a 'critical realist' space for the determination of 'truth'. White comments on Wright's position: 'To some extent we see eye to eye. We both agree that children should openly discuss the truth of religious and secular claims about the nature of reality.' However, White is unconvinced that this essentially philosophical-conceptual defence is (a) 'not enough to justify religious education as a separate curriculum subject studied on a compulsory basis as now from 5 until 16' since it 'would also have to be shown that such discussion has a priority over other candidates for curricular time for all those 500 periods'; and (b) 'that it is not enough to justify religious education as a separate compulsory subject even of a shorter duration, since the discussion could take place elsewhere; in personal, social and health education (PSHE), for instance'. In short, 'Compelling children to study this or that curriculum area for years on end is not something to be done lightly, and sound arguments are needed for it' (White, 2005: 22–3).

It is ironic that while global socio-political justifications for religious education proliferate, even this secular positioning of religious education is under attack. Despite, then, religious education's considerable accommodation to secularist positions – socio-political, moral, philosophical – it is deemed insufficiently distinctive to justify its compulsory place in the curriculum.

Summary

The arguments for accommodation in terms of the rationale for and pedagogies of religious education has taken more sophisticated forms than White gives the subject credit, and the range of religious education pedagogies which have emerged as religious education has separated itself from the religious life are examined in the next chapter. In the separation of religious education from the religious life, religious education has nevertheless faced considerable epistemological difficulties. But in political terms, as the subject has shifted to a liberal political justification – for example in dealing with issues of cohesion, diversity and pluralism – the religious educator has faced problems (perhaps unsurprisingly) similar to those of liberal political philosophy: how to make a constructive contribution to social cohesion in a context of cultural diversity and religious plurality in national and international contexts divided precisely by such difference. For the religious educator, a political problem takes necessarily pedagogical form. To many religious educators (teachers, policymakers and researchers), teaching about cultural diversity and informing about the grounds of religious pluralism will simply be sufficient to achieve such socio-political goals. But little credible evidence exists to show this is the case.

So, from some quarters, even the essentially political and certainly secular justification of religious education – through issues of social and community cohesion, and or cultural/religious diversity and pluralism – are themselves used as a means of arguing against the role of religious education. In England (the Ajegbo Report) and internationally (for instance, UNESCO, 2006, 2011), the rise of religious content in citizenship and related human rights education charts clearly the incursion of secular subjects on to the formerly exclusive territory of religious education. The core secular argument here is that there is nothing distinctive in religious education's contribution that could not or is not covered in other areas of the curriculum.

The ground for which so many religious educators have sought to justify their subject is being used against them by the very secular intellectual traditions with which they had sought to ally themselves. The next chapter looks precisely at these justifications in the form of six pedagogies of religious education.

Pedagogies of Religious Education: Teaching, Learning and Assessment

5

Introduction

To recount, the declining power of religion in Western political life dates not to the intellectual foment of Enlightenment but to the fracture of ecclesiastical authority wrought by Reformation. Newly enabled freedoms of the latter would thus facilitate the former. From the early Enlightenment onwards, political philosophy (Hobbes, Locke, Paine, Rousseau) radically intensified the process of social and political change. The effects of these political changes we live with today in the forms of democratic governance modelled on the political revolutions of the period, in differing ways in England, America and France (Himmelfarb, 2005). Enlightenment identified religious authority, with aristocratic and monarchical rule, as quite clearly as politically antiprogressive. In its wider intellectual currents, religion was associated with the perpetuation of economic and social inequality.

The following centuries witnessed such ideological critiques taking structural and institutional forms – not only in the seventeenth-century revolution in England, but also in the eighteenth-century revolutions in America and France. Communism in the nineteenth century considered these latter revolutions as only partial remedies to deeper seated structural injustices. Thus we witness those subsequent twentieth-century revolutions in Russia and China. Setting aside questions of historical causality, Fascism and Nazism soon emerged too, when political life was unrestrained by religious authority. The secularist counter-charge here is that ecclesiastical authority was and remains an example of autocracy , and that religious authority was itself a restraint, on individual and political freedoms, and the source of social inequality and economic injustice by its focus on the next world rather than this. What we can uncontentiously note is the forming of the United Nations in 1945 as a political move on an international scale to restrain the effect of ideological that is political and not religious extremes, enshrining the worldwide community in a political model of moderation: shared Enlightenment values of democratic citizenship, individual autonomy and wider social freedoms, all enshrined above all upon a notion that such values were human rights, inalienable and universal.

Enlightenment brought then a new confidence to secular intellectual outlooks beyond the political. The freeing of political power from religious authority would provide conditions for intellectual freedoms unhindered by ecclesiastical directive. This is marked in several distinct but overlapping currents in the history of ideas: (1) a direct and determined shift away from theological understandings of the world; (2) a rise in philosophical faith in human reason, aside from scripture and revelation as well as the theology which depended on these as first principles; (3) a flourishing of the natural sciences, most dramatically in nineteenth-century biological and geological sciences (theories of evolution being paramount) and in the twentieth century in the chemical and physical sciences; and (4) the emergence of new philosophical, psychological and social sciences. All disciplines desired to underscore rationalistic credentials by maintaining a critical distance from religion. The new philosophical, psychological and sociological sciences would take the intellectual critique in new and radical directions.

These emergent sciences sought to *understand* religion in order further to *dismantle* its intellectual influence, to show (1) how philosophical, psychological and social life had been formed by it; and (2) how philosophical thinking, human psychology and human society could progress beyond religion's personal and collective illusions, and ultimately harmful limitations. In order to dismantle the pervasive influence of religion in the present, these new disciplines would take pains therefore to analyse its origins. These new disciplines were founded on a critique of religion. Religion does not relate to supernatural realities, they made plain, but only displaced manifestations of political, philosophical, psychological or sociological forces, or combinations of them. To understand these forces was the foundational stage in transcending them. In this respect the explanations of religion are called 'reductive' or 'reductionist'.

If such disciplines studied religion in order to transcend it, a new and self-styled 'science of religion' sought not only to critique religion but embrace it as a worthwhile study in its own right. Mircea Eliade's (1957) *The Sacred and the Profane*, provides a still useful account of the late nineteenth-century origins and the subsequent chronology of the science of religion (in linguistics and the history of religions), a discipline which sought to study religion in its own right, without seeking to rid the world of it. Unlike the antipathetic spirit of other new sciences, the 'science of religion' was more sympathetic to the religious impulse, seeking to interpret (as 'science') without setting out to undermine it. In the mid-twentieth century, it is from this tradition that leading scholars such as Mircea Eliade himself (in the

United States) emerged, and a few decades later (in England) my former university tutor, Ninian Smart. In studying religion in its own right, religious studies, as the 'science of religion' has come more commonly to be known, would use a full range of historical, linguistic, philosophical, political, psychological and socio-anthropological approaches in order to understand religion.

All these developments would see the study of religion progressively separated from the religious life. Religion, where it was taught in schools and at least in state education, would *also* as a result and necessarily become increasingly separate from religious life. Further, many of the latter theories of religion would, as this chapter will show, become influential in shaping pedagogies of religious education. These pedagogies sought to identify neither with religious life nor theology, but with the very sciences which had critiqued religion. Baumfield's (2012) outline of the history of pedagogy as a term, traces its origins paedagogus as the slave who led the child to school, Baumfield suggests, 'Pedagogy retains this sense of the teacher as both the guide and servant of the learner' (Baumfield, 2012: 205) Paedagogus was however also the term used by wealthy Romans for the Greek slaves who educated their children!Clement of Alexandria's second century work The Paedagogus shows the adaptation of the term into Christian education.

'Paradigm Shift'

But in religious education, the nature of this pedagogy has, it barely needs to be stated, changed dramatically over past decades. In view of the association of these pedagogies with the new forms of enquiry, I use the term 'paradigm' to characterize specific and identifiable patterns from a broader and arguably seismic shift in the nature of religious education itself, its aims and purposes, and thus the inevitable impact on its pedagogy. Here, Thomas Kuhn's (1996) *The Structure of Scientific Revolutions* is a point of reference to explain why developments in religious education do justifiably merit the term, and represent indeed a 'paradigm shift'.

Kuhn describes how his ideas arose from time spent as a young academic in a university environment that spanned the natural and social sciences:

> Spending the year in a community composed predominantly of social scientists confronted me with unanticipated problems about the differences between such communities and those of the natural scientists among whom I had been trained. Particularly, I was struck by the number and extent of the overt disagreements between social scientists about the nature of legitimate scientific problems and methods. Both history and acquaintance made me doubt that practitioners of the natural sciences possess firmer or more permanent answers to such questions than their colleagues in social science. Yet, somehow, the practice of astronomy, physics, chemistry, or biology normally fails to evoke the controversies over fundamentals that today often seem endemic among, say, psychologists or sociologists. Attempting to discover the source of that difference led me to recognize the role in scientific research of what I have since called 'paradigms'. These I take to be universally recognized scientific achievements that for a time provide model problems and solutions to a community of practitioners. (Kuhn, 1996: ix–x)

The remainder of his initial essays and subsequent editions of his famous book are concerned with elaborating instances of paradigm and paradigm shift. He grounds his thinking in the concept of 'normal science', as meaning research 'firmly based upon one or more past scientific achievements, achievements that some particular scientific community acknowledges for a time as supplying the foundation for its further practice':

> Today such achievements are recounted, though seldom in their original form, by science textbooks, elementary and advanced. These textbooks expound the body of accepted theory, illustrate many or all of its successful applications, and compare these applications with exemplary observations and experiments. Before such books became popular early in the nineteenth century (and until even more recently in the newly matured sciences), many of the famous classics of science fulfilled a similar function. Aristotle's *Physica*, Ptolemy's *Almagest*, Newton's *Principia* and *Opticks*, Franklin's *Electricity*, Lavoisier's *Chemistry*, and Lyell's *Geology* – these and many other works served for a time implicitly to define the legitimate problems and methods of a research field for succeeding generations of practitioners. (Kuhn, 1996: 10)

Paradigms, he argues, in historical context shared 'two essential characteristics': 'Their achievement was sufficiently unprecedented to attract an enduring group of adherents away from competing modes of scientific activity. Simultaneously, it was sufficiently open-ended to leave all sorts of problems for the redefined group of practitioners to resolve.' These achievements he describes as 'paradigms'. Achievements that share these two characteristics I shall henceforth refer to as 'paradigms'. In choosing this term he refers to 'actual scientific practice – examples which include law, theory, application, and instrumentation together – provide models from which spring particular coherent traditions of scientific research': 'These are the traditions which the historian describes under such rubrics as 'Ptolemaic astronomy' (or 'Copernican'), 'Aristotelian dynamics' (or 'Newtonian'), 'corpuscular optics' (or 'wave optics'), and so on. The study of paradigms, including many that are far more specialized than those named illustratively above, is what mainly prepares the student for membership in the particular scientific community with which he will later practice' (Kuhn, 1996: 10–1).

Kuhn's conceptualization of paradigms has been cited and critiqued by an enormously wide literature, and its prevalence in such literature extends to not only (obviously) the history and philosophy of science but across the social sciences as well. Kuhn argues that to achieve paradigmatic status, 'a theory must seem better than its competitors, but it need not, and in fact never does, explain all the facts with which it can be confronted' (Kuhn, 1996: 17–18). Nevertheless, there are those 'who cling to one or another of the older views, and they are simply read out of the profession, which thereafter ignores their work. The new paradigm implies a new and more rigid definition of the field.' Those 'unwilling or unable to accommodate their work to it must proceed in isolation or attach themselves to some other group' (Kuhn, 1996: 18–19). Paradigms thus 'gain their status because they are more successful than their competitors in solving a few problems that the group of practitioners has come to recognize as acute' (Kuhn, 1996: 23). For Kuhn the advancement of scientific knowledge requires agreement on theoretical frameworks, the definition of unresolved problems and the methods for their resolution, and by such parameters is the paradigm, new and old, defined. The paradigm shift is a marked and decisive change in these. The new paradigm emerges from the old and is distinguished from it so that the latter's marginalization becomes progressively more affirmed.

The success of *The Structure of Scientific Revolutions* is shown by its application a range of fields. And while it has had many critics in the history of science as well as the disciplines which adopted the terms of his thesis, it has at least led to Kuhn's work receiving high prominence. As Bird (2011) comments: '*The Structure of Scientific Revolutions* is one of the most cited academic books of all time.' In Kuhn's opening comments about working across social and natural science disciplines, we see him bridging differing disciplines by a conceptual and methodological framework which potentially incorporated understandings of knowledge transformation across them all. The key discussions of such ideas were in the history of the natural sciences. It was an achievement to bridge the diversity of disciplines here with a plausible if contested framework. The application to disciplines outside the natural sciences adds further layers of potential difficulties. Not least because of another element of Kuhn's paradigm. This was the idea of 'incommensurability'.

Kuhn's conceptual framework was applied, then, in the first instance to natural sciences and a cycle of empirical observation and the theoretical frameworks and hypotheses:

> The standard empiricist conception of theory evaluation regards our judgment of the epistemic quality of a theory to be a matter of applying rules of method to the theory and the evidence. Kuhn's contrasting view is that we judge the quality of a theory (and its treatment of the evidence) by comparing it to a paradigmatic theory. The standards of assessment therefore are not permanent, theory-independent rules. They are not rules, because they involve perceived relations of similarity (of puzzle–solution to a paradigm). They are not theory-independent, since they involve comparison to a (paradigm) theory. They are not permanent, since the paradigm may change in a scientific revolution. (Bird, 2011)

'Consequently,' as Bird explains, 'comparison between theories will not be as straightforward as the standard empiricist picture would have it, since the standards of evaluation are themselves subject to change.' This difficulty in comparison of different theoretical perspectives is what is meant by 'incommensurability': 'Theories are incommensurable when they share no common measure.' If 'paradigms are the measures of attempted puzzle–solutions, then puzzle–solutions developed in different eras of normal science will be judged by comparison to differing paradigms and so lack a common measure' (Bird, 2011).

This idea cannot be applied easily to the history of ideas but really only the formal methods of enquiry which the history of ideas generated. For instance, there are difficulties in applying the notion of paradigm shifts to the history of ideas contexts per se. We cannot say from the Enlightenment there was a *paradigm shift* from religious to secular understandings of the world – though secularization theorists expected this – because both the religious and secular have persisted, with accommodations, tensions, etc. Neither straightforward nor particularly modern, such tensions defined modernity but are not 'paradigmatic'.

However, in the more defined context of our present topic, the Kuhn's terms can, with caveats, be usefully applied. Here I think the notion of paradigm and incommensurability is one way to interpret significant changes in the nature and purposes of religious education. This is the case especially where research in the field draws from the social scientific and other disciplines which are in the history of science paradigmatic. Religious education researchers, for example, use (paradigmatic) social science frameworks in order to delineate both problems and frameworks as well as methods for resolving them.

Evident 'incommensurability' emerged here. Changing the definition of the 'problem' (the aims and purposes of religious education) changes *methods* (pedagogies, models of teaching, learning and assessment) for addressing these changed. Deep incompatibility between old and new or incommensurability becomes apparent. This is where the history of ideas *does* remain important. Through this we view the broader intellectual sources and influences, religious and the secular, that have impacted the field. So, an example in religious education terms might be: where religious education was once related integrally to the religious life (Chapter 3), it is now in state religious education, increasingly dominated by agendas set by secularity (Chapter 4). There is a great deal of difference between a religious education committed to the development of a faith perspective and a religious education committed to the subject for its social and political usefulness, for example, in community cohesion, in ameliorating potential conflicts within and between religions, and so on. It is clear that many religious educators define themselves in such ways. 'Confessional' and 'non-confessional' is often used by those committed to state religious education as a way of distinguishing their practices from what has gone before. 'Incommensurability' is evident here: if the subject is defined in such different ways the methods (the pedagogies) by which the subject addresses its aims and purposes will change. The outline of models of religious education in Chapters 3 and 4 will share, of course, points of contact. Nevertheless, religious education related to the religious life will differ in fundamental ways with a religious education more closely related to secularity.

Paradigms of religious education

The word paradigm here is used here, then, advisedly to demonstrate major shifts in religious education pedagogy. Grimmitt's (2000) *Pedagogies of Religious Education* collected together a selection of approaches to teaching and learning, each chapter written by the originator of the pedagogy. They are described as research-based approaches to religious education in that the pedagogy was: (a) informed by scholarly reflection (Grimmitt, Wright); or (b) part of a programme of practitioner, classroom development (Cooling, Erricker and Erricker, Hull); or (c) was both (a) and (b) and supported by new empirical research (Jackson). Sterne's (2006) *Teaching Religious Education* took a similar range of pedagogies but emphasized these approaches as an opportunity for the religious education *teacher* to be a religious education *researcher*. The sense of the religious education teacher as researcher must really here be understood in senses of either (a) or (b) above and not (c).

Some of the approaches are so contextualized by the contributors to Grimmitt's volume, but neither volume sufficiently grounds religious education pedagogy as a whole in the intellectual traditions from which they emerged. These trajectories can be detailed as a series of 'paradigm shifts' in religious education. I propose six paradigms:

1. Scriptural-theological
2. Phenomenological
3. Psychological-experiential
4. Philosophical-conceptual
5. Socio-cultural
6. Historical-political.

The most easily identifiable paradigm shift was away from the scriptural-theological. The shift of religious education away from scripture and theology in Judaeo-Christian context reflects parallel political and wider intellectual currents. Whether the five identifiably new approaches to religious education are *themselves* paradigms (in the sense Kuhn uses the term) is debatable. But each approach, as we shall see, draws its intellectual inspiration from disciplinary developments that are. I thus identify pedagogic developments in religious education as paradigmatic to the extent that each shifts from a distinct emphasis on (1) scripture and theology towards alternatives whose ideas and approaches are rooted in other disciplines or forms of knowledge: (2) phenomenological; (3) psychological; (4) philosophical; (5) sociological; and (6) political. No discipline is so closely bounded; so these religious education pedagogies include interdisciplinary fusions.

In this context however, the scriptural-theological (1) is often pejoratively regarded as narrow, unreflective of modern educational thinking, the language of open critical thinking rational autonomy. The term 'confessional' religious education has been the common form of labelling. Indeed all subsequent paradigms (2–6) do this. By so doing, the intention is to distance a 'closed' religious education from an 'open' and 'progressive' one. As Kuhn notes, there are, nevertheless, those 'who cling to one or another of the older views'. What happens to them? According to Kuhn, 'they are simply read out of the profession, which thereafter ignores their work'. Those 'unwilling or unable to accommodate their work to it must proceed in isolation or attach themselves to some other group'. Is this the case with religious education? We can at the very least see a distinction between those approaches which retain the link between religious education and the religious life (as in Chapter 3) and those which have dissociated religious education from the religious life.

The scriptural-theological paradigm

In Western countries that retained religion as a curricular subject in state schools, the state attempted a studied neutrality to religious education, outside of which were schools divided along the Catholic and Protestant denominational lines formed by the Reformation. Where state religious education so existed, it produced, as in England, a dual system of church schools which provides religious education along the said denominational lines; and religious education in state schools which attempted to cater for children across this divide, by a non-denominational religious education. In the dual systems where the state provides some funding for schools with a religious foundation, these are also technically state schools, but I use the term 'state school' here to delineate state schools without a religious foundation.

Despite these nuances of foundation, in schools of both types within this dual system, religious education was formed and shaped on scriptural-theological foundations. Christian scripture and a nominal theological perspective were in England, for example, the only form of religious education until the 1950s. Today, the scriptural-theological approach is largely limited to schools of a religious character.

The involvement of the state in education did not involve then a paradigm shift in religious education, but it would facilitate such secular influences to flourish. We can trace this by examining the progressive decline in the Bible teaching in state religious education in England. What in European or American terms is remarkably late, is that the 1870 Education Act made elementary education, including religious education, compulsory. Religious education became compulsory in state schools only a decade after nineteenth-century Christianity was entering an intellectual maelstrom. For all the impact of wider intellectual currents of the eighteenth century, nothing would shake the foundations of Christian belief in the nineteenth century or since, than a theory of evolution which challenges the first book of the Bible and thus the foundations of the Bible itself.

That Darwin's 1859 publication of *Origin of Species* was a landmark challenge to biblical revelation is a familiar story. It provoked immediate and very public debate, as in the clash between Huxley and Wilberforce (Desmond, 1997). Subsequent accommodation and conflict in science and religion debates frequently centre on evolutionary theory and biblical accounts of creation. Darwin is seen here as a neutral scientific figure dispassionately uncovering the laws of nature, leaving others to comment on how such science might affect religious belief. *On the Origin of Species* made Darwin a focus for ecclesiastical mockery. But Darwin avoided adding personal voice to public controversy. Huxley and not Darwin engaged in the 1860 Oxford debate. However Darwin's late life autobiographical writings are insightful:

> Whilst on board the Beagle I was quite orthodox, & I remember being heartily laughed at by several of the officers (though themselves orthodox) for quoting the Bible as an unanswerable authority on some point of morality. I suppose it was the novelty of the argument that amused them. But I had gradually come by this time (i.e. 1836 to 1839) to see the Old Testament, from its manifestly false history of the world, with the Tower of Babel, the rain-bow as a sign &c &c, from its attributing to God the feelings of a vengeful tyrant, was no more to be trusted than the sacred books of the Hindoos [*sic*], or the beliefs of any barbarian.

His attacks on religion are then directed specifically to Christianity:

> The question then continually arose before my mind & would not be banished . . . By further reflecting that the clearest evidence would be requisite to make any sane man believe in the miracles by which Christianity is supported – that the more we know of the men at that time were ignorant & credulous to a degree almost incomprehensible to us – that the Gospels cannot be proved to have been written simultaneously with the events – that they differ in many important details, far too important as it seemed to me to be admitted as the usual inaccuracies of eye-witnesses – by such reflections as these, which I give not as having the least novelty or value, but as they influence me, I gradually came to disbelieve in Christianity as a divine revelation.

'I found', he writes, 'it more and more difficult, with free scope given to my imagination to invent evidence which would suffice to convince me':

> Thus disbelief crept upon me at a very slow rate, but was at last complete. The rate was so slow that I felt no distress, & have never since doubted even for a single second that my conclusion was correct. I can indeed hardly see how anyone ought to wish Christianity to be true; for if so, the plain language of the text seems to show that the men who do not believe, & this would include my Father, Brother & almost all my friends, will be everlastingly punished. (Darwin, 2008: 391–2)

He adds, with undoubtedly intended irony, 'And this is a damnable doctrine.'

The decade prior to the 1870 Education Act, though, featured highly charged debate between advocates of biblical revelation and Darwinian theories of evolution. The 1860 dispute between Bishop Samuel Wilberforce (son of the anti-slavery campaigner William Wilberforce) and Thomas Huxley (variously 'Darwin's bulldog', the 'priest of evolution' and the 'devil's disciple') did little to enhance for an informed Victorian public the credibility of biblical revelation. Held appropriately at the Oxford University library, now the Museum of Natural History, at the annual meeting of the British Association for the Advancement of Science, most accounts suggest Wilberforce was either ill-prepared or ill-matched for the meeting with Huxley. Wilberforce resorted to satire and scorn more than argument, infamously asking whether Huxley was related to the ape on his grandfather's or his grandmother's side. The reply by Huxley was: 'If then, said I the question is put to me would I rather have a miserable ape for a grandfather or a man highly endowed by nature and possessed of great means of influence and yet who employs these faculties and that influence for the mere purpose of introducing ridicule into a grave scientific discussion, I unhesitatingly affirm my preference for the ape' (Desmond, 1997: 279). Citing the absence of direct contemporaneous verbatim record of the meeting, this account is contested by those supportive of the fundamental veracity of biblical revelation: the biased and mutated accounts of this meeting, or perhaps because of them, history has come to regard this event as something of a turning point in the public acceptance of the theory of evolution (Grigg, 2009). Desmond (1999) himself gives credit to the mixed perceptions of victor and vanquished: Huxley considered himself the most popular man in Oxford for the next 24 hours, and Wilberforce might also have sensed himself and not Huxley as victor. Nevertheless, aside from the accuracy of the verbatim record of the disputation, growing public doubt over biblical revelation meant Christianity was not faring well against the new findings of biological science (Desmond, 1997; Desmond and Moore, 1992) also Gearon 2013a.

As if to look at ways of reframing the Bible to a mood of growing scepticism towards it, 1870 was also the year in which Bishop Wilberforce ordered a revision of the standard Anglican translation of the time, the King James or Authorized Version (Gearon, 2013, forthcoming). It was also a year of some conciliation from the other scientific side of the debate. Thus, in 1870 too Huxley expansively praised many of the contributions of the Bible to English culture, and in a paper written on the new school boards established by the 1870 Education Act. Huxley's essay praised the Bible's literary qualities in particular, and in this its educational merit (Huxley, 1870). Huxley's secular, cultural heritage argument was not of course a theological defence. We thus have a secular scepticism of biblical revelation matched by a secular admiration for the Bible's cultural merits, a perspective which is shared today by many secularists. It was marked in the 400th anniversary commemorations of the King James Bible. Even Richard Dawkins has described himself a 'cultural Christian' (Dawkins, 2007a; on the cultural reception of the Bible in secular context, see Hamlin and Jones, 2010).

For religious education, then, the 1870s was already an intellectual milieu growing sceptical of the text which was central to its teaching. At a time when few teachers had anything like university-level education, growing numbers of new church colleges for teacher education helped to raise standards of training for new teachers. And at least within the context of a Christian school, ethos, doctrine, religious authority and revelation had some *prima facie* justification. In fact, although the 1870 Education Act meant the provision of state schools (there were technically none before this date), it did not diminish but rather it did accelerate the demand for Catholic and Protestant schools. In the two decades following the act, the number of children attending church schools doubled to 2 million (Gillard, 2011). The 'dual system' was clearly providing a need unfulfilled by state provision, whether or not this related to religious education, we can only speculate.

In terms of state religious education, it meant some degree of ecumenical cooperation at least among Protestant denominations, as Bates puts it, the 'tradition of Christian instruction established in nineteenth century Anglican and Nonconformist elementary day schools was maintained in nondenominational form in secular "board" and "county" schools after 1870 and 1902'. Bates, writing from a perspective critical of biblical teaching, suggests that 'disputes between the churches prevented it developing beyond a dry, factual study of the Bible'. Given the absence of any empirical studies of biblical teaching in nineteenth-century schools, it is difficult to know from where Bates draws this conclusion. He is right however to point to evidence of improved ecumenical relations between the churches in the first half of the twentieth century: 'Negotiations between the churches and the LEAs [Local Education Authorities] to solve the problems of the "dual system" after the 1918 Education Act resulted in the churches having the major say in determining the official content of religious teaching in the rapidly expanding state school sector' (Bates, 1994: 6–7).

Religious education was here distinguished by Cowper-Temple clause (section 14 of the Act): 'No religious catechism or religious formulary which is distinctive of any particular denomination shall be taught in the school.' Nevertheless, how this non-denominational approach was to be achieved was never fully elaborated. The Cowper–Temple clause in this regard was in incipient form and masked a problem of pedagogical foundations to which it had been subject throughout its history: How can religious education be taught outside of a religious tradition? Even in religious education of a scriptural-theological approach, finding a pedagogy in content and method that would satisfy all denominations remained unresolved.

The pedagogical problems on 'non-denominational' scriptural-theological Bible teaching surfaced in *The Spens Report on Secondary Education* (1938). Its chapter 5 dealt exclusively with 'Scripture'. On scriptural knowledge, *Spens* comments: 'There are three main departments into which Biblical study in schools is likely to fall: the religious ideas and experiences of Israel, of which the record is to be found in the Old Testament, the life and teaching of Jesus Christ, and the beginning of the Christian church.'

Spens' optimism is apparent: 'We believe that there is a wide and genuine recognition of the value and importance of religious instruction and the teaching of Scripture in schools, and that the time is favourable for a fresh consideration of the place that they should occupy in the education of boys and girls of secondary school age. The subject has been hitherto admittedly difficult and sometimes controversial. No kind of religious instruction can fail to raise issues relating to the meaning of life and to human destiny which in the world outside the school are the subject of profound disagreement'. The problem remains 'largely . . . of finding an approach to the subject which can enlist the disinterested enthusiasm and give scope to the professional ability of teachers who may differ widely in their personal convictions'. Further, the report's authors 'believe that the present temper of public opinion is such that the educational issues involved in the teaching of Scripture may be faced fairly on their own merits, and that they are no longer obscured by past controversy'. Given the subsequent history of the scriptural-theological approaches, and the place of the Bible in religious education, such optimism seems somewhat misplaced.

Spens consciously rejects a cultural heritage argument, its justification, that is, as part of English language, literature, culture or history:

> It is often maintained that the study of the Bible should have a place in the curriculum for its literary value alone. We do not wish to underestimate that value. The English Bible is one of the glories of the literary heritage bequeathed to the English-speaking peoples. For that reason there is much to be said in favour of the inclusion of portions of the Bible in the syllabus of English literature. But it is also true that no boy or girl can be counted as properly educated unless he or she has been made aware of the fact of the existence of a religious interpretation of life. The traditional form which that interpretation has taken in this country is Christian, and the principal justification for giving a place in the curriculum to the study of the Scriptures is that the Bible is the classic book of Christianity and forms the basis of the structure of Christian faith and worship. The content of the Bible has, therefore, inevitably its own dignity and associations. It can neither be treated merely as a part of English literature, nor can it be merged in the general study of history. (*Spens*, 1938: 206–17).

The wider cultural appreciation of the Bible would be among its only surviving merits in the religious education that would form in the next decades (Hamlin and Jones, 2010).

The 1944 Education Act was a landmark for religious education in England which postponed the real decline of Bible teaching in English schools. What is invariably forgotten is that the framework for religious education now becomes not simply non-denominational but *secular* as well. The latter word appears repeatedly in the act. Albeit the section headed 'secular instruction' is seemingly in contrast to 'religious instruction', the former effectively frames the latter. Yet, despite *Spens* and the secularism of English religious education legislation, in the decades which followed the 1944 Education Act, locally agreed upon syllabuses (the legal framework for state religious education in England) followed a broadly biblical orientation advocated by *Spens* in terms of content (Copley 2004; Thompson 2004). The *Durham Report* (Ramsey, 1970) examining 'the fourth R' (religion) in education would take cognizance of psychological theories of religious education and the changing religious makeup of British society. But it would still place emphasis on the primacy of Christianity in religious education. Nevertheless, landmark as the *Durham Report* was, biblical and theological emphases in state religious education would from here on become marked.

Newer secular psychological frameworks for understanding children's attitudes to the Bible would however come to dominate. Harold Loukes (1961, 1963), Ronald Goldman (1964, 1965) and Edwin Cox (1971) were especially influential in their analysis of the role of the Bible in religious education. Their collective argument was that, bearing in mind their psychological development and prevailing sociological conditions, children lacked, to use the Loukes/Goldman term, 'readiness for religion'. It is opportune to recall Callum Brown's (2004) observation that, though long in gestation, these mid-twentieth-century decades were the true beginning of 'the death of Christian Britain'. Using a seemingly benign child-centred methodology and outlook, these religious education researchers particularly targeted the Bible as inappropriate for children (Hyde, 1990). Child-centred education was deemed to meet the children's needs in preparing for adult life, and such education increasingly took the curricula centre stage. Religious education in English schools increasingly became aligned to personal and social education. On the basis of a few influential researchers, Bible teaching declined. Readiness for religion research provided a ready-made excuse for educators already ill-equipped to teach the Bible to jettison it from the curriculum.

These child-centred approaches, soon seen as lacking content, were themselves marginalized. While more will be said of Ninian Smart's contributions, his then fairly unprecedented intervention as university professor into school education, marked a turning point for religious education, and arguably the real moment of decline for the scriptural-theological approach. In a 1969 edition of the American journal *Religious Education*, where we might note his explicitly secular allegiance, Smart writes: 'I am deeply committed to the secular principle in state education. That is, I am sceptical as to whether the present pattern of religious education in England, which assumes that for those who do not contract out on grounds of conscience, etc., the content of religious education shall be Christian, is right or viable' (Smart 1969a: 26).

The Schools' Council Working Paper No. 36 (1971), initiates moves to adopt Smart's phenomenological approach to religious. This (but then Smart was part of the working group) and to transform scriptural-theological religious education into the teaching of world religions. In 1985, an inquiry into the education of children from ethnic minority groups, chaired by Lord Swann, published *Education for All*. The *Swann Report* saw such teaching as making a potentially positive contribution to a harmonious 'multicultural' society. As Barnes (2001) notes, the *Swann Report* came down 'decisively in favour of a nondogmatic, nondenominational, phenomenological approach to religious education' (Barnes, 2001: 445). The idea was of its time. In a nation and a world more and more aware of religious diversity, the teaching of world religions in schools would now come to dominate religious education. In many respects it still does.

These factors shaped the 1988 Education Reform Act, the most significant piece of education legislation since 1944. Its implications for religious education were considerable, requiring in law that syllabuses for religious education in state schools 'shall reflect the fact that the religious traditions in Great Britain are in the main Christian whilst taking account of the teaching and practices of the other principal religions represented in Great Britain'. Despite this considerable shift away from scriptural-theological approaches, essentially the Bible to teaching world religions, the 1988 Education Reform Act was nevertheless charged by some as reactionary for giving Christianity the paramount place, which many considered was self-evident from historical perspective alone. Bates, acknowledging the 1988 Act's promotion of world religions in religious education, claims the act itself was 'inspired by reactionary thinking out of keeping with the ethos and needs of a multicultural society' (Bates, 1996: 85).

This phenomenological approach was consolidated by the Schools' Curriculum and Assessment Authority (SCAA, 1994; later the Qualifications and Curriculum Authority), *Model Syllabuses* and later, as we saw earlier, in the *Non-Statutory Guidance for Religious Education* (QCA, 2004) and in *Religious Education in English Schools: Non-Statutory Guidance 2010* (QCA, 2010). Ironically, a major report by school inspectors found one tradition whose serious weaknesses in learning and teaching in English state schools marked it out for special criticism: Christianity (Ofsted, 2010).

There was some rearguard action to shore up the subject teaching of both Christianity and the Bible. The Stapleford Project, for example, introduced 'concept-cracking' to give a philosophical-theological edge to teaching Christianity (Cooling, 2000). Specifically in regard to teaching and learning the Bible in religious education, Terence Copley and colleagues' Biblos project investigated attitudes and understanding of children of all ages to the Bible, and from this research produced a number of reports and curriculum recommendations (Copley 2008; Copley et al., 2001, 2004). Showing a laudable personal and professional commitment, such initiatives can hardly be said to have dented the consciously secular orientations of religious education which would emerge from the phenomenological teaching of world religions.

The phenomenological paradigm

In the last section, examining the scriptural-theological we saw the emergence of a genuine and, what would be wholesale, shift in approaches to understanding religion, and this had and continues to have a profound and worldwide effect on the teaching of religion. Ninian Smart exerted an immense influence on the study of religion. His groundbreaking book (Smart, 1969a) *The Religious Education Experience of Mankind* was an attempt to argue systematically the case for the non-confessional approach to the study of religion. In other words, in order to understand religious belief you didn't have to be a believer.

In this book he argued for a 'phenomenological' approach to the study of religion. The term derives from the philosophy of Edmund Husserl, and is a technical epistemological investigation of how we know the world of phenomena. Smart, in essence, took religion as a valid subject to study, as a phenomena. He was not of course the first by any means to do so, and Smart also builds on far more than the phenomenology of Husserl, drawing also on anthropology, sociology, philosophy, psychology and indeed theology (see Pals, 2008). Smart, then, synthesized the various branches of the study of religion into a system. Smart's late 1960s book is most famous in this regard for introducing the notion that religion has 'six dimensions': the doctrinal; the mythological (or narrative); the ethical; the ritual; the experiential; and the social. In a later work, the more inclusively titled *The World's Religions* (Smart, 1989), and elaborated in a subsequent book, *Dimensions of the Sacred: An Anatomy of the World's Beliefs*, Smart (1999) added a seventh dimension, the material, covering the aesthetic dimension, notably the arts, including architecture, but having wider reference to all aspects of what socio-anthropologists call 'material culture'. Smart acknowledged the debt of this thinking to the phenomenology of Edmund Husserl, particularly Husserl's work on consciousness, and how we know objects that we as human subject encounter in the world. This in turn had drawn from a distinction Kant had made between the noumenal and the phenomenal, the world of ideas and the world of phenomenon.

Smart took a complex discussion from philosophy, as it had filtered through 'phenomenology', and applied it very loosely to the understanding of religion as a *phenomenon*. Smart thus comments that to 'religionists' (those who study religion) 'it means the use of epoche or suspension of belief, together with the use of empathy in entering the experiences and intentions of religious participants'. This implies that 'in describing the ways people behave, we do not use, as far as we can avoid them, alien categories to evoke the nature of their act and to understand those acts' (Smart, 1996: 2). It was, however, Gerardus van der Leeuw (1938) in *Religion in Essence and Manifestation* who is acknowledged (by Smart, Eliade and others) as having applied this largely notional 'phenomenology' to the study of religion. Disliking the implied essentialism of van der Leeuw – 'essence' implies 'definition', and also the conceptualization of 'worldviews' (considered 'too cerebral'), Smart is more concerned with 'the attitude of informed empathy' which 'tries to bring out what religious acts mean to religious actors'. Smart's approach therefore presents 'a functional delineation of religion in lieu of a strict definition'.

However, the method of detached observation is only partially original. In the sense that scholars of religion, in attempting to delineate a field specific to them (see earlier, 'the science of religion') were keen to differentiate their field precisely from others who in other fields had studied religion, especially socio-anthropologists. That accepted, Smart also openly acknowledges his debt, and the debt of the 'science of religion', not only to the social sciences but also to psychology and psychoanalysis, explicitly and technically in *The Science of Religion & the Sociology of Knowledge: Some Methodological Questions* (Smart, 1973). In *Dimensions of the Sacred*, he explicitly contextualizes this study by relating the seven dimensions to the disciplines which had helped shape religious studies: textual and philological studies; anthropology and sociology; and psychology and psychoanalysis. But to understand the shock of this approach, we have to recall that university departments in England had not, to the same extent as in Europe and the United States, been as influenced by this 'science of religion'. In English universities, with exceptions, the study of religion meant the study of theology in the Judaeo-Christian tradition. The detachment in Smart's approach was not always welcome, especially when this detachment was applied to Christianity, most fully undertaken in *The Phenomenon of Christianity* (Smart, 1979).

Smart's approach to the study of religion, and active interest in schools as well as universities, showed his perceptiveness in seeing the importance of religion in the modern world, and the importance therefore of a wider understanding of religion in the modern world. Smart had the foresight to see (when very few other university scholars did) the significant potential of schools for addressing issues of religious pluralism in the global political context. It is this latter political context which, Smart had the foresight to see, would be one of the lasting justifications for the study of religion. Thus the final chapter of his *Dimensions of the Sacred* specifically addresses the 'political effects of religion'.

Smart left for religious education as well as religious studies worldwide an extraordinary legacy. Apart from his work in the study of religion within universities, Smart was and in many direct and indirect ways continues to be influential in advocating the practice of the study of world religion in school religious education. As noted, through the Schools Council (1971) *Working Paper 36: Religion in Secondary Schools*, the phenomenological approach to the study of religion thus begin to provide a link between the academic study of religion in universities and the teaching of religious education in schools.

Adjunct problems which the subject is wrestling with today were also identified by Smart. For example, which religions to teach, how much coverage is to be given and how to represent them them, and by whose account: 'Thus, in an important sense, the study of a religion involves *presenting* that faith, and so the exercise frequently involves considerable powers of sensitivity and imagination. But, it will be objected, only the member of a faith can effectively perform the presentation' (Smart, 1969a: 27). Smart disagrees. His principle of empathetic understanding, seeing the faith as an insider might, done well means that even an outsider to a tradition can make a faithful representation of it. Given Smart was himself presenting an account of the world's religions, he would have to hold to this position. The phenomenological position (van der Leeuw, Smart and so forth) attempts to differ from reductionist accounts by this faithful representation of religious tradition. There will also be tensions here: Smart had encouraged a multidisciplinary approach to the study of religion, as we have noted, and many of these were reductive in approach.

As for the limitation or defining of content in schools, Smart suggests the following sketch:

> It is implicit in my argument that a person who is going to undertake the teaching of religious studies should have knowledge of at least three areas. First, he needs a grounding in his 'home' tradition; and this means in turn that he should be able to handle problems in understanding the biblical material; second, he needs grounding in the comparative study of religion – in the sense that his course should include an immersion in some traditions other than the 'home' tradition; third, he should be aware of modern developments in religious and atheistic thought and the sociology of religion. The three areas are inter-related, since both Christian theology and biblical studies have been revolutionised in the 19th and 20th century, and it is also in this period that sociological and phenomenological studies of religion and the comparative study of religion have burgeoned. In brief, such a tripartite course will keep the student continually open to the methodological and philosophical problems surrounding the content with which he is working. It is to be hoped that through such a plural and critical course he will acquire both sensitivity and openness in dealing with the subject. (Smart, 1969a: 29)

Question marks remained (as they do today) over how such teachers would be supplied. University departments such as his own also served that purpose, and so there was some self-interest logic behind Smart's proposals.

A subsidiary problem was the supply of teaching and learning materials for such a curriculum. Half a century later, school textbooks, especially how and by whom religions are represented, remain a perennial issue as the curriculum research study *Materials Used to Teach about World Religions in Schools in England* suggests (Jackson et al., 2010).

The other issue was the anticipated response of Christian denominations to what Smart *explicitly* defines as a secularizing of the subject: 'How will churches and religious organizations react to a secularization of the teaching of religion?' Smart can correctly state this as he recognizes that the foundations on which the new religious education are to be based are indeed secular. But the subsequent claim that it is traditional religious education rather than secularity itself which has alienated 'younger people' from religion is unfounded, and so too then is his claim that such developments are good for the churches:

> It is probably not realized that a substantial cause of alienation from orthodoxy among intelligent younger people arises not from lack of 'religious instruction', but because of it – because, that is, of a suspected and often real lack of openness in the treatment of religion compared with other spheres of human experience. Paradoxically, what is good for the secular, pluralistic state is good for the churches. (Smart, 1969a: 30)

It is 'the secular state as neutralist and recognising pluralism,' he states, 'which rightly insists or ought to insist on a pluralistic approach to the teaching of religion'. Writing in the 1960s, he was one of a minority to challenge then prevalent notions of secularization. Dismissing it, cautiously – 'I am not sure that the emphasis on increasing secularization is really true to the facts about the world taken as a whole' – and then more confidently, 'things have not come to such a pass and I do not believe they ever will'. By such arguments he suggests religion can 'legitimately demand at least a significant share in the spectrum of subjects' (Smart, 1969a: 30). 'Revolutions in education,' he concludes, though, 'cannot be made overnight'. But in fact if not overnight then within a few short years, this approach had become embedded within religious education. Many subsequent developments in religious education are thus to some degrees also responses to Smart.

The psychological-experiential paradigm

Psychology of religion was the dominant scientific paradigm to influence the modern field of education, as Furlong and Lawn (Furlong and Lawn, 2010) outline in their overview of *Disciplines of Education* (also Furlong and Lawn, 2009). The role of educational applications of psychology was also pivotal in securing its role as a new discipline within universities (Crozier, 2010: 32). Though, as Crozier (2011) points out, the relationship between psychology and education has become less close and more contested, the remit of the psychology of education has been and remains of wide application: in assessment, cognitive development, intelligence, motivation and so forth, especially applied to theories of learning (Daniels and Edwards, 2004; Goodman, 2010). Here Piaget's theories of children's development informed much of the early work in psychology of education. In areas closely allied but distinguishable from religious education, later psychology of education researchers have applied Piagetian frameworks of children's moral development (Piaget, 1997) significantly to theories of moral development by Lawrence Kohlberg (Kohlberg, 1981; see Munsey, 1980). Robert Coles's (1986, 2011) work has spanned what he terms the 'moral archaeology of childhood' and the spiritual life of children. But unarguably, it is James Fowler (1981) who once again made fashionable the application to 'faith development' (see Francis and Astley, 1992).

Psychology of education developed in close conjunction with psychology of education, and in this regard had a strong impact on the subject, as noted earlier, through figures such as Colin Alves, Edwin Cox, Ronald Goldman, Kenneth Hyde and Harold Loukes, between the late 1950s and early 1970s. Given the predominance of Christian religious education at the time, these studies examined pupils responses to questions of theology and scripture, analysing their responses in terms of psychological developmental frameworks. Almost invariably, the shared conclusion was that such responses showed a low level of theological understanding and scriptural interpretation. Though the studies were relatively small scale, their impact was not. A sense of the inappropriateness of Christian religious education as it was then taught would lead to wholesale changes to religious education in the 1960s in particular, with increasing emphases on dealing with ethical and moral themes of relevance to young people and a limiting of the theological and scriptural content (see Kay, 1996; also Thompson, 2004).

There is still current and wide international interest in integrating Christian theology, faith formation and spiritual development with psychological theory (e.g. Estep and Kim, 2010) as well as in education (Alexander, 2001, 2004; DeSouza et al., 2009). There is also a widespread continued application of psychological theory and research to religious education (e.g. Francis, 2005; Francis et al., 2005). Francis in particular is responsible for a proliferation of psychological attitudinal studies, including attitudes to and effectiveness of faith schools (Francis, 2009). Nevertheless, as the phenomenological approach came to dominate school religious education in the 1970s, the psychology of education approaches to religious education dramatically waned in impact. These approaches would certainly never re-attain their impact on religious education as they had once done.

That said, there was a period in 1990s religious education when the impact of a, loosely to be interpreted, psychological influence on religious education pedagogy became evident. Though it had nothing like a profound effect on the wider curriculum, it was notable in focusing on spirituality, spiritual development and the 'experiential' aspects of religion and religious education. This emphasis was a direct response to and reaction against Smart's phenomenology of religious, as it was perceived to have become in schools. What was seen as dry and not-relevant teaching of Christianity through biblical and theological teaching had transformed, according to this view, into a superficial factual teaching of world religions.

This development was evidenced in the establishing, by Clive Erricker, Jane Erricker and Catha Ota, of the *International Journal of Children's Spirituality*. In pedagogical terms, it centred on a textbook for schools and teacher education: *New Methods in Religious Education: An Experiential Approach* (Hammond, Hay, Moxon, Netto, Raban, Straugheir and Williams, 1990). The title of the latter shows the twin influences of Smart (*The Religious Experience of Mankind*) and William James's *The Varieties of Religious Experience* (James, 1985). In the former case, though this new spiritual development emphasis is generally assumed to be a reaction again phenomenology, it can also be seen as regaining for religious education the experiential emphasis seen be lost when such was translated to schools. But Smart saw classrooms as places for the study, not for generation of religious and spiritual experience. This is where the new approach can be distinguished from Smart, for this is precisely what these new approaches in broad terms favoured, classrooms as places where students could be opened directly to spiritual experience.

The psychologist William James's 1902 Gifford Lectures in Edinburgh were the source of a book which is still the basis of understanding the psychology of religion today, *The Varieties of Religious Experience* (James, 1985). James begins with definitional issues, aware that definitions are 'so many and so different from one another'. From this lack of definitional consensus, James asserts that religion 'cannot stand for any single principle or essence, but is rather a collective name'. Seeing in such attempts at definition an unavoidable 'oversimplification' – 'the root of all that absolutism and one-sided dogmatism by which both philosophy and religion have been infested' – James suggests to his audience that we should not fall 'immediately into a one-sided view of our subject, but let us rather admit freely at the outset that we may very likely find no one essence, but many characters which may alternately be equally important to religion' (James, 1985: 26).

It is religious experience (the 'religious sentiment'), itself diverse in object and interpretation – allied to 'the feeling of dependence' or 'a derivative from fear' or 'sexual life' or a 'feeling of the infinite' – that interests James:

> There is religious fear, religious love, religious awe, religious joy, and so forth. But religious love is only man's natural emotion of love directed to a religious object; religious fear is only the ordinary fear of commerce . . . in so far as the notion of divine retribution may arouse it; religious awe is the same organic thrill which we feel in a forest at twilight, or in a mountain gorge; only this time it comes over us at the thought of our supernatural relations; and similarly of all the various sentiments which may be called into play in the lives of religious persons. As concrete states of mind, made up of a feeling *plus* a specific sort of object, religious emotions of course are psychic entities distinguishable from other concrete emotions; but there is no ground for assuming a simple abstract 'religious emotion' to exist as a distinct elementary mental affection by itself, present in every religious experience without exception. (James, 1985: 27)

There is 'no one elementary religious emotion' but rather 'a common storehouse of emotions upon which religious objects may draw, so there might conceivably also prove to be no one specific and essential kind of religious object, and no one specific and essential kind of religious act'.

One way to mark it out easily 'is to say what aspects of the subject we leave out'. At the outset, he states, 'We are struck by one great partition which divides the religious field. On the one side of it lies institutional, on the other personal religion . . . one branch of religion keeps the divinity, another keeps man most in view': 'in these lectures I propose to ignore the institutional branch entirely, to say nothing of the ecclesiastical organization, to consider as little as possible the systematic theology and the ideas about the gods themselves, and to confine myself as far as I can to personal religion pure and simple.' He addresses the question about whether 'religion' should 'be reserved for the fully organized system of feeling, thought, and institution, for the Church, in short, of which this personal religion, so called, is but a fractional element': 'But if you say this, it will only show all the more plainly how much the question of definition tends to become a dispute about names. Rather than prolong such a dispute, I am willing to accept almost any name for the personal religion of which I propose to treat. Call it conscience or morality, if you yourselves prefer, and not religion – under either name it will be equally worthy of our study.' He does in the final lecture bring in 'theologies and the ecclesiasticisms' and of their relation to the religious experience. But he persists with his view that 'at least the personal religion will prove itself more fundamental than either theology or ecclesiasticism': 'Churches, when once established, live at second-hand upon tradition; but the *founders* of every church owed their power originally to the fact of their direct personal communion with the divine. Not only the superhuman founders, the Christ, the Buddha, Mahomet [*sic*], but all the originators of Christian sects have been in this case; so personal religion should still seem the primordial thing, even to those who continue to esteem it incomplete' (James, 1985: 29–30).

Religion, James states, shall therefore 'mean for us *the feelings, acts, and experiences of individual men in their solitude, so far as they apprehend themselves to stand in relation to whatever they may consider the divine*. Since the relation may be either moral, physical, or ritual, it is evident that out of religion in the sense in which we take it, theologies, philosophies, and ecclesiastical organizations may secondarily grow.' The 'divine', James insists, we do not take 'in too narrow a sense': 'There are systems of thought which the world usually calls religious, and yet which do not positively assume a God. Buddhism is in this case' (James, 1985: 27).

William James remains critical to modern discussions of religious experience. James influenced to some degree all subsequent psychology and much philosophy of religion. In the third lecture on the 'reality of the unseen', we see strands of the thinking of Rudolf Otto's *The Idea of the Holy* and Mircea Eliade's *The Sacred and the Profane*. The psychotherapy of religious experience remains still indebted to James's analysis of the 'religion of healthy-mindedness' (Lectures IV and V) and the 'sick soul' (Lectures VI and VI).Presaging the work of Carl Jung is James's chapter (Lecture IX) on 'The Divided Self, and the Process of Its Unification'. James gives considerable attention to 'saintliness' (Lectures XIV, XV, XVI and XVII) and mysticism. Philosophy itself is given relatively short shrift, identifying, as the preceding chapters intimate, 'primacy of feeling in religion, philosophy being a secondary function'.

The title of James's *Varieties of Religious Experience* is reflected in Smart's *The Religious Experience of Mankind*. James was an important subliminal influence on the late 1980s and early 1990s backlash against what were seen as the pedagogical *results* of Ninian Smart's phenomenology on religious education, described at the time as a 'Cook's Tour' of world religions, leading to superficiality in treatment of the complexities of religion. One especially ironic charge here was that Smart neglected the spiritual and experiential. This of course he precisely did not do, as the title of Smart's (1969a) most important book makes clear. From the 1990s, the work of Clive and Jane Erricker, with Cathy Ota and others thus achieved prominence with emphases on spirituality in education, including, as noted, the establishing of the *International Journal of Children's Spirituality*.

Debates, however, reached a vitriolic high point early in the 1990s within the *British Journal of Religious Education*, centred on a textbook for schools and teacher education: *New Methods in Religious Education: An Experiential Approach* (Hammond et al., 1990). *New Methods* presented the case for a greater experiential and even 'spiritual' development emphasis in religious education. The approach was based on the supposed experiences of the 'transcendent' by ordinary people in everyday life, pioneered in England by the Religious Experience Research Unit (later the Alister Hardy Research Centre), but part of a much wider field of psychological enquiry, including work on the moral and spiritual life of children (Coles, 1986, 1990). The sorts of exercises the team of *New Methods* authors advocated included 'stilling' exercises, 'guided fantasy' and empathetic tasks such as quiet 'meditative' walking.

The approaches were given seemingly legal sanction by the way in which the term 'spiritual development' was enshrined in the 1944 and 1988 Education and Education Reform Acts, respectively:

> The curriculum for a maintained school satisfies the requirements of this section if it is a balanced and broadly based curriculum which
> (a) promotes the spiritual, moral, cultural, mental and physical development of pupils at the school and of society; and
> (b) prepares such pupils for the opportunities, responsibilities and experiences of adult life (HMSO, 1988: 1).

In Copley's (2000) historical account of spiritual development in English schools, he demonstrates its transformation from Christian formation to a more generalized notion of psychological self-knowledge. Though Hammond and Hay (1990) root their experiential approach as 'new methods in religious education', many saw little explicitly and nothing systematically religious about the 'techniques' espoused. The book provoked unprecedented criticism:

> *New Methods in Religious Education* makes dozens of suggestions for exercises or techniques which aim to get children 'going inwards', looking at what is going on 'inside themselves'. Typical is imagining 'watching a cat dozing in the sunshine' and then asking 'What was it like for you?' A common justification for requiring children to undertake these activities is that people's experience is 'always and inevitably *subjective*'. Therefore to understand the experience of another, it is necessary to penetrate into their inwardness or subjectivity. But this claim only compounds the confusion. If the claim is just that all human experiences are had by human subjects, then the claim is both true and trivial. But if the claim is being made that experience necessarily requires an inner world where some series of internal events parallels some series of external events, then this claim is clearly based on a philosophical dualism which lacks credibility. (Thatcher, 1991: 22)

Thatcher adds to his philosophical critique with an educational one: 'It is hard to see how these practices can be justified in the name of religious education. Many are so tangential to religion that politicians, heads, teachers, school governors . . . and children will rightly wonder why they are being practised at all. Is this the best use of the restricted timetable time for religious education?' (Thatcher, 1991: 26).

Hammond and Hay (1992) made a robust but curiously Christian theological response, curious in the sense that *New Methods* contained so little Christian theological content. In a paper which draws on the New Testament – ' "When You Pray" Go To Your Private Room' A Reply to Adrian Thatcher' – Hammond and Hay cite a number of biblical texts, including the passage from which the paper's title is derived:

> Not a word from their lips can be trusted, deep within them lies ruin. (Ps. 5.9)
>
> God create a clean heart in me, put into me a new and constant spirit. (Ps. 51.10)
>
> Man's spirit is the lamp of Yahweh, searching his deepest self. (Prov. 20.27)
>
> This is the covenant I will make with the house of Israel when those days arrive – it is Yahweh who speaks. Deep within them I will plant my Law, writing it on their hearts. Then I will be their God and they shall be my people. (Jer. 31.33)
>
> But when you pray, go to your private room and, when you have shut your door, pray to your Father who is in that secret place, and your Father who sees all that is done in secret will reward you. (Mt. 6.6)

A broader defence derives from the idea of withdrawal from the world in the religious life:

> Retiring to a place of solitude for the conduct of religious exercises has been central both in the personal lives of the founders of the great religious traditions represented in this country and in what they advocate for their followers. Jesus retires to a lonely place to pray, Muhammad retreats to a cave in the desert, the Bhagavad Gita urges the yogi to go into the forest to meditate. Nor is the necessity to withdraw less recognized by religious people in our own day, as the current mushrooming of the retreat movement demonstrates. At issue is the contention that such behaviour is a form of escapism, avoiding the glaring evils in the environment around one. (Hammond and Hay, 1992: 145–6)

The core issues centre not on whether such practice occurs in religious traditions but whether such practice, or an imitation of it, is appropriate to the classroom.

Such approaches would not however have made headway if English legislative contexts had not required education to contribute to the 'spiritual, moral, mental and physical development' of children. Yates (1999) characterized the relationship between legal framework and spirituality as little more than 'the bureaucratization of spirituality'. There were attempts to distinguish between had attempted to make a 'spiritual development' as 'educational in intent' and 'relevant for all' as compared with 'developing spirituality' as 'catechetical in intent' and 'therefore inappropriate for some' (Meehan, 2002: 291). This cannot be said to be successful. What begins with an attempt to resolve the confusion of terms simply adds to it. It does not address a more fundamental question, as to why is spiritual development educationally valid *at all* in state school context except insofar as law provided the justification.

The psychological-spiritual paradigm has a multitude of roots. These are first and foremost, in England and the West, rooted in the Judaeo-Christian tradition. The emphasis here is upon children's experience. Trond Enger's (1992) 'Religious Education between Psychology and Theology' suggests that one of 'the most significant features within theology over the last two decades is the renewed emphasis on experience' which 'renewed theological interest for religious experience is, of course, also reflected within religious education' (Enger, 1992: 435). He describes this 'renewed interest in experience in theology and religious education – not to speak of the psychology of religion where it, at least since William James, has played the main part' as 'legitimate' for several reasons. First: 'Experience is that dimension in religion without which no other dimensions would have existed. The scarlet thread through the whole of the history of the church is nothing but a continuous process of experience and a continuous process of story-telling – a continuous narrative of a person's experience with God. The church is nothing but an experience – and narrative-community . . . The central place of the experience is true not least of the Bible. What is the Bible but a grandiose narrative about human experience with God – attempts to put these experiences into words?' Second: what 'makes this renewed concentration on religious experience legitimate, in fact absolutely necessary, is the obvious gulf so many people find today between the experiences of God they read about in the Bible and the world of their own experiences. God has for too many today become nothing but a meaningless and incomprehensible concept, because they do not any longer find proof of God in the experiences of their everyday lives. That is why experience once again has to be placed on the agenda in theology and religious education and in a way where the theologian and religious education-teacher must concentrate on opening up and creating new possibilities for experience of God' (Enger, 1992: 435–6).

Between religious experience and religious education, vis-a-vis, for example, Hammond et al.:

> The recognition of the basic role of experience in Christianity (as in all other phenomena that deserve the name of religion) is, of course, not without problems as far as the teaching of Christianity and religion in schools is concerned. It is partly a question of whether the concentration on the experiential dimension of religion is compatible with the aims and objectives in a secularized school with its non-confessional religious education. And partly it is a question of whether religious experience, experience of what we call God, has anything at all to do with the learning process, whether religious experience can be learned at all. The answer to the last question also gives most of the answer to the first one . . . Experiences of God always have a prehistory, they always build on certain conditions. It is on this point that religious education can and ought to do something: to contribute to the creation of these conditions for religious experience, so that the student's horizon can be widened and kept open. (Enger, 1992: 436–7)

Enger argues for the need to focus on the *substance* of the religious experience, to ask questions such as: 'What *sort* of religious experience do we want to expose students to? What *sort* of religious experience do we want to prepare for?'

Carr's (2005, 2006) philosophical treatment suggests the term 'spirituality' has diverse meanings across religious traditions and beyond them. This breadth of terminology, definition, reference points, and so forth, are what made understanding spirituality beyond religious traditions difficult. Even within single or particular religious traditions, spirituality is itself contested. For this reason, attempts do derive an educational, useable and explicitly 'secular spirituality' (Newby, 1996) have been largely unsuccessful, as a number of philosophers of education seem also to have suggested (Carr and Haldane, 2003; Hand, 2003). When spirituality has been adopted by and into secular contexts, it has less well defined and less easy to determine and more diffuse senses (take the range of diffuse uses and applications in Best, 1996). For example, when adopted into this humanistic context, it has meaning to those who adopt it. Spirituality is thus widely used now as a general sense of disillusionment with perceived strictures and inhibitions of 'organized religion', but prefer the term 'spirituality'. Hammond et al. (1990) as a basis for their experiential approach in *New Methods*. Where *state* schools are required to provide for 'spiritual development' – and surely English state schools are increasingly in this matter a minority – a necessarily pluralistic sense of the spiritual of course needs to be adopted, and this will incorporate religious and secular models, however confused such adoptions are. In practical terms, busy schools pay far less attention than they once might have done a decade and more ago, when there was intense debate about spirituality in education.

When spiritual development in such educational-legislative contexts can refer to any form of search for meaning and represent any form of meaningful self-development, the problem of definition becomes, conceptually, an acute one. And, as many have argued, this conceptual impasse is irresolvable, the definition of spirituality in education is so diffuse as to become ultimately *meaningless*. The close association of spirituality and religion however means it remains an issue for religious educators. As for the wider school context, in subject specific settings, confusion over spirituality development marks a lingering, now residual and once meaningful relationship between religious education and the religious life.

The notion that spiritual development can be rooted anywhere outside of religious traditions is recent. It can be traced to responses within Romanticism, responding to what it perceived to be the Enlightenment's overemphasis on rationality. Romanticism's emphasis on self-expression and creativity led to some of the great literary achievements of the late eighteenth century: It would also lead many artists and writers to see creativity as a replacement not only for rationality but religion as well. Among the most systematic critiques of phenomenological *and* 'spiritual' approaches to religious education emerged from philosophically informed pedagogies, most notably identified with 'critical realism', but which I identify as the philosophical-conceptual paradigm.

The philosophical-conceptual paradigm

Andrew Wright and Philip Barnes are the most notable of those scholars who have formulated a philosophical pedagogy for religious education: 'critical religious education'. Religious education here, it is argued, should be characterized not by studied phenomenological neutrality or autonomous and undisciplined 'spirituality' but as a search for 'truth' (Barnes, 2006, 2007; Wright, 1994, 2001, 2005). Wright states: 'Critical religious education constitutes a disciplined liberal education.' It follows Hirst and Peters (1970) – to oversimply a debate which half a century later continues to provoke discussion (Marples, 1999) – in emphasizing knowledge and truth, and what became a contested core of curriculum 'subjects' to convey this knowledge and truth. Hirst and Peters put this in near apocalyptic terms in *The Logic of Education*: humanity's 'survival depends largely on their ability to master a vast heritage of knowledge' (Hirst and Peters, 1970: 115). Hirst and Peters and their emphasis on knowledge acquisition are often portrayed, to an exaggerated degree, as anti-progressive, preferring the imposition of knowledge rather than a kindling of children's experience.

'Critical religious education' thus tends to emphasize on following similar, though distinguishable, paths, also knowledge and especially 'truth' in religious education. However, for a critical realist, the inculcation of religious 'facts' should give way to the cultivation of the critical insights of the philosopher and theologian. Knowledge of religion should be the gateway to the truth about them.

Philosophical-conceptual models of the religious therefore become important. Critical religious education thus rejects any phenomenological setting aside or sometimes called 'bracketing out' of truth claims in religious education. Critical religious education also rejects the vacuous pursuit of 'spiritual' experience without 'a direct critical engagement with the substance of religious truth claims' (Wright, 2003: 281).

Does this mean an overemphasis of philosophy in religious education? Wright suggests critical religious education is often misinterpreted in two main ways. The first temptation is to reduce such thinking 'to the level of a serviceable technique' rather than as 'a foundational disposition that drives the entire pedagogy of the subject'. The second is to 'mystify critical thinking by turning it into some kind of esoteric skill accessible only to the more insightful and imaginative teacher' (Wright, 2004: 281). Indeed, despite the technical framing of critical religious education, at its root is 'the relatively mundane process of asking intelligent and interrogative questions'. Wright argues that 'this proposal is simply an attempt to recover the original vision of the Schools Council of a form of religious education in which children are taught to think philosophically, logically, scientifically, sociologically, psychologically, historically, ethically, aesthetically and – by implication at least – theologically about religion' (Wright, 2003: 282).

The 'questioning of the existential relevance of academic knowledge has its roots in the Enlightenment's ideal of a pure objective knowledge untainted by the vagaries of subjective opinion'. Wright identifies how the

> Enlightenment engendered a purely rational approach to religion in the form of a natural theology that, in concerning itself primarily with the 'God of the philosophers' at the expense of the 'God of Abraham, Isaac and Jacob', produced a deistic theology in which God functioned merely as the first principle or source of order in the universe, rather than as the object of veneration and worship. (Wright, 2003: 283)

The 'Protestant reaction to this reified natural theology took the form of religious revival driven primarily by an appeal to religious experience, generally – though not exclusively – dislocated from cognitive reflection'. In support is cited the Great Awakening in America, the growth of non-conformism in Britain, the emergence of Pietism on the Continent.

It was Schleiermacher in his late-eighteenth century-work *On Religion: Speeches to its Cultures Despisers* who identifies how Enlightenment emphasis on reason had led to a neglect of religion: 'It may be an unexpected and even a marvellous undertaking, that any one should still venture to demand from the very class that have raised themselves above the vulgar, and are saturated with the wisdom of the centuries, attention for a subject so entirely neglected by them' (Schleiermacher, 1799). As noted at the end of Chapter 1, he saw as paltry any reduction of religion to its social or political usefulness. But he acknowledged the insights that the Enlightenment of his time had done to challenge the theological and metaphysical claims of Christianity. What remains untouched by this rationalistic onslaught is the fundamental sense of a Christian theological worldview in which creatures are ultimately dependent on their Creator, and from this sense of dependence emerges a religious spirit unalterable by reason.

Wright interprets Schleiermacher in arguing that 'in this scheme of things, religious doctrine, being no more than a secondary reflection on primary religious experience, is stripped of any significant cognitive content'. In Schleiermacher's case, this is not entirely accurate, for his later work, for example, *The Christian Faith*, Schleiermacher encourages not simply the experiential sense of dependence but a doctrinal account of it. If we take Wright's other examples – the Great Awakening, British non-conformism, continental Pietism, and again Schleiermacher himself – this notion that 'religious experience . . . is stripped of any significant cognitive content' can hardly be supported. Rational assault on Christianity did result in a renewed emphasis on religious experience but it was not a wholesale stripping of doctrinal content; it could hardly be so.

Wright is correct to identity an emergent contrast in emphases rather than exclusive dichotomy 'between rational theology and experiential religion' (Wright, 2003: 283). The critical realist thus seeks a reunification, embraces 'a realistic understanding of truth and as such its fundamental concern is with how things actually are in the universe, with the ultimate order-of-things, with that which exists regardless of our ability to perceive it'. Whether, for example, God exists or does not exist makes a fundamental difference to our understanding of the world. Further, the choice between '(say) theism, atheism and agnosticism is avoidable only by the most dubious and strenuous act of mental gymnastics'. It follows therefore that 'the more reflective, considered and educated the choices we make the better'. Is this 'confessional' religious education? Wright argues not: 'What distinguishes this concern for truth from forms of confessional religious education is that it approaches the question of truth with an open rather than a closed horizon . . . Where confessionalism seeks to transmit one particular answer to the question of ultimate truth, the critical approach is concerned to equip pupils to engage intelligently in the quest for themselves.' Though 'critical religious education is fundamentally concerned with questions of realistic truth it recognises the importance of a critical engagement with alternative understandings of "truth" ' (Wright, 2003: 286).

In attempting to rehabilitate the question of truth, critical religious education claims not that the question of truth has been ignored ('the problem is not that religious education has no concept of truth') but that such religious education is tacitly 'behind a rhetoric of neutrality' imposing 'neutrality' in a 'confessional manner', thereby defeating its own claims to objective evaluation of religions (Wright, 2003: 287). This conception of religious education risks replacing 'a Christian confessionalism with a liberal confessionalism' (see also Copley, 2006; Felderhof et al., 2007). As we noted above, a liberal democratic assessment of this would be that 'education based on democratic principles seeks to reduce particularistic influences to a minimum' (McLaughlin, 2011: 81). Either case is difficult to 'prove': either that secular religious education represents then a form of secular indoctrination or that religious education epitomizes the closed and the indoctrinatory.

Wright argues that the 'truth' encountered within modern forms of liberal religious education operates on two levels: immanent and transcendent. In the former case, it is a 'pragmatic approach to truth, in which religion is taught not as an end in itself, but as a tool for encouraging tolerance and mutual understanding in a culturally divided society'. We have seen there is a strong case for this, and wide international evidence to show the emergence of such aims in religious education. Whether as Wright suggests, however, that such an approach is concealing a 'hidden' truth, covertly converting students' perspectives to a position of relativity is easy to countenance but difficult to prove: such a view may even be prevalent among students, but it is difficult to assert either that they come to religious education with this attitude formed (if indeed they have it), or whether they are formed in this attitude through religious education. Where limited empirical evidence exists for such views and attitudes, we can cannot generalize on this limited evidence. Dan Moulin's notion that religious education classrooms contain a 'silent minority' of students resistant to such relativism – perhaps an implied 'silenced' minority – cannot be substantiated beyond the valid claims that some schools might contain such exemplars (Moulin, 2011: 313–26).

The second definitional level of truth with which Wright is concerned is the transcendent: 'On the level of transcendence concerns for social cohesion have often led to the conclusion that, insofar as religion is viewed as a human response to transcendence, the only valid theological option is that of a universal theology in which all traditions are regarded as being equally true' (Wright, 2003: 287–8). We have remarked on the increasing international prevalence of such instrumental, political uses of and justifications for religious education. The critical realist perspective here correctly shows the close inter-relationship between the political and the epistemological. Though the instrumentalist position rightly affirms likely epistemological undercurrents, it cannot be categorically affirmed that the former necessarily affirms the latter.

The greater counterweight to the critical realist position is arguably more fundamental, resting as it does on a conceptual-philosophical framework. Although critical realism encourages and incorporates a wide range of disciplinary approaches to religious education, a flaw is its internal logic: in correctly identifying a persistent post-Enlightenment rupture between reason and experience (or rationality and theology; or fact and value), its approach as a pedagogy actually seems to shore up the first of these dichotomies. We can make a simple case on the basis of its own examples from the history of religions around the time of the Enlightenment: the American Great Awakening, British non-conformism and Continental pietism. First, critical realism seems here to be asserting itself a difficult-to-substantiate charge against of each of these post-Enlightenment movements: each actually contains strong emphasis on experience, yes, but always underpinned by a doctrinal framework for this experience. Second, critical religious education's interpretation here, and the philosophical-conceptual more generally, neglects *pre*-Enlightenment emphases on experience in the religious life: an example of this neglect is the desert and monastic traditions which provide the spiritual sources of much medieval Christian mystical prayer, writing and reflection. Religious education focused on a critical realist interpretation of religious education as the search for truth in the classroom risks overconceptualizing religion, making it too philosophical. In other words, the philosophical-conceptual paradigm risks not only shoring up the very Enlightenment divide it seeks to overcome, but also the very misrepresentation of religion it seeks to avoid.

The socio-cultural paradigm

Socio-cultural approaches to religious education are a sympathetic re-working of Smart's phenomenology but placing more emphasis upon the socio-anthropological method. The key work here is Robert Jackson's (1997) *Religious Education: An Interpretive Approach*, having had immense international impact on educational thinking about the wider roles of religion, in schooling, education policy, and research, across Europe and worldwide. The interpretive approach was the method informing research and pedagogical thinking in the REDCo project:

> Drawing on methodological ideas from cultural anthropology, it recognizes the inner diversity, fuzzy edgedness and contested nature of religious traditions as well as the complexity of cultural expression and change from social and individual perspectives. Individuals are seen as unique, but the group tied nature of religion is recognized, as is the role of the wider religious traditions in providing identity markers and reference points. Pedagogically, the approach develops skills of interpretation and provides opportunities for critical reflection in which pupils make a constructive critique of the material studied at a distance, re-assess their understanding of their own way of life in the light of their studies and review their own methods of learning. (Jackson and O'Grady, 2007: 182)

The interpretive approach aims to help children and young people find their own positions within the key debates about religious plurality (Jackson, 1997, 2004; Willaime, 2009). Its most recent and influential manifestation has been in the REDCo project (see earlier, Chapter 2). Although 'there are some differences in these pedagogical approaches, they all share closely related stances on the analysis of cultural and religious discourse and views about the agency of pupils': 'It is advanced as a pedagogical and research tool and a contribution to various debates and has never been intended to be seen as the pedagogical approach to the subject . . . it is complementary to various other approaches and lends itself particularly to the study of contemporary religious practice' (Jackson, 2011a: 190).

The origins of this approach lie in the founding sociological work of Emile Durkheim and especially in *The Elementary Forms of the Religious Life* (Durkheim, 2001). Durkheim at root saw religion as the highest form of society's representation of itself. From Durkheim's analysis of what were then regarded as religion's 'primitive' origins, it was surmised that religion itself originated in society's self-deification. E. E. Evans-Pritchard's classic survey sets such socio-anthropological theorizing in the context of related *Theories of Primitive Religion* (Evans-Pritchard, 1966). Most prominent contemporary sociological theories of religion dispense with connotations of the 'primitive' or preoccupation with religious origins. In religious education, the most influential adaptation of socio-cultural frameworks has been via the ethnographical work of anthropologist Clifford Geertz, especially *The Interpretation of Cultures* (1975). The ethnographic method examines manifestations of culture in the minute detail of its own settings. In educational context, ethnographic studies in religious education have similarly focused on children in their own communities (e.g. Nesbitt and Arweck, 2010), or as Arweck and Nesbitt (2010) neatly put it, 'plurality at close quarters'. Ethnographic method thus forms the empirical and methodological basis for later curricula and pedagogical frameworks, establishing a 'close link between the activity of the ethnographic researcher, working on field research, and the activity of the learner in the classroom, attempting to understand religions in the contemporary world' (Jackson, 2011a: 190).

The interpretive approach, consciously attending to research and pedagogy identifies three levels of operation: representation, interpretation and reflexivity:

> The interpretive approach is concerned with how religions are represented, for example, by practitioners, the media, and by resources for religious education. It takes a critical stance towards Western, post-Enlightenment models of representing world religions as homogeneous belief systems, whose essence is expressed through set structures and whose membership is seen in terms of necessary and sufficient conditions. (Jackson, 2011a: 191)

A critique of this approach is that it removes boundaries which make the traditions identifiable as integral wholes. This is generally denied by claims that the interpretive approach is avoiding oversimplification in representation. Drawing on socio-cultural models which assert the complexity of representation (ethnographers focus on *detail*), the approach is also critical of attempts to 'essentialise or stereotype religions' (Jackson, 2011a: 191). A religious tradition is thus seen 'as a contested whole'. Religious traditions are researched and, in the pedagogy based on this, taught in all their 'complexity and internal diversity', raising awareness of the lived experience of the traditions in communities (Jackson, 2011a: 191).

The second feature of *interpretation* is also influenced by Geertz, and consciously distanced from theology: 'The interpretive approach is not derived from theology.' The approach it is claimed is not relativistic in relation to truth, acknowledging varying and often competing truth claims. Jackson contrasts this with the phenomenology of religion, 'in which researchers or learners are expected to leave their presuppositions to one side, the interpretive method requires a comparison and contrast between the religious symbols, concepts and experiences of those being studied and the nearest equivalent concepts, symbols and experiences of the researcher or learner (whether religious or not)'. Sensitivity to the perspective of the other is however a necessary condition of this approach with the claim that 'genuine empathy' is 'possible once the concepts of the others' discourse have been understood'. The socio-cultural and specifically ethnographic approach to religion as an aspect of (though it is claimed not reduced to) culture is apparent in the implications of all this; 'a basic aim' for religious education is 'to develop a knowledge and understanding of the grammar, the language and wider symbolic patterns used by people within religious traditions, so one might understand better their beliefs, feelings and attitudes' (Jackson, 2011a: 192).

Reflexivity is understood as 'the relationship between the experience of researchers/ students and the experience of those whose way of life they are attempting to interpret'. Three aspects of reflexivity relate to religious education: 'Researchers/learners are encouraged to review their understanding of their own worldview in relation to what they have studied (edification). They are helped to make a constructive and informed critique of the material studied at a distance, and they are involved in reviewing their own methods of research/study.' In the interpretive approach, 'the term edification is used to describe this form of learning'. In practice, 'such reflexive activity is not easily separable from the process of interpretation'. Interpretation 'might start from the other's language and experience, then move to that of the student, and then move between the two'. Thus, 'the process of understanding another's way of life is inseparable, practically, from considering issues and questions raised by it'. Teachers cannot guarantee all this will happen but they can facilitate teaching and learning so that it might (Jackson, 2011a: 192–3).

The REDCo project incorporated these three aspects as both research method and pedagogical approach. In a project including researchers 'steeped in a range of epistemological and theoretical positions and methodological approaches, it was considered appropriate to use the interpretive approach not to impose any uniformity in theory, epistemology or method, but as a stimulus to theoretical thinking in relation to field research methods and to pedagogy' (Jackson, 2011b). In successive discussions by the REDCo project team, the interpretive approach was summarized as a series of questions to be reviewed as research and pedagogical development proceeded (Jackson, 2011b). The questions 'apply equally to the research process (in which the interpretive approach was itself rooted) and to the development and review of pedagogical processes'. Each group of questions corresponds to one of the three key concepts of the approach (i.e. *representation*, *interpretation* and *reflexivity*).

On *representation*, the REDCo researchers ask, as researchers and developers of pedagogies:

- How well are we portraying the way of life of those we are studying so that we avoid misrepresentation and stereotyping?
- Are we presenting religions in too monolithic a way?
- Are we giving sufficient attention to diversity within religions?
- Are we considering whether individuals might be drawing on a wider range of spiritual or ethical resources than are reflected in traditional portrayals of religions?
- Are we showing awareness that individuals might be combining elements from a religion seen in traditional terms with values and assumptions derived from a more postmodern outlook?
- How far are we aware of the perceived relationship (or lack of relationship) of individuals studied to background religious and cultural traditions?
- How far does the use of power by relevant authorities/actors (national, regional, local) affect the representation of others and self/own group/tradition?

On *interpretation*, the REDCo researchers ask, as researchers and developers of pedagogies:

- How far are we giving attention to the religious language/concepts/ symbols used by those whom we are studying/representing?
- How well are we translating the other person's concepts and ideas (or comparing the other person's language/concepts with our own nearest equivalent language/concepts) so we have a clear understanding of them?
- How far are we able to empathize with the experience of others after we have grasped their language/concepts/symbols?
- Have we considered the relationship of individuals to groups to which they belong (e.g. sub-tradition, sect, denomination, movement, caste, ethnic group) and of these groups to their background religious and cultural traditions?
- Have we considered the impact of power relations on processes of interpretation?
- How far have we considered issues of translation (linguistic and cultural) in relation our use of religious language?

On *reflexivity* the REDCo researchers ask, in relation to research:

- How far are we aware of the impact of our own cultural background/values and beliefs/gender/ research role/power, etc., on the research process or development of pedagogical ideas?
- How far are we relating the data of our research to our own current understandings of difference?
- How far are we giving attention to the evaluation of our research methods?

On *reflexivity* the REDCo researchers ask, in relation to pedagogy:

- How far are we enabling students and teachers to reflect on their own assumptions/presuppositions/prejudices in relation to studying those with different religious/cultural beliefs/practices?
- How far are we giving attention to issues of enabling students and teachers to relate material studied to their own ideas and values?

- How far are we giving attention to issues of motivation in relation to reflexivity?
- How far have we enabled students and teachers to make a careful, sensitive and distanced critique of new ideas studied? (Jackson, 2011b: 194–6).

It has, Jackson suggests, 'been a fruitful approach in generating new knowledge and insights into relationship of children and religion'. Its ethnographic method 'seems to show considerable diversity within and not simply between religions. It has produced too the unexplored nuances of family relationships where a mixture of faiths are represented, the impact this has on children, and its implications for religious education.' One of the latter implications is that 'children often do not recognise the religions they are taught in school as being representative or at worst seriously misrepresentative of the faiths they experience in family and community'.

This misrepresentation, accordingly, it is claimed, finds its way into school textbooks (Jackson et al.). Correlative to the interpretive method are the findings by the proponents of this approach that religion as taught in schools often does not appear as it does not only in community but also in textbooks. One empirically valuable contribution of this approach has in fact been a large-scale analysis of materials used for the teaching of world religions in school textbooks. Apart from clear misrepresentation of 'fact', the core problem here of course is at what stage would one recognize a 'representative' or 'true' portrayal of the tradition? Again, these findings in relations to textbooks can be seen in *Materials Used to Teach about World Religions in Schools in England* (Jackson et al., 2010).

The interpretive approach, in its use of ethnographic method, has increased our knowledge of the complexities of representation of religion, in education but especially by looking at the lived experience of children and their communities. It places much less emphasis on world religions as easily bounded systems of tradition which can be taught in neat segments of history, and more on internal and external diversity of religion, the plurality within the religions themselves. Thus the multilayered complexities of religion should, it is argued, be set forth in teaching religious education. These findings arose from an ethnographic approach which placed high priority on the views of students in relation to the religions they knew. As the earlier extracts from the REDCo research show, it is ethnographic insights gleaned from children which are the basis for the view that religions are not the bounded traditions they are portrayed to be.

As an exercise in ethnography, this breaking down of bounded traditions may be epistemologically and methodologically sound, but it raises or rather I think *creates* problems which are *themselves* misrepresentative of religion. These problems add too unnecessary a complexity to a subject that already has enough. Besides, arguably, teachers and students do already and have always engaged with the complexity, diversity and plurality of religion. Teachers in schools who approach world religions by necessity already incorporate diversity into the teaching of different religious traditions and within traditions themselves. I know for example of no conceivable instance where Christianity is ever taught without reference to denominational difference and or to the historical circumstances which brought this difference about.

I think the more significantly troubling facets of the approach are those which derive from its use of socio-cultural, that is, ethnographic method, namely, its conclusions drawn from an emphasis on fuzziness, the indeterminacy of boundaries. If we can accept that fuzziness is very difficult to teach, more importantly if the ethnographic method really *is* attempting to be a faithful representation of religions, then a very simple counter to their conclusions is that this fuzziness is not something which religions themselves recognize. The ethnographic approach is in this regard, itself, even wary of the term 'tradition'. But the notion of tradition, if we are concerned with a faithful representation of religions, is something which the majority of religions are themselves are comfortable with and regard as critical to their self-understanding.

There are methodological issues here too. As noted, it is ethnographic insights gleaned from children which are the basis for the view that religions are not the bounded traditions. At a rather obvious level, if you are asking schoolchildren to define their traditions, it is hardly surprising that a portrayal of the tradition is not the best informed and is likely to be religion at its most 'fuzzy'. Some religious traditions have less emphasis on authority than others, allowing much greater individual freedom; those which do have well-defined and rigorously imposed authority structures – and this is the majority of religions – simply could not accept the finding of the ethnographic approach. If its rationale is based on a truer representation of religions, then, this presents a rather insurmountable problem for its religious education pedagogy. In examining in minute detail the views of children with regard to the views of religion, this on its own is arguably an inevitably flawed source of (authoritative) representation.

In terms of the aims and purposes of religious education so researched and taught, this interpretive notion of edification shows how its socio-cultural methods reflect socio-cultural intentions:

> Edification need not only result from studying religions or cultures other than one's own. The study of one's own ancestral tradition, in religious or cultural terms, can also give new insights in re-examining one's sense of identity. In the case of religious education, young people might see religions, including the one of their own history, from a new perspective Edification does not imply the adoption of the beliefs of followers of a religion being studied, but does recognise similarities and differences between all humans and of the relationship between the identity of each person and the manifestation of differences. (Jackson, 2011a: 193)

But the aims and purposes of edification seem, from my reading, to be directed primarily to towards meeting the challenges of such religious diversity; 'it builds upon a positive attitude towards diversity, recognising the encounter of people with different beliefs and cultural practices as enriching in principle', and so forth.

Nevertheless, in and through these socio-cultural emphases, the ethnographic approach has been a key mover in the development of programmes of religion in education internationally, not least because, as we have seen, of its political applications.

The historical-political paradigm

The historical-political paradigm emphasizes understanding present-day uses of religion in education as a means of achieving broad political goals. These are largely secular in origin and in language. Religion in education serves the principles of liberal democracy in responding to a culturally and religiously diverse populace. Teaching and learning in this model is directed towards ameliorating any potential conflicts inherent amidst such pluralism. The philosophy for this originates directly from political liberalism; its validation for enforcement is in those legal frameworks which underpin liberal democracies, particularly through human rights frameworks which stress equality under these laws, which though constraining (as laws do) are also guided by the principle that the law should not overly restrict individual and collective freedoms. Any conflict is translated politically into the processes of democratic decision making. In pedagogical terms this approach stresses dialogue. Political efforts to achieving cohesiveness among the citizenry are mirrored in religious education efforts to do the same. Political principle thus underpins pedagogical principle (see Gearon, 2008). The international pervasiveness of such models was made apparent through earlier chapters. The words which compose the REDCo project – European in origin, international in impact – perfectly illustrate this approach.

This paradigm is always necessarily *historical* because in seeking legitimacy it invariably looks to the past. It is plain that such legitimacy is rooted within a specific legal-political tradition of the Enlightenment. Citizen educators however are keen to intimate a longer and more ancient tradition for these ideas. They do so by tracing a genealogy of Enlightenment back further to the Greek city state and the like. Dewey, Crick and Heater demonstrate this move, as do Enlightenment historians like Gibbon. The *Toledo Guiding Principles* (OSCE, 2007) take a slightly different but still historical approach to such justifications by rooting a genealogy of tolerance to Toledo itself. The genealogy here is thus less specifically secular. The religions themselves can model tolerance. But the foregrounding of tolerance as a principle of religion or politics is one which really only emerges consistently from the Enlightenment, and Rousseau's' 'civil religion' aptly illustrates this in the way Rousseau suggests 'tolerance' to be the one virtue among all others in the social contract. The close association of the historical-political with the socio-cultural paradigm is evident in those models in their theoretical modelling of religion as a source of social bonding and identity, and Durkheim (2001) presents the preeminent example of this in arguing that religion was a representation of society itself.

Presentation of REDCo findings at the European Parliament seem to provide some credence to a view that such approaches are supported by young people in schools. To reiterate, while acknowledging contextual differences between and within the participant countries, students 'wish for peaceful coexistence across differences, and believe this to be possible', for students 'peaceful coexistence depends on knowledge about each other's religions and worldviews'; students 'who learn about religious diversity in school are more willing to have conversations about religions/beliefs with students of other backgrounds than those who do not', and so forth (Weisse, 2009a,b).

The rights justification here is doubly confirmed by the legal-political emphases on the voice of the child. The 1989 Convention on the Rights of the Child is of paramount importance here. In religious education terms this convention framed not only the rights of children to education, but to religious education, and here the learning of 'civilizations' and religions other than their own are regarded as pedagogically foundational (Jawoniyi, 2012). In the REDCo project context, however, we might reflect on the extent to which children's views are a key determinant of pedagogy. I can think of no other subject in the curriculum where pupil or student voice is given such precedence. Comments made in regard to the socio-cultural paradigm apply here: the primacy of student voice is arguably not an entirely authoritative source for the representation of the religions themselves.

The growing worldwide political impetus for teaching religion in education (often used as a term more neutral than religious education) is by the nature of its influence *political*, but it is also and of absolute necessity *historical*. One of the problems in implementation was that we have the politics without the history: the acceptance (and clearly many European students have) of certain liberal democratic values as the core rationale for religious education. Religious education here, as noted, risks limiting religion to its public and political face.

The other problem is that we have history with too much present-day politics. The Ajegbo Report (2006) was commissioned to examine issues of citizenship and diversity in the context of British history, but its view (or rather its chronology) of British history is one which seems to begin in 1945. Where we do have the history we see it used, as history so often is, as a means of the past justifying or answering the problems of the present. The Ajegbo Report labours this less than does the *Toledo Guiding Principles* document, but both share the joint need for historical and political justification.

These historical-political approaches arguably underplay historical and contemporary conflict and difference, emphasizing commonalities in order to reach the political liberal goal of tolerance and understanding. The problem of political liberalism has thus in education found one of the means to achieve its aims. Arguably, though, historical-political paradigm use of historical for political purposes can be open to question. Barnes's (2006) addresses the question of what such an approach does to the representation, or, in Barnes' view, the misrepresentation of religion in education. By failing to take such profound differences serious, these political rationales for religious education fail in the very thing they hold most dear: for, Barnes argues, only in taking difference seriously can differences be seriously addressed. For critical religious education, it is especially a failure to take differences in religious truth claims seriously. The difficulty of difference for the historical-political approach is that to overemphasize differences of course also risk a failure of political-pedagogical objective. To emphasize difference is to risk not cohesion but conflict.

Political liberalism though makes on the surface no claim to judge between truth claims. It holds, within the bounds of law, the need for religious plurality to be respected. It is to remind us what Willaime calls the 'double constraint of law and sociology': under the law religions are equal, and the given sociological circumstances of all societies are religiously plural. In this context one religion it is deemed cannot have social or political priority over any other religion. Though far from the political realities in many countries, where freedom of religion is negligible, or severely restricted, as an educational ideal it has its appeal. Given the close relationship between politics and pedagogy, it should be no surprise that a problem in modern-day democratic politics becomes a problem presented for liberal education to solve.

The philosophical-theological counterpart of political liberalism in regard to religion is a theological notion of religious pluralism in which all religions represent cultural variations of one ultimate reality. There cannot logically, he argues, be more than one ultimate reality; for there to be more than one ultimate reality or ultimate truth would be a contradiction. This position was espoused by John Hick (1989) in *An Interpretation of Religion*. But this seemingly radical view of the essential truth of all religions is one which, after some past decades of curricula experimentation, has come to be held by many religious education professionals and religious education policy. Political liberalism – as the political counterpart of this theology – though it is unconcerned with religious truth(s), operates de facto as if all religious traditions were equally true; or rather as if the adherents of these traditions are legally entitled to hold that the truths of their traditions are true. The philosophical-theological position which asserts the essential truth of all religions, and if not their truth their equal educational validity, is given force then by political circumstance. The growing correlation of religion with terrorism and violent conflict, with extremism, has simply given an additional rationale to the political liberal motivations for the teaching of religion in schools. It accounts for the present-day dominance of the historical-political paradigm. Negative aspects of this are not only the manipulation of historical analysis for narrowly conceived political aims through education, but a limitation of the representation of religion in education to its public and political aspects.

Assessment

Each of the pedagogies considered in this chapter will in assessment terms be framed by what is prioritized as achievement and attainment in religious education. In sketching this position, I do not however propose here to go over the ground of practical assessment, including lesson planning in relation to aims and objectives, differentiation, examination assessment, pupil self-assessment, and so forth, in religious education which a range of colleagues have already addressed extensively (in particular, Rudge, 2008; Wright, 2008; or Aldrich, 2012; Blaylock, 2012; Brooks and Fancourt, 2012; Fancourt, 2005, 2012).

But I do want to draw out one general principle of assessment which religious education pedagogy seems to present its present diversity: pedagogies of religious education seeking paradigmatic status imply an assessment model. As Stern (2006: 63–79, 2007) convincingly outlines, philosophies of pedagogy determine models of assessment; but institutional contexts can also determine this – schools can determine the way religion is represented, taught, assessed, as Homan in large measure suggests when discussing the 'construction' of religion in schools and classrooms (Homan, 2012). Thanissaro (2012) presents an interesting case study of this, attempting to demonstrating how in a London school, attitudes to religious education are improved by different approaches to teaching and learning: 'experiential' (visits oriented, discussion based) rather than 'knowledge and test' ('banking') models are seen as more beneficial in developing attitudes to religious education and religion.

Thanissaro favours an experiential model of teaching and learning, and the assessment outcomes of this have more favourable attitudes to not only religious education, but also religion. Thanissaro is illustrative of a general principle: pedagogies of religious education seeking paradigmatic status imply an assessment model. Each of the pedagogies considered in this chapter will thus in assessment terms be framed by what is prioritized as achievement and attainment in religious education. Thus the psychological-experiential paradigm might *emphasize* learning about and from religions and beliefs that which might contribute to spiritual development; the conceptual-philosophical paradigm might *emphasize* learning about and from religions and beliefs that which might contribute; the historical-political paradigm might *emphasize* learning about and from religions and beliefs that might contribute to the democratic values which religions share; and so forth.

One influential model of religious education assessment permeates many: the notional two 'attainment targets', that is, by the distinction between 'learning from religion and belief' and 'learning about religion and belief'. The popularity of these attainment targets is near pervasive outside formal public examination (where religious education is more often called religious studies). If we apply the two attainment targets model to the pedagogies discussed, we can see its flexibility. Each paradigmatic model selects from or determines what it is important to learn about and learn from religion.

A statement of terms of the two attainment target model of assessment in religious education can be found in Grimmitt (1987, 225–6):

> When I speak about pupils *learning about religion* I am referring to what the pupils learn about the beliefs, teachings and practices of the great religious traditions of the world. I am also referring to what pupils learn about the nature and demands of ultimate questions, about the nature of a 'faith' response to ultimate questions, about the normative views of the human condition and what it means to be human as expressed in and through Traditional Belief Systems or Stances for Living of a naturalistic kind. When I speak about *learning from religion* I am referring to what pupils learn from their studies in religion about themselves – about discerning ultimate questions and 'signals of transcendence' in their own experience and considering how they might respond to them. The process of learning from religion involves, I suggest, engaging two though different types of evaluation. Impersonal evaluation involves being able to distinguish and make critical evaluations of truth claims, beliefs and practices of different religious traditions and of religion itself. Personal evaluation begins as an attempt to confront and evaluate religious beliefs and values . . . becomes a process of self-evaluation. (1987, 225–6, emphasis in original)

Geoff Teece (2010), who worked with Michael Grimmitt, writes one of the most insightful commentaries on how the distinction has been misinterpreted and misunderstood. The title of Teece's paper says much about its orientation, and the subject's disorientation: 'Is it learning about and from religions, religion or religious education? And is it any wonder some teachers don't get it?'

The terms *learning about religion* and *learning from religion*, states Teece, 'have become widespread'. He argues for 'second-order explanatory frameworks of religion' if we are 'to organise the religious education curriculum'. 'Organising,' he argues, 'the phenomena of religion into curriculum structures necessarily requires some form of reductionism.' Teece attempts to make the distinction between the two possible forms of reductionism – *descriptive reductionism* and *explanatory reductionism*. According to this distinction, *descriptive reductionism* is the failure to identify a religious experience by which the subject identifies it. *Explanatory reductionism* offers an explanation that mig ht be accepted within the tradition. Teece asks whether second-order frameworks 'can appropriately account for the phenomena of religion'. He argues a case 'could be made for *learning about religion* in terms of a second-order explanatory framework'. Smart's typology is set as an exemplar. Here: 'Second-order frameworks for religion can be useful, especially if such a framework interprets religions in the context of what, for the adherents, their religion teaches about what it means to be human.' Teece then refers – in support of this idea about 'what it means to be human' – 'two categories of concepts' (Teece, 2010: 100). These are concepts which are 'common to religious and secular experience'. But what are these and how can the religious educator determine them? What are these concepts that are 'distinctive of particular religions' which would enable the religious educator to organize the curriculum? Learning about religion is relatively easily framed when set against the challenges of assessing what students might be expected to be learning from religion.

The epistemological hole is dug deeper: 'It might be more helpful to adopt a second-order explanatory framework that interprets religion as distinctive phenomenon with its overriding characteristic being its spiritual dimension as understood as human transformation in the context of responses to the transcendent' (Teece, 2010). But what does this mean? Why do we *need* these commonalities? Such a framework, it is claimed, 'might enable teachers and syllabus compilers to select appropriate content from the *religions* that pupils could beneficially learn about and from' (Teece, 2010: 102). But this is going beyond a second-order category. Would such a move not be a forcing of categories on both religious and secular perspectives which ultimately risk not being justly selected 'commonalities' *but impositions of them*? Or, what would be as bad, teacher-manufactured versions of commonalities? In a secular context where the first principles of faith are abandoned, Teece is naturally right to point out the need for second-order frameworks, but the real problem is in the selection of *what* second-order frameworks.

In state religious education contexts, the separation of religious education from the religious life makes the selection of second-order framework no easy matter. Even the scriptural-theological approach had its problems here in the early non-denominational context of state religious education where a scriptural-theological still predominated. As for the subsequent, reactive range of paradigms considered here, the nature of what students learn from religion will invariably be determined by the second-order frameworks of the respective paradigms. As noted, the psychological-experiential paradigm might emphasize spiritual development; the conceptual-philosophical paradigm understanding of ideas; the historical-political paradigm the democratic values which religions share; and so forth.

The assessment of *what* children are supposed to be *learning from* in religious education would be a real problem if teachers were not more often concerned with teaching within the framework, especially in the later years of schooling, of public examination syllabus. I take a pragmatic view here. At least these syllabi provide a reasoned body of knowledge, provide opportunities for the development of children's understanding of this knowledge and some scope in (what is often called) evaluation for them to balance arguments for and against what they have learnt, to test the application of the traditions in view of challenges they face. Examination board requirements do change, but not constantly, and provide the most rigorous guide to assessment in religious education without the tendentious overtones of much religious education pedagogy. Many of the latter approaches of course would be resistant to both the presentation of religion, aims and objective of study, and the aims of assessment presented by examination boards. The approach seems to me clear and uncluttered:

> Assessment objective 1: Demonstrate knowledge, understanding and analysis
>
> Describe, explain, analyse, using knowledge and understanding
>
> Assessment objective 2: Use of evidence, evaluation and argument
>
> Use evidence and reasoned argument to express and evaluate personal responses, informed insights and differing viewpoints. (OCR, 2012)

These are taken from one examination board and are well-stated unambiguous principles of assessment objectives which are applied to the study of world religions, including textual studies, and options in ethics and philosophy. Other examination boards offer similar frameworks. They all also offer a range of support material relating to reading, syllabus content and design, examination papers and reports and so on. These specifics provide one of the key sources of guidance for effective *religious studies*. The shift from religious education to religious studies has long been attested to by government inspection and examination results that the standard in the subject are much higher when taken as part of a formal examination curriculum with clear guidance on structure and assessment.

The pedagogies of religious *education* outlined in this chapter, all, by contrast, attempt to reach beyond such reasoned approaches to religious knowledge. The alternative paradigms all suggest seemingly sophisticated alternatives, from spiritual development to critical thinking through to cultural understanding, and from this political harmony. For this reason, each has a correspondingly less-than-coherent model of assessment: it is difficult to determine if any of the grander claims made by such pedagogies could even be reasonably or meaningfully assessed. And this is a core difficulty, for all their supposed rootedness in the scientific rationales.

Limited groundbreaking empirical evidence currently exists which seems to support this view. Research which questions the effectiveness of religious education in terms of its more 'high-blown' aims begins by asking a seemingly simple question: Does religious education work?

Does religious education work?

Does religious education work? 'An Analysis of the Aims, Practices & Models of Effectiveness in Religious Education across the UK' was a funded project of the Economic and Social Research Council (ESRC) and Arts and Humanities Research Council (AHRC) of the major Religion and Society Programme. At a programme meeting, Linda Woodhead, the programme's director, presented *Does Religious Education Work?* project as a model of a good research question. On the surface, the questions appears simple. As the preceding chapters have shown, whether the subject 'works' or not is both epistemologically complex (and often made more complicated than it needs to be) and also, at an existential level, possibly even unanswerable. As we have seen in reviewing the pedagogies in this chapter, the answer to that question will depend on the understanding of the aims and purposes of religious education. Even concealing as it does by its seeming simplicity, the research question nevertheless produced some extremely interesting findings.

The Does RE Work? project (Conroy, 2011a,b; also Baumfield et al., 2012) was the single most comprehensive study to date of the state of religious education across the United Kingdom unpacking 'the various kinds of claims made with respect to Religious Education in the very different contexts of England and Wales, Northern Ireland and Scotland. Using a combination of philosophical, theological and detailed ethnographic approaches, we intend conducting a study of the local (school-focused) social, cultural and pedagogical practices which shape the delivery of Religious Education'. Central to the aims were the 'charting of religious education from conception to delivery through to social impact'. To achieve this, the project attempted to 'secure our geographical and disciplinary spread as well as interdisciplinary and generational cohesion'. At the outset of they described their aim was 'to map different definitions and means of testing the effectiveness of Religious Education':

> In any school context ideas about the aims and effectiveness of Religious Education will go hand-in-hand. In faith-based schools these aims are likely to differ in major respects from those of a non-denominational school. It is likely that effect ive Religious Education in the former will lay claim to certain developmental features of children's spiritual needs. In the latter case, it may be that Religious Education is intended to serve specific civic needs and purposes. This raises questions as to the definition of such needs and the investigation of how Religious Education teachers, as a matter of pedagogical practice, imagine they meet such needs and purposes. (Conroy, 2011a)

As we have seen, since the inception of religious education in the state-maintained sector, such questions have been asked continually. The project's timing was important since it could review with critical hindsight the radically changing aims and purposes of religious education to examine what sort of impacts they have had in the classroom.

It conducted the ethnographic work in 24 schools across the United Kingdom, a total of 240 days of observations, and around 500,000 words of field notes, besides transcripts of pupil and teacher focus groups, photographs, recordings, questionnaire results, examples of teachers' schemes of work and pupils' work samples, and the outcomes of teachers' own practitioner enquiry research projects (Conroy, 2011a). The study showed a picture of religious education classrooms with more complex policy and academic literature credits.

If these were the emergent themes, what then were the findings? The principal investigator, James Conroy presented these in positive and negative terms as follows:

Positive religious education:

- is often led by highly committed and thoughtful teachers;
- teachers are often highly regarded by students;
- makes a positive contribution to multicultural awareness;
- is often shaped around local demographic and cultural needs and expectations;
- occupies a threshold place in the school – this has positive and negative aspects – allows religious education to be different but sometimes those differences allow headteachers to marginalize it;
- in some cases emphasizes skills of debate, reflection and creative discussion in contrast to an increasingly exam-driven curriculum in other subject areas;
- stands as a counter-cultural influence within the school (even religiously sponsored schools); and
- departments tha t are fortunate to have a significant body of staff in religious education would appear to offer many advantages in coping with the myriad entailments and expectations of the subject.

Negative religious education:

- does not, in the main, make students religiously literate;
- sees pupils demonstrate widespread ignorance of basic religious concepts;
- suffers from
- too many coming;
- limited time allocations;
- placing examination and non-examination pupils in the same class; and
- being too dependent upon local conditions and the disposition and skills of the teacher.

Findings concerning teachers were that they:

- feel under a lot of pressure, underconfident and in many cases undervalued;
- struggle to find a pedagogic middle path between allowing pupils to develop their own values and offering more substantive accounts of particular values/claims/doctrines;
- are not infrequently underqualified, with the result that their coverage of a given subject can be limited; and

- find themselves caught between the goals they want to pursue in helping students explore the big questions of life, and the increasing need to teach to the test in order to secure resource and status.
- What was noted as particularly 'unclear':
- promoting community cohesion through inter-religious understanding (DCSF 2010);
- RE is witnessing something of a shift away from the study of substantive religious doctrines and practices to something more philosophical, which doesn't require more than minimal assent around generalized principles; and
- places enormous emphasis on discussion (Conroy, 2011b: 3–4).

Conroy asserts that with wider onslaughts on religious belief in general, there is little room for complacency in the teaching of religious education.

Given the ground covered in this and other chapters, these challenges are far from new; they have, however, seemingly intensified. Lundie (2010) makes in this regard a noteworthy comment: 'Given the statutory nature of school-based religious education in a culture which boasts some of the lowest rates of religious practice in the world but retains strong rhetorical attachments to the religio-spiritual impulse, there are indeed interesting questions to be asked about the status and efficacy of religious education in schools.'

The Does RE Work? research Conroy states, 'is likely to be argued over for some time'. He is right. If requiring confirmation through a larger sample of schools, the project findings, certainly on the evidence at hand, have uncovered some important questions about the impact – positive and negative – of the effectiveness of pedagogic innovation in religious education over the past half century. But the very posing of the question in this way – does religious education work? – is symptomatic of a more general malaise identified by educational researchers (see Oancea and Pring, 2008), which has infected and limited the aims and purposes of religious education when its aims and purposes are confined to purely secular and especially narrow utilitarian aims and purposes.

Summary

The chapter has examined six 'paradigms' in religious education:

1. Scriptural-theological
2. Phenomenological
3. Psychological-experiential
4. Philosophical-conceptual
5. Socio-cultural
6. Historical-political

The latter five emerged from the first and in reaction to it. There are broad correlations between these pedagogies of religious education paradigm and the intellectual disciplines from which they emerged, hence to some extent justifying the term 'paradigm' and the notion 'paradigm shift' or 'paradigm shifts' in religious education pedagogy. The latter five are however largely united in the acknowledgement that a scriptural-theological basis for religious education is no longer tenable in modern secular societies (denigrated as 'confessional' and 'an anachronism').

However, are these developments paradigmatic? As noted, paradigms 'gain their status because they are more successful than their competitors in solving a few problems that the group of practitioners has come to recognize as acute'. At the close of this chapter a review of research impacts on classrooms that there is rather some epistemological confusion among teachers about what the subject should now be achieving. So we cannot say that there is any degree of paradigmatic acceptance of any of the religious education pedagogies presented in state religious education.

Dominant aspects of these religious education pedagogies are, however, a varied synthesis of aspects of each of these rationales: (i) in schools of religious character the scriptural-theological still predominates, where religious education remains coherently related to the religious life (whether we accept the framework or not); (ii) the subject's focus on the study of world religions (the phenomenological paradigm) is prevalent in both religious education and examination-level religious studies; (iii) the psychological-experiential paradigm persists in both the legislative requirement for schools to contribute (where they do) to children's spiritual and moral as well as intellectual development, though what *is* spiritual development in these contexts is particularly problematic; (iv) the philosophical-conceptual increasingly appears popular, mirroring and embodying some of the fundamental Enlightenment's critical, that is philosophical methods for approaching religion; (v) the socio-cultural paradigm provides, in England and internationally, justifications for the subject in terms of cohesion, diversity and plurality; and shares with (vi) the historical-political paradigm, these same socio-cultural goals but reified within a particular reading of post-Enlightenment political history, and orients religious education to identify with a particular model of governance, that of democracy, and adjunct theories of political liberalism.

Kuhn argues that to achieve paradigmatic status, 'A theory must seem better than its competitors, but it need not, and in fact never does, explain all the facts with which it can be confronted.' The pedagogies of religious education outlined in this chapter are paradigmatic in their identification with distinctive academic disciplines but are not, we might conclude, paradigmatic in the sense of having achieved an unambiguous consensus. Though such consensus may be emergent, if we look at international contexts of religion in education, and the dominance of political agendas for research. Yet the weakness of this and other models is apparent and threefold: weak models of assessment for grandiose goals; a lack of evidence to show that religious education, given these influences, 'works'; and a more fundamental difficulty in conceptualizing in psychological, political or socio-cultural terms how success might be envisaged. In reacting against the dystopian realities of religious conflict – locally, nationally and internationally, in historical and contemporary milieu – these idealist pedagogies of religious education seem to be envisaging utopian alternatives. But it is difficult to see these as realist subject goals for religious education taught, in pragmatic terms, for perhaps an hour a week.

In Kuhn's terms, there are those 'who cling to one or another of the older views, and they are simply read out of the profession, which thereafter ignores their work'. Those 'unwilling or unable to accommodate their work to it must proceed in isolation or attach themselves to some other group'. Commitment to the scriptural-theological paradigm exists here most clearly, and I think with at least logic consistency, in faith schools across all traditions.

This amounts, however, to some degree, a rejection of a central tenet of liberal education's notion of autonomy. Acceptance say of the Bible as revelation (however one interprets it) is contrary to Kant's (1784) definition of Enlightenment itself:

> Enlightenment is man's release from his self-incurred tutelage. Tutelage is man's inability to make use of his understanding without direction from another. Self-incurred is this tutelage when its cause lies not in lack of reason but in lack of resolution and courage to use it without direction from another. Sapere aude! 'Have courage to use your own reason!' – that is the motto of enlightenment.
>
> Laziness and cowardice are the reasons why so great a portion of mankind, after nature has long since discharged them from external direction (naturaliter maiorennes), nevertheless remains under lifelong tutelage, and why it is so easy for others to set themselves up as their guardians. It is so easy not to be of age. If I have a book which understands for me, a pastor who has a conscience for me . . . and so forth, I need not trouble myself. I need not think . . . others will easily undertake the irksome work for me. (Kant, 1784: 1)

Schools of a religious character accept or share with political and educational liberalism a privilege of choice in religious education and schooling: in schools of a religious character the choice is for an acceptance of scriptural and broader, religious authority from tradition. The secular counter-argument of course, as we have seen – especially where critiques of religious schools and religious education are conjoined – is that neither religiously oriented schools nor their religious education *do* offer free choice. But rather, by the nature of their education (in institutional and curriculum terms) they actually deny individual autonomy. This form of education is also deemed ultimately damaging to society as a whole.

Thinking for oneself, defined universally in liberal education, as 'autonomy' has become the rationalist basis for teaching and learning in religious education. Some element of this exists even in those schools where scriptural revelation retains its hold as the source of ultimate truth: to reiterate (though it is contested that they do) schools of a religious character also hold to many liberal educational principles. In the 'dual system', such schools' rationale for religious education can be said to be in tension with notions of liberal educational autonomy. For this reason: an education in religion which begins with belief as a foundation cannot place faith in autonomy as the highest educational ideal. The counter-charge by those from faith traditions is that secular state religious education and state education itself in permeating its ethos and education with secular goals also do not really offer freedom or true autonomy. At the extreme, such arguments take the form that state religious education is a formal of secular, liberal indoctrination. The extent to which religious education in state schools or schools of a religious character facilitates educational autonomy remains open to debate.

What we can say, however, is that in schools of a religious character it is faith and not reason that remains the ultimate educational foundation. Their educational environment is created to link religious education with the religious life. This is arguably a modern-day re-statement of Anselm's role of reason as 'faith seeking understanding'. Faith is the starting point. *By contrast* religious education in state schools begins not from the starting point of faith but of reason. Its pedagogical justification for learning about religion is that of reason seeking an understanding of faith. There are in this (state religious education) context no epistemological grounds on which to assume the a priori basis of religious truth. This leaves open the study of the phenomenon of religious truth as declared by the religious traditions, but neither acceptance of it, nor (actually) the means for the adjudication on such truth. In practice there is a presumed sceptical neutrality of reason in relation to religion, but state religious education rather perpetuates a version of what Ricoeur (1970) called the 'hermeneutics of suspicion'.

The challenges to which the religious life has been chronically subjected are now acutely apparent in modern, secular pedagogies of religious education. We see that the epistemological foundations of these pedagogies emerge directly from those new 'scientific' disciplines which had their very origins in the critique of religion. Religious education is in part defined by its rejection or accommodation of these.

But there are yet other currents of aesthetic as well as intellectual currents which have impacted religious education here, and I consider these next, in the framework of a lecture given by C. P. Snow, late in 1950s Cambridge.

Religion across the Curriculum: Arts, Humanities and Sciences 6

Introduction

Contemporary religious education reflects one part of a wider disputed territory around the role of religion in public life. The foregoing chapters have demonstrated how political agendas often now determine the aims and rationale of religious education. We might conclude that these factors continue to reinforce (what in plural contexts is') a separation of religious education from the religious life. The faith context for schooling has not made this separation; contemporary secular religious education arguably (as it caters to students from diverse backgrounds) needs to, but this separation provides the subject with problems as to its epistemological ground and thus pedagogical foundations. It is for this reason that the post-9/11 emphasis on religion in global governance has been swiftly taken on as a justification by the subject, despite the essentially political nature of such justification. Indeed, as high-profile projects like REDCo indicate, such moves have given religious educators what is an unparalleled public profile.

The tensions which draw religious education in often conflicting directions are not only political. We saw how many modern religious education pedagogies have been shaped by largely secular, social scientific and psychological paradigms which had their origins in critiques of religion. Religions can be said to be framed, then, by a series of political (what Willaime calls the 'legal' and 'sociological') and epistemological constraints.

This chapter examines how these epistemological issues are present in the wider school curriculum, particularly in the arts, humanities and sciences, and how they afford (cross-curricular) opportunities for religious education.

'The Two Cultures'

C. P. Snow's (1959) Cambridge lecture 'The Two Cultures' highlighted a conflict between the arts and the sciences which emerged in acute form in the eighteenth-century Enlightenment, and particularly in responses to it by the movement which came to be known as Romanticism. The Romantics reacted against the perceived rational excesses of the late eighteenth and early nineteenth-century life, and against the disenchantment of the world brought about by an overemphasis on rationale thought. Thus, if the Enlightenment philosophers had sought truth through reason, the Romantics saw this as falsely excluding other, and to them higher forms of truth which could not be defined through or limited by reason. In his 'Engraving of the Lacoon', for William Blake 'Art is the tree of life. Science is the tree of death.' To Samuel Taylor Coleridge, the Enlightenment, 'this French wisdom' 'has purchased a few brilliant inventions at the loss of all communion with life and the spirit of nature' (Coleridge, 2005: 347). Keats's famous identification of truth with beauty epitomizes this, in the final lines of his 'Ode to a Grecian Ode' (1819):

> Thou, silent form, dost tease us out of thought
> As doth eternity: Cold Pastoral!
> When old age shall this generation waste,
> Thou shalt remain, in midst of other woe
> Than ours, a friend to man, to whom thou say'st,
> 'Beauty is truth, truth beauty,' – that is all
> Ye know on earth, and all ye need to know.

The debate then was not new. The conflicts between 'rationalism' and 'romanticism' arose from eighteenth-century Enlightenment. Both, we might note, saw a similar shift from a theological orientation: both rationalism and Romanticism were looking for new ways of seeing the world which had lost religious certainties. Put simplistically, we might suggest that the rationalists celebrated the loss as liberation; the Romantics recognized the loss but lamented it.

Richard Holmes (2008) in *The Age of Wonder* outlines an artistic image of this eighteenth-century Enlightenment divide, one seen by Whelan (2009) as 'the prequel' to the 'two cultures' debate two centuries later. Holmes thus uses Benjamin Haydon's 'Christ's Entry into Jerusalem'. It is a painting, the original naturally, which becomes the source of debate at a dinner party with an enviably distinguished guest list including William Wordsworth, Charles Lamb and John Keats. Holmes narrates the scene:

Describing the increasingly rowdy dinner-table discussions that developed, the painting provoked a debate about the powers of Reason versus the Imagination. The destructive and reductive effects of the scientific outlook were mocked. Warming to the theme, Lamb, mischievously described Newton as a 'fellow who believed nothing unless it was as clear as the three sides of a triangle'. Keats joined in, agreeing that Newton had 'destroyed all the poetry of the rainbow, by reducing it to a prism'. Haydon jovially records: 'It was impossible to resist them, and we drank "Newton's health, and confusion to Mathematics." ' (Holmes, 2008: 319; also Whelan, 2009: 13–18)

Mary Shelley, obviously one of the Romantics, can be said to have done much to create the emergent genre of science fiction. Her *Frankenstein* can be interpreted as Romanticism's attack on the monstrous potential of science. Other science fiction of course celebrated science's critical role in the future of humanity. Later, H. G. Wells, one-time student of Thomas Huxley, is a paramount example of the latter, and one who also, as a former teacher himself, recognized the critical importance here of education. Indeed, Wells (1938) described history itself as 'a race between education and catastrophe'.

The theological currents of the debate were obviously not entirely lost even in the late nineteenth century. They came into sharp focus in the late nineteenth century after Darwin's *On the Origin of Species* and *The Descent of Man* had confirmed through scientific conjecture scepticism towards religion which many intellectuals already felt. In wider cultural terms, the 1880s saw two opposing views of high culture (the art and humanities, classical and Christian), looking essentially to the past and to tradition, and the emergent pleas for science as the key to progress, looking, that is, decisively, to the future. The former had dominated (this being 1880, at least public school) education; the latter had to fight for its space within the curriculum, in universities as much as in schools. Whelan comments: 'With the arts and science now occupying separate camps, the battle for control of the school curriculum could begin. There was no problem about mathematics, which had been at the core of the classical curriculum for hundreds of years, but there was a definite unwillingness to take valuable classroom time from Virgil and Homer and give it to physics and chemistry' (Whelan, 2009: 17–18).

The nineteenth-century version of the 'two cultures' debate crystallized between Matthew Arnold (poet, critic, school inspector and son of Thomas Arnold, headmaster of Rugby) and Thomas Huxley (scientist, commonly known as a defender of the then new evolutionary theory, as 'Darwin's bulldog'). It was Arnold who argued for 'culture' as a bastion against 'anarchy' and who defended the traditions of the school curriculum so oriented not only merely as a means of cultural enrichment but as a guide to character and good conduct (Arnold, 1974, 2009), and Huxley (2011) advocate of science. In *Unmapped Countries: Biological Visions in Nineteenth Century Literature and Culture*, Swierlein (2005) shows though how deep were the broader effects of the new biology in particular on the arts and humanities. Nineteenth-century debate, polarized as it often was, was not always vituperative. The exchanges between Arnold and Huxley were relatively good natured, certainly good mannered. Arnold was happy to concede sciences social advantages, and Huxley had himself benefitted from a classical education. He simply wanted more room for science in the curriculum. Indeed, Huxley (1870), in the year of the foundational Education Act in England, writing on the new school boards, was happy to write in praise of the cultural wealth if not the theological truths of the Bible.

There were long-standing and deep historical undercurrents to the debate which Snow re-ignited, but they were also specific to what Furedi calls 'the temper of the times'; Snow's '1959 lecture spoke to a growing mood of unease with Western society's cultural and intellectual inheritance. Economic and technological change appeared to call into question the traditions that still influenced the key institutions of public life. Britain's cultural elites felt estranged from the very institutions into which they were socialised. There was a growing consensus that Britain's traditional values and institutions were suffocating society.' The response of the 'Establishment' 'was to distance itself from its past and to look for an alternative source of authority'. 'By the time C. P. Snow delivered his lecture British society was more than ready for his forceful and passionate affirmation for the project of modernisation as well as his scathing attack on traditional authority' (Furedi, 2009: 61).

C. P. Snow had a foot in each of the 'two cultures', which is why he felt a dual sense of authority to comment on both: 'By training I was a scientist: by vocation I was a writer' (Snow, 1998: 1). A fellow of Christ's College, Cambridge (where Darwin had been an undergraduate), Snow was also a bestselling and (in his day) celebrated novelist, renowned and enriched by the *Brothers and Strangers* series of novels. Novels like *The Masters* (Snow, 1951) narrated the rivalry for academic succession in a Cambridge college. Another of his novels coined a phrase of abiding use *Corridors of Power* (Snow, 1964). Aside from a skill at pithily framing an idea, to his critics, neither his scientific nor his literary achievements have been long-lived. The phrases 'two cultures' and 'corridors of powers', by the harsh assessment of one, 'are essentially what remain of the once towering reputation of Sir Charles Percy Snow' (Kimball, 2009: 31).

Snow's scientific career was certainly short-lived and at one point traumatic. His apparent 'discovery' of a way to synthesize Vitamin A in the 1930s – widely publicized and published in the prestigious scientific journal *Nature* – was also very publicly discredited. Snow's disillusionment led him to literature. Snow published his first novel in 1932. He continued to be involved in science as a government advisor, notably during the Second World War. By the 1950s, his literary success had far outstripped any limited scientific interests. He nevertheless remained a committed admirer of science. His key interest was in what science and technology could achieve in terms of the betterment of humanity. *Two Cultures* was concerned with, then, more than simply identifying an epistemological fissure between science and the arts. The work, as published, is divided into four sections: 'The Two Cultures'; 'Intellectuals as Natural Luddites'; 'The Scientific Revolution'; and, surprising to those who might not know Snow's work, a fourth section, 'The Rich and the Poor'. Snow's intentions in highlighting the divisions between the arts and the sciences were pragmatic. He had a vision that science and greater scientific knowledge, brought about by greater education in primary and secondary schools, could alleviate what he felt to be in the modern age an inexcusable level of inequality between the rich Western world and the impoverished other. He makes a conscious link between scientific and technological development, sees the rich world with the latter and the poor without it. Education, especially in science, is seen by Snow as the solution. His many critics seem to forget that Snow was not presenting an either or. He took the criticism of 'high culture' commentators well. It never led him to despise his critics when he might well have, or disregard high culture when he could easily have dispensed with it and those of its proponents who so castigated him (Leavis, 1962; Trilling, 2001).

Snow's lecture was given at the height of his fame. A self-confident breezy authority is evident, certainly in the early part of *The Two Cultures*. Though he states that 'my personal history isn't the point now', he traces the personal origins of his perspective, including a rather cursory summary of his scientific career: 'I came to Cambridge and did a bit of research here at a time of major scientific activity.' But Snow accepts he was privileged to be at Cambridge at a time of immense advances especially in the new physics, a 'ringside view'. Critics did not take to Snow's casual, chirpy and chance-laden account. Tinged with just the hint of self-importance, after the two lines that summarize his Cambridge career his continued involvement in science reads like an incident in one of his novels (where events occur like this): 'And it happened that through the flukes of war – including meeting W. L. Bragg in the buffet on Kettering Station on a very cold morning in 1939, which had a determining influence on my practical life – that I was able, and indeed morally forced, to keep that ringside view ever since.' 'So,' he says – in what we must remember was originally a lecture – 'for thirty years I have had to be in touch with scientists not only out of curiosity, but as part of a working existence.' He is as equally casual about his writing career (and we need to remember that in 1959 Snow was a bestselling author whose star was still on the rise – *Corridors of Power* still to be published): 'During the same thirty years I was trying to shape the books I wanted to write, which in due course took me among writers' (Snow, 1998: 1–2).

Snow writes with assuredness about moving freely between two groups of literary and scientific intellectuals. Not describing himself as such, but giving to critics an annoying sense of Snow's self-projection as polymath: 'There have been plenty of days when I have spent the working hours with scientists and then gone off at night with some literary colleagues. I mean that literally.' This easy moving among all hues of intellectual elite is from where Snow of course gets his big idea:

> I have had, of course, intimate friends among both scientists and writers. It was through living among these groups and much more, I think, through moving regularly from one to the other and back again that I got occupied with the problem of what, long before I put it on paper, I christened to myself as the 'two cultures'. For constantly I felt I was moving among two groups – comparable in intelligence, not grossly different in social origin, earning about the same incomes, who had almost ceased to communicate at all, who in intellectual, moral and psychological climate had so little in common that instead of going from Burlington or South Kensington to Chelsea, one might have crossed an ocean. In fact, one had travelled much further than across an ocean – because

after a few thousand Atlantic miles, one found Greenwich Village talking precisely the same language as Chelsea, and both having about as much communication with M.I.T as though scientists spoke nothing but Tibetan. For this is not just our problem; owing to some of our educational and social idiosyncrasies, it is slightly exaggerated here, owing to another English social peculiarity it is slightly minimised; by and large this is a problem of the entire West. (Snow, 1998: 2–3)

His knowing references to scientific South Kensington and literary Chelsea with their American parallels show a man at home in the higher sophisticated echelons of England and America.

F. R. Leavis was probably among the most well-known of literary critics at the time. His 1948 book *The Great Tradition* argued for the civilizing power of literature. And he did see Snow's argument for bridging the gap between science and the arts as part of this civilizing process. But it was the man Snow and not his ideas that Leavis attacked. Leavis's diatribe is memorable for the cutting elegance of his prose. Leavis describes Snow as adopting 'a tone of which one can say that, while only genius could justify it, one cannot readily think of genius adopting it' (Whelan, 2009: 7).

The *attack* on Snow was by any standards ferocious, and was almost as much discussed in subsequent decades as the lecture itself. As Tallis (2009) has it, 'Even at this distance, Leavis' sneers have the power to shock, to anger and to disgust. The immediate result of his lecture was that the question of the "The Two Cultures" ceased to be a subject of serious debate and became instead a delicious scandal' (Tallis, 2009: 44). As Collini (1998) comments, 'Leavis' contempt was total'. Leavis understood that Snow's commentary on the 'two cultures' arose of personal experience. It is precisely this which Leavis attacks. Leavis, in order words, gets personal. Leavis was on particularly strong ground as a literary critic to attack Snow as a man of letters. Snow is 'intellectually as undistinguished as it is possible to be'. The two cultures lecture exhibits for Leavis an 'utter lack of intellectual distinction and an embarrassing vulgarity of style': 'Snow is, of course, a – no, I can't say that; he isn't. Snow thinks of himself as a novelist [yet] as a novelist he doesn't exist, he doesn't begin to exist. He can't be said to know what a novel is. The nonentity is apparent on every page of his fictions' (Collini, 2009: xxxiii–xxxiv).

The debate was more than about an exchange of arguments eliding into insults. Leavis and others perceived Snow as representative of and partly responsible for a degeneration of British culture. Like Arnold's *Culture and Anarchy*, in Leavis's estimation, high culture was a bastion against nothing less than civilizational decline, and now modern popular culture, the mass media, the arts themselves, were contributory to instead of defences against it:

That Snow's novels enjoyed, in the late 1940s and 1950s, a considerable réclame in the London literary world was, in Leavis's eyes, further damning evidence of their meretriciousness. And that world, the world of 'literary London', of smart cocktail parties, of reviews in the Sunday papers, of the latest 'view' propounded in the New Statesman or on the BBC's Third Programme, was a world in which Snow had come to move easily and with increasing fame. But Snow was also a technocrat, a spokesman for what Leavis regarded as the 'technologico-Benthamite' reduction of human experience to the quantifiable, the manageable. (Collini, 1998: xxxiii)

Snow 'had blundered across one of the most sensitive terrains in twentieth-century English literature: the assessment of the human consequences of the Industrial Revolution', 'the Romantic versus the Utilitarian, Coleridge versus Bentham, Arnold versus Huxley' (Collini, 1998: xxxv). The Industrial Revolution to its advocates (including Snow) saw science and industry as *the* means of human progress; to its detractors (Romantics who found a modern ally in Leavis) such progress was at a terrible dehumanizing cost. The latter view has many present-day defenders:

> The contemporary relevance of this argument can hardly be overestimated. We live at a moment when 'the results of science' confront us daily with the most extreme moral challenges. Abortion on demand, nanotechnology, the prospect of genetic engineering – the list is long and sobering. But more challenging than any particular application of science is the widespread assumption that every problem facing mankind is susceptible to technological intervention and control . . . In this situation, the temptation to reduce culture to a reservoir of titillating pastimes is all but irresistible . . . Culture is no longer an invitation to confront our humanity but a series of opportunities to impoverish it through diversion. (Kimball, 2009: 41)

'There is only one way out of all this: it is, of course, by rethinking our education' (Snow, 1998: 18): 'Yet one would underestimate the national capacity for the intricate defensive to believe that that was easy. All the lessons of our educational history suggest we are only capable of increasing specialisation, not decreasing it' (Snow, 1998: 19). Yet there are, we are generally told, no concrete proposals for education within *The Two Cultures*.

Though Snow delineates the problem well – otherwise it would not be being discussed after its sixtieth anniversary – he more presents rather than practically unpacks a solution. In the space of a short lecture, it would have been unreasonable to expect more. Few single lectures have provoked as much thought, and this was the intention. Snow had a common-sense, one might say no-nonsense, view of education. Science was there to serve and transform society, arts and humanities were to enrich understanding not simply entertain. He not only approved but considerably influenced the Robbins Report (1963). Its recommendations facilitated the general expansion of higher education in England which, as Snow did, saw universities as critical to social progress, in the arts and sciences. The Robbins Report, like Snow, held in esteem the arts and humanities and the sciences, and a view of knowledge as valuable in itself but also pressing on those with learning to serve the needs of the society which had provided them with it. The teaching profession benefitted enormously, from the greater flow of graduates of both arts and humanities as well as sciences into the profession. The development of programmes of religious studies within universities in England was a direct result of Robbins. Development of teacher education programmes sought to embed a number of academic disciplines to the field: history, philosophy, sociology and psychology of education became integral to, not optional within, teacher education. But this also meant some drift from the subject or curriculum discipline in teacher education. But this development also opened the subjects to these disciplines.

Snow's common-sense or no-nonsense approach would have had little time for the educational *theory* which emerged in the decades following his lecture. Despite the furore his lecture caused and the debate and initiative, especially in higher education, it stimulated, Snow was very much a traditionalist, ironically, like his Leavisite opponents. Though this educational theory often went under the guise of social or psychological science, Snow had little patience with them as scientific. Snow's view of education was that teaching and learning in science were determined by science, they did not need a theory of learning or a theory of teaching. The curriculum was a matter for the subjects themselves. He would see these emerging in an organic Kuhnian sense – trial, error, experiment, communities who shared knowledge and ideas. In science, Snow's passion was the practical application. The arts he saw as a source of personal enrichment not social transformation. They also provided insight into the human condition in ways which science could not. His tastes in reading were serious. His passion was for Russian literature above all else. Though he later had a preference for Tolstoy, from age 20, Snow declared Dostoevsky his favourite author, *The Brothers Karamazov* his favourite novel. Education in the arts and humanities involved reading as essential as science involved experiment. Without reading, learning was impossible. If teacher education had a role, it would be in devising a curriculum for arts and humanities and the sciences in schools, not devising new theories of how these subjects were learned.

This after all was a time characterized by a sense of competitive urgency. The very names of the space race, the arms race suggest this. Leavis wrote *The Great Tradition* 3 years after the explosion of the first atom bomb, Snow's lecture was given in some of the most dangerous years of the Cold War. There was little time for unnecessary *theories* of teaching and learning when there was so much teaching and learning to be done. The intensity of the argument perhaps masked a closer alignment than Snow and Leavis would likely admit. In teaching and learning both were traditionalists, and despite Snow's egalitarian rhetoric, both were in their own ways elitists (see Ortolano, 2009; Whitmarsh, 2012). There was also a quietly understated but prominent secular tone on either side of the divide.

Religion across the curriculum: arts, humanities and sciences

Religion thus featured nowhere in the two cultures debate of the 1950s, certainly to a far lesser degree than in the Arnold-Huxley debates in the 1880s. Yet recent decades have seen a resurgence of religious aspects of the two cultures debate which would have surprised both. Science–religion debates are an aspect of one side; and there, admittedly much more diffuse, are a plethora of examples where religious tradition is a major objector to culture, especially in matters around blasphemy, other perceived offences and wider debates on freedom of expression (Gearon, 2002). Religion, then, has surfaced in all sorts of ways, in debates about public and political life, but has also critically surfaced on both sides of the two cultures, again in ways which might have surprised and dismayed Snow and Leavis.

For the remainder of this chapter, I want to provide examples of the ways in which religious education relates not in obvious ways directly to the two cultures debate, but on the one hand to the arts and humanities, and on the other to the sciences. I show that this cross-curricular dimension to religious education reflects a much wider relevance of religion in spheres far beyond the school. Then I wish to draw from this cross-curricular sketch some conclusions about the broader issues of religious education's identity. These are illustrated by religious education's cross-curricular range. This is a strength of the subject, I argue, and a weakness, an ambivalent advantage then. Yet there is concealed here a deeper level of ambivalence which shows the impact of and relationship between school religious education and university-level study of religion in education.

Arts and humanities

The history of the visual arts shows a pattern evident in all the arts, in music, literature, theatre. This is a distinctive shift, at least in the Western context, in subject matter and orientation of the artist. The Sainsbury Wing of the National Gallery houses medieval art from the period 1250 to 1400. It is exclusively Christian and exclusively religious. It is a reflection not only of what Smart calls the material dimension, but such art also embodies in pictorial form – God the Father, the Son, and the Holy Spirit, the earthly life of Jesus, the apostles, the Church Father and the lives of saints in later era. The paintings are as much as any written document, a window to medieval religious life, showing how these people perceived and placed into perspective a short earthly life. The brevity of this fallen existence on earth was set before ever-present reminders of the 'four last things' – death, judgement, heaven and hell. In this eschatological lens, saints were those who showed how the right path might be steered through the snares of this world. There were eternal consequences for consciously taking the path offered by the devil. The pictorial representation may have changed but it would be an error, and one commonly made, that the theology and worldview entirely disappeared after the medieval period. The doctrines of judgement, heaven and hell remain intact in all but the most liberal Christian theology; and, of course, life expectancy may have increased since the Middle Ages, but the facts of death have not.

The medieval collection in the National Gallery, from 1250, is however a time when alternative views to this medieval Christian worldview began to emerge. In England this date represents the century in which the universities of Oxford and Cambridge were founded, and across Europe the middle of the thirteenth century was also, arguably, the beginning of Renaissance and the 'new learning'. It was thus, too, the beginning of a time when the shared worldview would begin to fragment. First, this would happen through the Renaissance itself. From then, the fragmentation would continue through Reformation and, as we have seen, to Enlightenment to our 'advanced' present. Suffice to say though that in the middle of the thirteenth century, such developments were matters for a very small scholarly elite.

In the medieval period represented by the Sainsbury Wing collection, then, the visual art incorporates and reflects all other dimensions of the religious life. If we takes Smart's dimensions of religion: (1) In experiential terms the art represents the lives of the latter apostles and saints, struggles with temptation, the eschatological context of a short early life confronted by the eternal and the judgement which would decide on that eternal fate, heaven and hell. (2) The narrative and mythic is clearly also and obviously represented by the art, it tells the story of Christian faith, but the paintings very often also portray the text of the Bible itself, particularly notable in portrayals of St Jerome, the translator of the Bible into Latin. (3) The doctrinal and philosophical is obviously incorporated too, for portrayals of the Trinity and the work of God on creation and the lives of fallen mankind, are visual statements of theological understanding. (4) In ritual, we can note that the majority of the paintings of this period were designed for devotional purposes, and, apart from those paintings commissioned by wealthy patrons of the arts, were generally painted not only as visual representations of faith, but placed in the context of worship, in this case the Mass in Catholic churches, where the paintings were, with the altar was the focus of devotion. (5) The social dimension shows the close relationship not only between religion and art, but religion and society, portrayals of New Testament life or the lives of the saints, often (and often not so subtle) contemporaneous portrayals of that society and the donors who commissioned the art. The latter point is important. We do not know the names of many of the artists – some of the famous ones of course we do – because for the most part the artist was less important than what was portrayed. (6) As has been regularly commented on in the history of art in this period, in a society in which the majority of the population, the poor and landless, could not read or write, the paintings not only told the Christian story, the story that is of their salvation, but of the commandments which were there to guide them on this path, and the Heaven that would be their reward, but also portrayals of the Last Judgment and of Hell, the punishment which would be theirs if they did not. (7) The 'material' or aesthetic dimension thus in the context of the history of medieval art at least contains all others.

The galleries which follow the period past the 1450s, that is, the beginnings of the modern world, show the emergence at the time of the Renaissance of the artist, of the individual genius which we know or conceive in romantic or idealized terms today. It is from this period that we do come to know and celebrate the names of individual artists. The religious still predominates, as does the emphasis upon commissioning and commissioning for the purposes of religious, that is, Christian worship. However, the Reformation marked the great shift not only in theology and ecclesiology, but also art. Not only were many of the medieval representations of Catholic art regarded as unscriptural (the communion of saints, purgatory) but also the notion of pictorial representation (especially of God) was seen by many Reformers as blasphemous of the many who had come to regard this Catholic art as idolatrous, based on a literal interpretation of the Exodus 19, the command against idolatry. European art as a result suffered the single greatest destruction of an irreplaceable cultural heritage, not witnessed in prior history, or since. Parallels between the destruction in England first of the monasteries, of the art of Catholic religious life, and later, under Puritan influence, of modern day book burning and, especially in the Soviet Union and Communist China, of the destruction of religious buildings may be distasteful but they are apposite. For what we see in the Sainsbury Wing, or in galleries of a similar nature worldwide, is the tiniest fragment of a European heritage lost forever.

Artists still existed, of course, but their skills where Reformed Protestantism dominated were no longer needed. Some fled to Catholic countries. Others remained in their native lands. In these instances, the portrayals of religious life disappear in such contexts. What emerges are more allegorical portrayals of the same existential context – belief in the terrible consequences of the Last Judgement if anything intensified. The Reformation thus had a profound effect not only on European theology but on European art as well.

If each period of art is thus, as art critics tell us, not simply a painting but a window into the world, during the eighteenth-century Enlightenment, artistic preoccupations also reflect this, not only a renewal of interest in the classical world, which had been evident half a millennia earlier in the Renaissance, but also an artistic representation of science. Such portrayals, though there are some notable ones, were not prevalent. It is here where Snow's articulation of the divide between science and arts is particularly significant. For the response of Romanticism to the perceived intellectual sterility of the Enlightenment, science, and new technology, provoked an artistic response in which emotion and not reason, individuality and not the steady march of scientific and social progress predominated. If we remain in the National Gallery – any world-leading gallery of Western art will show a similar development – we see, then, the disappearance of religious imagery which predominated in the medieval period (at least where the Reformed rather than Catholic interpretation of Reformation predominated). The consequence was more allegorical representations of Christian faith.

The Enlightenment provokes further responses. But here the artist, perhaps by the nature of the work, in general sided with the Romantic response and reaction against Enlightenment. If we follow the galleries to the nineteenth and early twentieth centuries (where the collection ends) we see the emergence of the artist as the supreme example of the individual, and with this, as happened in the Romantic response to Enlightenment, the predominance of the idea of the often-tortured genius. The story of the history of art does not of course end (nor begin) with the National Gallery. Along the river, the National Gallery and the Tate Modern portray, as galleries of modern art worldwide portray, an ineluctable move towards abstraction. Religious imagery makes here an often curious and sometimes (intentionally) disturbing reappearance, in Francis Bacon's Crucifixion. In all, in the wake of Enlightenment, the arts did not return to the old content and formal, representative means of expression. It took on board the Enlightenment rejection of religion. But from its rejection too of Enlightenment reason, it aligned in favour of emotion and experience. For Romantics this opened up an entire arena of a spirituality without the formal constraints of institutional Christianity, the effects of which were for a time apparent in a short-lived emphasis on the spiritual development in state schools. It was from this period too, the eighteenth century and progressively into the nineteenth, that alternative traditions, especially those of the East, and particularly India, were sought. In terms of the role of the artist and the nature of art, the fact that there was a 'role for the artist' and debates about the nature and 'function' of art demonstrates from the late eighteenth century onwards, that both art and the artist (in all its material forms) were beginning (in some quarters) to supplant religion as a source of (highly individualized) meaning. This has had a subtle and profound on religious education in a number of ways. Probably one of the most profound has been in the emphasis on the importance of individual experience, a correlative of the Enlightenment principle of autonomy from inherited authority, but one which can be traced to the Renaissance. In simple terms, we can see the latter as a rebirth of classical learning, and its influence on philosophy we see as a re-emergence of a tension evident in early Christian centuries. But the Renaissance was also critically a rebirth of classical approaches to aesthetics, the pursuit of experience and sensual enjoyment through the arts. We saw in the patristic era, a range of approaches to classical philosophy and early Church Fathers who rejected classical philosophy and would usually, invariably, reject classical approaches to the arts. Of all authors, Augustine, and again in his *Confessions*, is by far the most plain in this, and he plainly rejects not only the classical philosophy of his own education but also the arts, the amphitheatre and the literary competitions of which he and his friends were so enamoured.

We are dealing with large themes here, but we can see how there is a strong lineage between the Renaissance recovery of an aesthetic sense and sensuality and the Romantic sense that this is where meaning itself was to be found. Keats's poetic aphorism affirms this. To see how artistic appreciation in the nineteenth century made the link between Renaissance and Romanticism many examples could be provided. In art history terms, Walter Pater's influential Studies in the History of the Renaissance was credited with providing the historic justification for this aestheticism. At his trial, Oscar Wilde even cited Pater as having been formative. Throughout the visual and literary arts from late eighteenth-century Romanticism to early twentieth-century modernism, artistic endeavour was the paramount quest for meaning by men and women who rejected Enlightenment rationalism, the industrialization it spawned, but who were also in large part in a world not provided with the old religious certainties. Blake, Coleridge, Wordsworth are often torn here between the relationship between artistic and religious experience, and might be distinguished from later modernist models where the aesthetic becomes a replacement for religion (see, e.g. Clack, 1999).

These reflections might seem distant from religious education but they have directly impacted it: in the emphasis on the individual interpretations of religious tradition, often framed as all equally valid, and characterized by the vacuities of 'learning from' religion without any sense of what framework this 'learning from' is in; and, perhaps above all, this approach to experience as paramount is found in explicit terms in the psychological-experiential paradigm.

The sciences

To say that books on religion and science have proliferated in recent decades would be an understatement. Treatment of these topics is not of course new at all. Classic cases are, of course, Galileo and Darwin, and not least because what was at stake was so fundamental. These are cases we see Kuhn take up as genuinely paradigm shifting. From the Cambridge Studies in the History of Science series, John Hedley Brooke's (1993) historical essay provides some sense of the historical depth of the literature (see also Brooke and Maclean, 2005; Grant, 2006). Many offer very scholarly treatments of religion and science (Dixon, 2008; Harrison, 2010; McGrath, 2011; Polkinghorne, 2011; Ward, 2008). These offer dispassionate accounts which are relatively free from either scientific or theological polemic, even if there is usually an underpinning exposure of sympathy usually to religion, often expressed as arguments which charge that there is no real epistemological breach between religion and science. The most polemic extend to debates about religion, science and the 'new atheism' (Dawkins, 2006; McGrath, 2007a) are no less scientifically informed or theologically knowledgeable for that. This is what probably accounts for their enduring popularity. Inevitably, few authors have sufficient grasp of one side or the other to satisfy their adversaries. The fact that one side or the other misrepresents or inadvertently uncovers some naive understanding of science or religion leading to further exchanges in lively vitriol is some indication that some people still care about ideas. Many of the works of science in this area make their arguments about religion by implication, and they often have more force for that, evidenced by Stephen Hawking and Leonard Mlodinow's (2011) *The Grand Design*. Science here does not argue against religion, it simply makes theological argument superfluous to explaining the way things are. Hawking's (1996) *A Brief History of Time* had famously/infamously said that modern cosmology was revealing 'the mind of God'. Snow would have approved at least of the ways in which many of these writers contributed to an understanding of scientific 'culture'.

Michael Poole (2011, 2012) is one of the few educators with significant experience of science and religion in the classroom and lecture hall. The term 'science' he uses to mean mainstream science. As we have seen, this is what Kuhn refers to as 'normal science'. Its origins and emergence result from paradigm shifts within the scientific community. As the mainstream or normal science developed a body of knowledge accepted by the scientific community, its insights have often been in long struggle with the pre-scientific worldview, that is worldviews, notably religious worldviews which emerged prior to the public acceptance of modern science.

Poole (2011) identifies three key foundational areas in the development of science which have come into conflict with the scientific. They are: (1) the nature of science; (2) the data of science; and (3) the applications of science. Poole provides a shorthand checklist:

(1) *The Nature of Science:* Strengths and limitations of science; influence of the worldview of the scientist, with its beliefs and values, on the interpretation of science; scientific laws and the possibility of miracles; the philosophy and history of science; views on the relationships between religion and science and the persistence of the 'conflict thesis'; unpacking the Galileo affair and the Wilberforce/Huxley encounter; the theological concept of Creation, its difference from young-Earth creationism and from scientific theories of origins; reductionism and emergence; evidence and proof; facts, faith and reason; presuppositions necessary for science; the plurality and potential compatibility of different types of explanations; 'God of the gaps'; the use of language in religion and in science and how models and metaphors enable discourse about what is (i) new (ii) invisible and (iii) conceptually difficult.

(2) *The Data of Science:* Earth, its existence, age, status, position in space and in our solar system; cosmogony, Big Bang, Anthropic Cosmological Principle (Goldilocks Effect), eschatology, multiverse; the portrayal of Charles Darwin in the recent 'Darwin Year'; evolution, evolutionism and the role of chance in design. The distinction between traditional views of design, with supporting arguments, and the claims of the 'Intelligent Design Movement' and their arguments; the behavioural sciences; the social sciences.

(3) *The Applications of Science:* Issues of ethics and integrity; foundations of morality; environment; animal welfare; technology/alternative technology; nuclear power; medicine; military; space exploration; bio-engineering; nanotechnology (Poole, 2011; also 2012).

Across these three broad domains, no other force has shaped society so much in the past two or three centuries. If we examine this in terms of Smart's seven dimensions we could note – as we did for the arts – an absolutely seismic shift away from cognizance let alone conformity to a religion. No other form of knowledge has through its technologies had the spectacular transformative effect on the material culture of human civilizations. In terms of the other six dimensions – experiential; narrative; doctrinal and philosophical; ritual; social; ethical, moral and legal – science has continued to effect direct challenges to religion. In religious experience, psychologists can reduce what is described as religious experience to something else which does not relate to the divine or any transcendent reality. These terms are indeed no longer required to form an explanation of people's experience when they say they have had a religious or (as is common when there is antipathy to institutional religion) a spiritual experience. In narrative, let us say biblical narrative, the challenges began in the most pronounced way, as we noted earlier, by Darwin, and a whole tradition of evolutionary biology which leads to the highly influential figure of Dawkins today. In doctrinal and philosophical terms as well the ritual dimension, these were first to be systematically challenged by all Enlightenment philosophers; one of the perhaps unforeseen consequences of the Protestant Reformers was that their challenge of Catholicism would open the intellectual floodgates to that which, even in the less ritualized forms of Protestant Christianity, is foundational, the Bible. As for the social and the ethical (including moral and legal) dimensions of religions, these too had been systematically challenged by Enlightenment philosophers, with religion no longer seen as a sufficient foundation for ethical, moral or legal guidance and constraint, new foundations were needed, though as has been well-documented and acknowledged by moral and political philosophers themselves, the search for such moral foundations have proved elusive.

Religious education affirms the importance of different religious traditions approaching such issues from their own theological perspectives. There is a tremendous range of scholarly and education organizations which address this interface, including the International Society for Science and Religion; the European Society for the Study of Science and Theology; and the Faraday Institute for Science and Religion. There are too a number of specifically Christian networks which address the questions, methods and applications of science from an explicitly theological perspective, including Christians in Science; Counterbalance; the John Ray Institute; and the Science and Religion forum (see Poole, 2011). The rise of science and a public presence so pervasive has shown its influence on religious education of the natural sciences. From nineteenth-century Darwinian theory to twenty- and twenty-first century advances in biology, chemistry, physics, and cosmology, discoveries in the natural sciences – insofar as they challenge religious and theological discourse – are now an accepted part of religious education.

However, the most significant influence of the natural sciences upon religious education has been the inclusion of scientific topics rather than scientific method in religious education. The real methodological influence on the subject has been from the social sciences, but with the emphasis upon science, 'the science of religion', religious studies and religious education researchers wishing, understandably to underpin their work with the credibility of knowledge that is warranted by science.

Religion across the curriculum

An idea which pervades Smart's work is precisely the breaking down of such boundaries between religious and secular worldviews. As he states in *Dimensions of the Sacred*, 'I believe there are sufficient affinities between religious and secular worldviews (such as applied Marxism and nationalisms) to include secularism in the scope of this work' (Smart, 1999: 2). This approach has enabled religious educators to open up their perspectives, and others' perspectives of it, embracing historic challenges from arts, humanities and science, as curricular opportunities.

However, we need to remind ourselves in this regard how far such moves have shifted religious education from its scriptural-theological roots, and in so doing the impact this has had on its identity as a discipline. In moving from the biblical and Christian origins to socio-political concerns (often shifting it closely to citizenship), religious education has weakened not only its theological identity but its place within the arts and humanities. Through the influence of social, psychological and political sciences in its interpretation of religion – not to mention phenomenology – religious education researchers have also attempted to imitate scientific understandings of religion. These socio-cultural methods have begun to have political-pedagogical impact in classrooms across Europe – and worldwide. At its worst, religious education here manifests through its social and political emphases an often naked utilitarianism. Now even the research questions framed to inquire of

the subject are utilitarian. There can be no better utilitarian framing of the aims and purposes of religious education than the question, Does religious education work? However,
as researchers seem to be showing, teachers are themselves increasingly unsure of *what is*
supposed to be working in religious education.

Religious education can, then, loosely still be said to be a subject that fits within the curricula context of the arts and humanities, but it has been shaped not by these by the sciences
and the social sciences. In terms of epistemology, then, the subject faces two ways, to the arts
and to the sciences. And in terms of practical pedagogy, the subject also faces in these two,
not necessarily conflicting, spheres of knowledge. We see this most clearly in the emphases
on teaching religion as a subject of genuine cross-curricular concern. There are real and
satisfying possibilities but also dangers here. Religious education – like the definition of
religion itself –spread too widely (or thinly) risks weakening its very identity as a subject.

A theoretically rich for teaching and learning in religious educators, a core problem with
this approach is in part the breadth of subject knowledge required. Though rich in material, no other subject in the curriculum asks of much breadth of knowledge of its teachers –
knowledge of world religions in and of itself is a task, mastering knowledge of one tradition
is to set a lifetime achievement. When added to the religious effects on culture, the breadth
of knowledge required of religious education teachers is daunting.

A reminder of the time allocated to the subject provides some realistic and practical
perspective. Over a 5-year period, religious education in primary or secondary school may
be taught for around 200 hours, more if taken as an examination class in the later years
of secondary education, but all the same around 200 hours. Thinking of these 200 hours
in holistic terms may be a rather down to earth way of managing some of the subject's
otherwise daunting complexity. It allows too for a fairly precise overall grasp of progres-
sion and continuity within and between years, a structure which checks overly ambitious
aims but which nevertheless allows for personal enrichment of children's knowledge of
religion.

In practical terms, however, there are numerous resources where expert subject knowledge
does exist. I would highlight three. First, there is the school context itself. Cross-curricular
approaches provide the single most significant opportunity for collaboration between religious educations and those subjects which are reflected by the 'two cultures' debate. Second,
there are, as noted above, specialist peer-reviewed (online and other) resources. These draw
on the expertise of those who have specialized in the interface of the arts, humanities and
sciences. Third, the use of museums, galleries and cultural centres seemingly not concerned
with religion provide opportunities for religious educators (including, as with point one,
other departments) to connect with the education departments within such centres. All
larger museums and galleries now have these as part of their own brief to widen public
access, and facilitated through initiatives such as Learning outside the Classroom. Indeed
to do this, is to open perspectives on the vast influence of religion across the curriculum, in
the arts, humanities and sciences.

'The Two Cultures' revisited: the study of religion and the disciplines of education

Reading Snow's 'Two Cultures' lecture now the tone *is* dated, as critics have mercilessly said of his novels. Yet there is also admirable idealism to what he had to say (felt compelled to say), and his novels still exude a warm nostalgic glow from a world in which such idealism was still conceivable. Even Snow's Cold War geopolitics is a reminder of a time when the planet could be neatly divided. And his analysis of the injustice of global economic and educational inequality still reads as heartfelt. When Snow revisits 'The Two Culture' lecture 4 years later to evaluate its impact, to my reading, we see graciousness in the face of bare personal affront:

> During the arguments so far, there has been one unusual manifestation, which I shall mention just to get it out of the way. A few, a very few, of the criticisms have been loaded with personal abuse to an abnormal extent: to such an extent in one case, in fact, that the persons responsible for its publication in two different media made separate approaches to me, in order to obtain my consent. I had to assure them that I did not propose to take legal action. All this seemed to me distinctly odd. In any dispute acrimonious words are likely to fly about, but it is not common, at least in my experience, for them to come anywhere near the limit of defamation. (Snow, 1998: 56–7)

Snow is a man of modesty and humility, surprised by the attention:

> It is over four years since (in May 1959) I gave the Rede Lecture at Cambridge. I chose a subject which several of us had been discussing for some time past. I hoped at most to act as a goad to action, first in education and second – in my own mind the latter part of the lecture was always the more pressing – in sharpening the concern of rich and privileged societies for those less lucky. I did not expect much. Plenty of people were saying similar things. It seemed to me to be a time when one should add one's voice. I thought I might be listened to in some restricted circles. Then the effect would soon die down: and in due course, since I was deeply committed, I should feel obliged to have another go. (Snow, 1998: 53)

The 'two cultures' may today seem simplistic, but there resonates still some truth in an old Enlightenment divide.

It is only in the review of the lecture's impact that he defines more the terms of 'culture' which he had presupposed by the seeming obviousness of the divide:

> The term 'culture' in my title has two meanings, both of which are precisely applicable to the theme. First, 'culture' has the sense of the dictionary definition, 'intellectual development, development of the mind'. For many years this definition has carried overtones, often of a deep and ambiguous sort. It happens that few of us can help searching for a refined use of the word: if anyone asks, What is culture? Who is cultured? the needle points, by an extraordinary coincidence, in the direction of ourselves. But that, though a pleasing example of human frailty, doesn't matter, what does matter is that any refined definition, from Coleridge onwards, applies at least as well (and also as imperfectly) to the development a scientist achieves *in the course of his professional*

> *vocation* as to the 'traditional' mental development or any of its offshoots. Coleridge said 'cultiva-
> tion' where we should say 'culture' – and qualified it as 'the harmonious development of those
> qualities and faculties which characterise our humanity'. (Snow, 1998: 62–3)

Snow draws out here and refines the educational import of this to a point of distinction between number and letter:

> Curiosity about the natural world, the use of symbolic systems of thought, are two of the most
> precious and the most specifically human of all human qualities. The traditional methods of mental
> development left them to be starved. So, in reverse, does scientific education starve our verbal
> faculties – the language of symbols is given splendid play, the language of words is not. On both
> sides we underestimate the spread of a human being's gifts. (Snow, 1998: 62–3)

No side is untarnished. Science as the means of human progress has it many defenders today, more perhaps than in modern science's infancy. The vision though has been blemished by abuses too obvious to restate, but which are integral to a more general disenchantment with an Enlightenment view of progress. The Romantic's vision of art, experience and the autonomy, the ultimate freedom of each individual is still perpetuated in liberal education. Arguably, the last great flowering of the vision was in the 1960s counter-culture. The 1969 moon landing is possibly where rationalist and romantic sides of an Enlightenment divide met. But subsequent decades scarcely demonstrated the sustaining adequacy of Keats's 'Beauty is truth, truth beauty.' The scarcity of genius is rarely recognized by those who aspire to it. Few except those who practice them as a profession share the faith once invested in the sciences as the vehicle for 'progress'.

Yet it was these failing secular hopes which were promoted as the future of religious education. Though her work has been much criticized, few have traced the recent secularizing trends in religious education (in England at least) more effectively than Thompson (2004), particularly in tracing this trend through shifting policy agendas in recent decades. Baumfield et al. (2012) have shown that this plethora of shifting aims and purposes for religious education over several decades accounts for a heavily guarded ambivalent answer to the question, Does religious education work? Another and I think unaddressed explanation for this ambivalence derives in part from these initiatives, but at a 'deeper' epistemological level, one which is mirrored in those influences from which religious education sought regeneration.

Snow's dichotomy holds here some evident truths about a general cultural divide but has some less than self-evident insights not only of religious education but more generally educational research itself.

In simple curricula organization terms, religious education is aligned with the arts and humanities. In the research community, we see an orientation to a range of particular social sciences. So we see something of a subtle arts/humanities and science divide already.

Yet our survey of religious education pedagogies demonstrates a lack of consensus in a secular *treatment* of the subject. As a response to what Willaime identified as a double – legal and sociological – constraint, we see the subject internationally responding to political demands, especially religious pluralism. There is considerable and growing orientation towards, broadly to be interpreted, secular political goals. It is a lineage from Rousseau to Rawls (the language at least of tolerance permeates both) which allows us to identify a pedagogical model mirrored in political liberalism.

The trajectory of this leads inexorably back to when Smart (1969a) argued for a reorientation argument of religious education in schools. Religious education should cease being religious education. It should become religious studies. In so doing it should model itself on university curriculum of religious. Religious education remains religious education where it is a non-examined subject in state schools in England but when it is examined it is called religious studies; but what is religious education in name is religious studies in practice. This would, as it did, involve religious education shifting from a Christian scriptural-theological orientation to the study of world religions utilizing a range of disciplines which had themselves shaped religious studies. The ground for this had already been prepared by the psychology of religious education which declared children ill-prepared for the nuances of biblical study. Smart's argument was entirely different. There is no sense in which he felt children would be ill-prepared for such scriptural or textual studies: how could he, if he was advocating not simply the study of Christianity but a diversity of traditions? Further, as Smart's dimensions of religion made plain, no religion could be studied without attention to its foundational narratives, its scriptures. But a mere religious studies professor from what was then a very new university could hardly have effected the change he did unless the ground was prepared in other ways. The idea, as we have noted, was of its time. The roots of Willaime's double legal and sociological constraint lie there too. It was the decade when the UN promulgated the Convention on Civil and Political Rights as well as the Convention on Social, Cultural and Economic Rights (both 1966; Chesterman et al., 2007). The global rights to religious freedom implied an international recognition of religious pluralism (Marshall, 2000). England in the aftermath of Empire was itself a nation and a world more and more aware of religious diversity (Parsons, 1994). Religious education was found to be an ideal curricula area to address matters of multiculturalism (Swann, 1985). The 1988 Education Reform Act which followed 3 years after Swann enshrined Smart's approach de facto phenomenology into law. Subsequent decades would see an intensification of religion in politics, and this would be mirrored in education systems not only in England but worldwide, as earlier chapters have shown. The pedagogical shift from the scriptural-theological was and is now near complete in state religious education.

The great pedagogical shift, as we have seen, was rooted in a school subject formerly aligned – in its use of history, of text, of theology – to the arts and humanities. This period of shift, considered already in some detail, represents a disciplinary or epistemological one. While in schools it remains prominently within humanities, there has been a discernible epistemological identification of researchers of religion in education beyond the arts and humanities towards the social and political sciences. And increasingly religious education (and in examined religious studies) now has a heavy orientation toward social and political issues, whether explicitly to social and political contexts or through ethics and philosophy.

This pattern of development and influence can be seen in the academic study of religion itself. As Eliade (1957) notes, as we did above, that the 'science of religion' began within historical and linguistic analyses of the subject. The new psychological and social sciences did much to shift this ground. Pals's (2008) *Eight Theories of Religion* remains the most useful starting point for those unfamiliar with what is otherwise an extremely disparate cross-disciplinary literature of long historical gestation. In terms of original contribution even as a secondary footnote Smart does not appear in Pals's overview. Smart in other words can be regarded as making less of an original contribution to a specific aspect of religious studies (even the phenomenological approach he accepts was van der Leeuw's initiative), than providing a synthesis and delineation of the field. Even Smart's six and then seven dimensions are rarely if ever cited now in the academic literature, except as part of an historical note. Yet his synthesizing efforts in the study of religion were nevertheless profound, particularly in demonstrating (not least at Lancaster) how disparate arts, humanities and (at least social and psychological) sciences could be utilized in the study of religion. The international significance of this was evidenced in his role shortly before his death as president of the American Academy of Religion. Smart's achievements have been structurally rather substantively impactful on the study of religion in universities as well as schools. The changes to school religious education we have noted throughout, but the change on university departments was also considerable, marking a distinct shift from theology to religious studies approaches, reflecting in part a disciplinary complexity but also, as we have also noted, a shift in norms expected of someone wishing to study religion. They are expected to believe in religion only insofar as they believe it to be worth studying. The shift of the theology to religious studies within many universities marks another stage of theology's history as a discipline. When McGrath (2007a) describes the establishment of the medieval universities as 'perhaps the most important moment in the history of theology as an academic discipline' he is also highlighting a lost time when theology was foundational to the formation of secular disciplines which dominate universities today (MacIntyre, 2009). The two cultures' faultline runs through religious education and research on religion in education.

The same faultlines run through educational research. In 'The Disciplines and Discipline of Educational Research', David Bridges's (2006) starting point is that of 'the early 1970s at which educational theory and research was temporarily structured under the "foundation" disciplines of psychology, sociology, philosophy and history of education'. He narrates an intellectual enrichment of educational research but argues that hybridization and interdisciplinarity have engendered fragmentation, even 'postdisciplinarity'. Bridges argues, however, 'that without discipline, in the sense of a shared language, a rule governed structure of enquiry – something "systematic" – we lose the conditions that make a community of arguers possible'. Further, 'we lose the basis for the special claim which research might otherwise make on our attention and on our belief'.

He thus traces the development from foundation disciplines to said 'postdisciplinarity':

> The organisation of educational theory and research under the 'foundation' disciplines of the philosophy, sociology, psychology and history of education dominated the functioning of teacher education and of the educational research community in the UK and in many other parts of the English speaking world in the 1960s and through to the 1980s . . . For a while these foundation disciplines appeared to offer: differentiation between different kinds of enquiry (R. S. Peters had recently complained of the current condition of educational theory as 'undifferentiated mush'); coherence in terms of the internal consistency of any one of these forms; and the 'systematic' or rigour of enquiry, which raised such enquiry above the level of popular or received opinion – the discipline of the discipline. (Bridges, 2006: 259)

However, these foundation disciplines 'only ever provided provisional forms of coherence, temporary alliances, between what were often radically different traditions': 'The sociology of education, for example, contained everything from traditional hard data survey people through ethnographers, neo Marxists and critical theorists to postmodernists and social relativists. Psychology spanned neurophysiology, behaviourism, cognitivism and constructivism through to psychoanalysis.'

Fractures between the arts and sciences became evident in the foundation disciplines as new alliances of intellectual communities emerged: 'This diversification and hybridisation was encouraged too as the educational research community was enriched by people coming into it with a much wider repertoire of methodologies and informing theory, drawn from literary and cultural studies, ethnography, feminist and post colonial theory, etc., etc.' The 'ideological and methodological differences' were, however, intensifying and were 'at least as great as anything they might have in common' (Bridges, 2006: 259–60).

Bridges concludes with where he started, on the need for discipline among the disciplines. If 'intellectual progress requires a context in which there is relatively close agreement on theories, methods of enquiry and the requirements for the initiation of newcomers into the discipline'. Where there is a kind of methodological pluralism evident, advances in educational research are as inhibited as they would be in science. And so Bridges closes: 'The educational research community has taken on board in the last 25 years a rich repertoire of forms of enquiry and representation. Perhaps in the next phase of the development of educational enquiry, we should focus on understanding and refining the conditions – the discipline – under which these are conducted' (Bridges, 2006: 272).

We have noted similar disciplinary pluralism in the study of religion, from relatively well-defined scriptural-theological limits to far more undifferentiated multidisciplinarity informing emergent pedagogies of religious education. It is a tension between the art and humanities' epistemological roots of the subject and the new influences of diverse scientific paradigms, in other words, the same intellectual influences which affected education (the Arnold–Huxley debate in the nineteenth century; the Snow–Leavis nexus in the twentieth). Though I used the word 'paradigm', and contextualized this within the Kuhnian uses of the word, I also questioned whether the 'paradigm shift' has resulted in a paradigmatic consensus. I think not. However, with scriptural-theological principle abandoned, state religious education has sought and is still seeking epistemological foundations. Though it remains within the humanities in the school curriculum, the pressures on the subject in pedagogical and research terms come from the (initially the psychological and now predominantly the social) sciences. What foundations there are, remain insecure. Where religious education sought these foundations was from disciplines that had ironically begun with critiques of religion. Yet it is for this reason that developments in religious education *can* in limited ways be called paradigmatic: they consciously identify with a discipline, and even the methods of that discipline. Some approaches are more systematic, rigorous and thus potentially significant than others (one may not like the 'socio-cultural' paradigm but its influence is undeniable); others (in the psychological-spirituality paradigm) seem to make rejection of the systematic a point of principle.

Again, the disciplines which transformed religious education have parallels in 'mainstream' educational research. But the ascendancy of these disciplines here is itself under threat. Furlong and Lawn (2009, also 2010) identify the disciplinary rise and decline of psychology, sociology, history and philosophy of education as foundational in educational research:

> What these broadly different disciplinary approaches [still] have in common . . . is that each of them recognises the importance of both an 'epistemological' dimension (questions of theory, of method, debates about the nature of evidence, and how it should be represented and defended) and a political or 'sociological' dimension which examines their struggle to establish themselves within their field. (Furlong and Lawn, 2009)

From the 1920s to the 1950s, they suggest, 'The main discipline in education was psychology; subjects of study, training, careers and publications were defined by the dominance of psychology in education.' As Bridges noted, from which Furlong and Lawn draw, from the 1960s to the 1970s, 'The disciplines in education grew in range and scale.' History and philosophy acted as a (humanities) disciplinary counterpoint to the social and psychological sciences. From the 1970s to the 1980s, 'a rapid massification and expansion of universities and teacher training colleges saw a range of new subjects of study and ways of understanding or defining them'. The Open University's influence 'in redefining educational studies (particularly in the sociology and psychology of education, and in new areas, like educational administration and management and curriculum studies) was crucial in the expansion. Both macro-theoretical and micro-case study research crossed the borders of the disciplines and even fostered the growth of determinedly non-disciplinary based study'. Here, 'Education as a field of study is (no more than) a particularly acute example of changes that have overtaken higher education more broadly.' The changes are identified as themselves 'sociological' and 'epistemological' in origin. In regard to the former, Furlong and Lawn note increased pragmatic, economic emphases of neoliberal policies. The new 'sociological' market and instrumental emphases have shifted the focus from studies of education away from the epistemological, away that is from an emphasis on what these disciplines can contribute to new knowledge to what they can contribute to new global economic situations. Furlong and Lawn (2009, 2010) thus lament the formerly foundational disciplines of education as ghosts of a lost past.

The reasons for this have been explored in a wide literature: the milieu of practical, policy-driven pragmatism of educational research. It was a process which educational researchers were aware of, themselves charting a decline of disciplinary influence on policy formation. A 1990s UK debate about the need for teaching to be a research-informed profession (Hargreaves, 1996) within a short space of time became an unprecedented critique of the relevance of educational research not only to educational practice (notably, Hillage et al., 1998; Tooley and Darby, 1998). Educational research, it was claimed, was ideologically driven, tendentious, failed to address the practical needs of the profession (teachers, practitioners as well as policymakers), was often small scale and fractured, lacking a large and sufficient enough evidence base to be described as methodologically rigorous, in all thereby undermining not only its rigour but also its significance, especially to the teaching profession. Added to these voices were those from government: if educational research was not relevant to the teaching profession, it lost its legitimacy to inform educational policy (Blunkett, 2000; for a review of these criticisms of educational research, see Oancea, 2005; also, Oancea, 2011). The medical and health professions were compared unfavourably to education (on the education-health comparison, see Pring, 2004). The former had historically used rigorous, large-scale studies to provide firm scientific foundations for its research findings. Resulting from this, and to address questions of rigour, method and significance, was increased emphasis on evidence-based educational research, modelled on the medical model, notable in 'systematic' and 'professional' research reviews (BERA, 2012; EPPI, 2012) and an emphasis on large-scale systematic research (TLRP, 2011).

Responses by educational researchers were of limited capitulation to the criticisms levelled at it by the economic instrumentalism of government and critically funding sources. The response was met with some resistance, especially of what was perceived as an academically confining 'new orthodoxy':

> At best, the assumptions about method, objectivity and research quality that underpin these approaches are controversial, and the form of that controversy is ironic. For one of the premises at the heart of the new orthodoxy is that research should build carefully upon previously established findings. This is central to the EPPI approach . . . However, if this approach were adopted with regard to what is known about research methods and research quality, fundamental difficulties with what is proposed in the new orthodoxy would surface. For . . . at least within social and educational research, it is now widely accepted that there is no possibility of theory-free knowledge or theory-free observation. Thinkers and writers about research methods differ significantly in their response to this fundamental issue, and no resolution or way forward is remotely close to being universally accepted. (Hodkinson, 2004: 10–11)

Much as Bridges (2006) would call for 'discipline' amongst the 'disciplines of education', Hammersley's (2005) response to Hodkinson argues too for disciplinary boundaries: 'Currently, educational research is not a series of well-bounded communities having some overlapping membership, but rather a site where there is a complex and constantly shifting web of networks or alliances that have varying degrees of boundedness, these promoting a plethora of purportedly distinct approaches through the use of terms whose reference is often vague and uncertain.' This need not be methodologically restrictive:

> Rather than the laissez-faire approach he [Hodkinson] seems to favour, I believe what is required is a form of liberalism that does not lay down specifications about method, but is concerned with holding the ring both to prevent deviation outside the boundaries of what counts as educational inquiry and to ensure fair competition among competing approaches within. So, contrary to Hodkinson, I see some self-policing of the educational research community as unavoidable: it has to have boundaries to defend itself not just from researchers who want to write imaginative literature, poetry, or political tracts, and pretend that these are research, but also from external agencies engaged in sham inquiry designed to serve commercial or political goals. Hodkinson's relativism leaves us weak not only against the reformer but also against internal and external forces whose stock-in-trade is precisely the telling of persuasive stories. (Hammersley, 2005: 152)

In this wider educational research context, the emergence of the different paradigms in religious education (pedagogy and research) is a reflection of similarly loosely conjoined epistemological developments and disciplinary alliances. In religious education we can say they have emerged from cross-fertilizations between the study of religion and the disciplines of education.

The same disciplines which so profoundly impacted education also had, as we have seen, a direct impact on the recent decades past development of religious education. If, as Furlong and Lawn note 'the main discipline in education was psychology', we can see direct parallels in (in the 1960s in particular) psychology's impact on religious education ('readiness for religion' and related research emerged from this). The influence of psychology of religious education has declined just as the psychology of education has declined as a discipline within education studies. Furlong and Lawn (2010) trace this by way of the emergence of other competing disciplines – sociology, philosophy, history of education – and hybridization between and the creation of new disciplines, and religious education has been so impact, but from two directions: the disciplines of education and the study of religion And the very multidisciplinarity and hybridity noted in educational research was apparent – and much earlier – in the study of religion. Smart's brand of 'phenomenology' encouraged a multiple range of approaches to the study of religion. Prominent were historical and linguistic approaches (which as Eliade reminds us were the origins of the 'science of religion') and the social and psychological sciences (sociology of religion, anthropology of religion, socio-anthropology of religion, psychology of religion).

If we take Furlong and Lawn's (2010) analysis, though, the very disciplines to which religious educators have turned for epistemological ground (after rejection of the scriptural-theological) are themselves under threat (at least as disciplines of education). Religious education and research on religion in education, like educational research itself, are subject to diverse external pressures beyond the subject and the disciplines. Furlong and Lawn (2009) identify these as sociological and epistemological, in broad terms neoliberal economic and market emphases. Religious education has not been subject to anything like the same degree of market or economic pressures in terms of performance. But there are nevertheless unequivocally similar instrumental pressures. Willaime has identified these pressures on religious education in Europe – but with demonstrated worldwide parallels – as a 'double constraint' of the 'sociological' and the 'legal'.

There is another twist to the story. Religious education's turning to the disciplines of education for epistemological legitimacy does not seem to have been reciprocated by an acknowledgement from those disciplines of education. Furlong and Lawn's (2010) *Disciplines of Education* makes not even an index reference to religion or religious education. This might be difficult to explain given the continued global influence of religion from secular political interest to, of course, the traditions themselves. On the other hand, it is an easily understandable neglect. The disciplines themselves originated by distinguishing their field of enquiry from the separation of rationality, empiricism, scientific method, etc., from religion or by a range of reductive accounts of it (again, Pals, 2008). The natural sciences played their part from nineteenth century onwards. Within a decade of Darwin's *On the Origin of Species*, the 1870 Education Act came into legal force the same year as the Huxley–Wilberforce debate on evolution. It is the same context which Richard Dawkins (2007) in *The Greatest Show on Earth* rightly uses as the centrepoint of his attack on Christianity, and a more wholesale attack on religion per se in *The God Delusion* (Dawkins, 2006). But the roots of other legal, political, psychological and sociological scientific questioning of religion's legitimacy lie in the late eighteenth century. After all Kant (1784) makes plain that an explicit break with religious authority would underpin all subsequent post-Enlightenment enquiry, in philosophy and natural sciences, of course, but also in the new disciplines generated. These disciplines not only shared this sceptical perspective, they presupposed it.

It is these collective epistemological challenges to religion's legitimacy which we find embraced by many religious educators and researchers in religion in education. And yet in mainstream educational research, there remains an epistemological and methodological distance, and if we take Furlong and Lawn's (2010) overview, to the point of erasure. This is curious given the present-day prominence of religion in the social and political sciences, all the more inexplicable given the international focus on religion in education. Religious educators should not be concerned by this marginalization within educational research. The disciplinary tides of the social and political sciences as well as arts and humanities are testimony to the vigour of religious education, religious studies and theology. There remain nevertheless disciplinary uncertainties in religious education.

If we take Snow's simple dichotomy, with all its simplifications, we find religious education with a dual disciplinary face: one facing the arts and humanities, one facing the sciences. In this regard, the study of religion has been accepted, has achieved renewed vigour, in a range of disciplines – in the political and social sciences especially – and this in turn has renewed its international academic relevance for religious education underpinned by religious studies and theology. Post-Enlightenment natural and the psychological, political and social sciences of course will inform this process. Such disciplines now often dictate the framework. The tensions and knowledge emergent from within religious tradition and knowledge derived outside of it can be traced, at least in Western Christian terms, to antiquity. The nature of religious education can be judged according to a fundamental, defining alignment with either the religious life or secularity. This dichotomy may seem oversimplified when both sides of it are informed by the other. Religious education imbued with secular aims and purposes needs still to draw on the frameworks of religion and theology, when it does not it is no longer religious education, but some other subject, citizenship or philosophy or sociology. Religious education related to the religious life, to that life which presented a theological worldview, a way of not simply arguing about but being in and seeing the world, will of course draw on secular frameworks but it is not dominated by them. But it remains nevertheless a valid distinction. The nature of religious education can therefore be judged in fundamental, defining ways with alignment to either the religious life or secularity.

Summary

This chapter positioned religious education in relation to a 'two cultures' debate reinvigorated by C. P. Snow's 1959 Cambridge lecture. It has looked at this as a positive pedagogical opportunity by looking at religion's place across the curriculum, in relation to the arts and humanities as well as the sciences. It might be argued that religious educators are teachers of *religion* and not these other subjects or curriculum areas. The core counter-argument here is that its wide cross-curricular potential relates to the uniquely contested place of religion in the modern world. Is this seeking cross-curricular relevance simply to cling on to religion's now residual relevance? The answer in part yes, but there are reasons why such an approach is critical. Since we live amidst an historical heritage where culture (arts, humanities) and religion are inseparable, as well as there being continuing reactions *against* such a heritage (science, new forms of cultural expression), cross-curricular approaches are not only valid but a necessary part of any religious education. Naturally, the various ways in which these conflicts and accommodations continue today are themselves also critical in demonstrating religious education's contribution to wider debates across the arts, humanities and sciences.

In more deep-seated ways, religious education finds itself in a not impossible to resolve identity crisis between the art and humanities on the one hand and the sciences on the other. This can also be related to the 'two cultures' dichotomy, by examining the multifaceted but in general terms twofold influences on religious education and research on religion in education: the study of religion and the disciplines of education.

When we see the cross-curricular range of subject matter, religious education can potentially cover, we, or I at least, can see a great many strengths to the traditionalist argument of teaching and learning proffered in distinct ways by both sides of the Snow–Leavis divide. Religious education can offer bridges over the divide. It offers a cohesive if constantly contested interpretive framework. However, when religious education loses its foundational focus, on the relationship between religious education and the religious life, knowledge of religion and the traditions of the religions is lessened. The disciplines of education have in this regard added much to the subject, but such additions have also often involved a confusion of aims and purposes simply by the competing multiplicity of them.

If the nature of religious education can be judged in fundamental, defining ways with alignment to either the religious life or secularity, in either case, only in knowing the traditions through reading them – their texts, their histories, their interactions and responses to the modern world – can students learn from religion. Reviewing the emergent pedagogies of religious education it can be intimated from their effects that they have at best been limited, at worst obfuscating. It is for this reason that religious studies as a subject examined according to clear guidance set by examination boards often produces the most consistent quality in terms of the development of subject knowledge and understanding as well as students' capacity to interpret and evaluate them, personally and in relation to the contexts of religion in post-Enlightenment modernity.

Religious education needs to be, and is, more than about *knowledge* of religion, but the plethora of new aims and purposes – phenomenological, psychological, philosophical, socio-cultural and above all political – has, to the extent that each has narrowed interpretation, also narrowed the subject range, risking a distortion of religion itself. The most fundamental distortion of all is the limitation of religious education to socio-cultural goals imposed by political directive.

Recent religious education pedagogy, it can be argued, has been shaped less by religious traditions than by the disciplines which have emerged to interpret them. The emergent, 'paradigm shifting' pedagogies of religious education have added complexity where simplicity of approach would have sufficed, tangential theory added before students have grasped the rudiments of a religious tradition, or its interdisciplinary complexities, and above all added political *agendas* before even the most basic understanding of political-theological context. Religion has so much more to offer.

Conclusion: Context, Aims and Limitations Revisited

The introduction glimpsed those centuries after the fall of Rome and of Britain's slow but progressive conversion to Christianity. The unique historical account of this, on which secular historians too depend, is Bede's early eighth-century *Ecclesiastical History of the English People*. So that in the open paragraphs he can declare:

> The island at present, following the number of the books in which the Divine law was written, contains five nations, the English, Britons, Scots [Irish], Picts, and Latins, each in its own peculiar dialect cultivating the sublime study of Divine truth. The Latin tongue is, by the study of the Scriptures, become common to all the rest. At first this island had no other inhabitants but the Britons, from whom it derived its name, and who, coming over into Britain, as is reported, from Armorica, possessed themselves of the southern parts thereof. When they, beginning at the south, had made themselves masters of the greatest part of the island, it happened, that the nation of the Picts, from Scythia, as is reported, putting to sea, in a few long ships, were driven by the winds beyond the shores of Britain, and arrived on the northern coast of Ireland, where, finding the nation of the Scots, they begged to be allowed to settle among them, but could not succeed in obtaining their request. Ireland is the greatest island next to Britain, and lies to the west of it; but as it is shorter than Britain to the north, so, on the other hand, it runs out far beyond it to the south, opposite to the northern parts of Spain, though a spacious sea lies between them. (Bede, 1999: 9)

A little under 200 years later, King Alfred's late ninth-century unification of England was achieved not simply through military victory but by religious conversion of Viking invaders. The dominance of religion in the Middle Ages is nowhere better encapsulated by the term 'Christendom': and the ultimate subjection of political power to ecclesiastical authority. To be outside the church, and thus salvation, by either excommunication or interdict was considered by monarchs a worse fate than losing an earthly kingdom.

The European Reformation fractured any unity and thus force of ecclesiastical authority. On many levels, it was this which facilitated in the sixteenth, seventeenth and eighteenth centuries formal separations of 'throne' and 'altar'. The eighteenth century also included revolutions which removed both 'throne' *and* altar' from the governance of newly emergent nation-states. The political and intellectual freedoms which these seismic shifts in European power unleashed were the beginnings of the modern world.

This book has really been about the subsequent shape of state religious education in this vast aftermath of still living history.

Chapter 1 examined the post-Cold War resurgence of religion in global governance and as a result the certainly surprising interest in religion and even a practical interest in religion in education from a range of political and some surprising security sources including the OSCE and the CIA. I concluded that what is new in these modern uses of religion in education is the transnational application of variants on a similar political theme. In the modern world, where religion is seen as a potential source of cultural and social disharmony or, worse, violent conflict, religion in education is being consistently used to address a pressing problem for political liberalism. Political agencies have here sought education as a means of partly resolving the issues raised by religion and religious extremism: a political problem I argued had become a pedagogical problem.

Chapter 2 showed how researchers of religion in education have sought to uncover potential resolutions of these political-pedagogical issues. Using case studies of initiatives in Europe and America, and the global impact of these, I showed how such political-pedagogical problems have become research agendas, and arguably are coming to *dominate* research agendas around religion in education.

Chapter 3's analysis showed however that the historical link between religious education and the religious life is not entirely broken, for example in schools of a religious character. In England such schools are part funded by the state. Even in those countries where such funding was not available (for instance, in France and America) private faith schools continued to exist, those which retain the link between religious education and the religious life. In countries like England where state funding for schools of a religious character exists, I showed how the dual system has been directly impacted in distinctive ways by the logic of Willaime's double constraint of legal framework and sociological conditions. In terms of sociological conditions, religious plurality has meant that an increased demand from diverse religious communities be met for their own schools. In law, though state funding is available for Catholic and Protestant schools, such state funding for other religious traditions has now also been met now. In all these faith school contexts, religious education remains an integral part of the religious life. If the arguments for and against faith schools are different from those for and against religious education, we saw how they have come to be often closely related.

Chapter 4 thus examined attacks on religious education that have often been jointly targeted by secular sources on both faith schools and religious education. In particular, how arguments over the role of religious education in addressing issues of cohesion in the midst of cultural and religious plurality have been challenged – as to whether religious education is necessary if such matters can be incorporated into the secular orientation of citizenship. The core secular argument here is that there is nothing distinctive in religious education's contribution that could not or is not covered in other areas of the curriculum. It was concluded that the grounds on which so many religious educators have sought to justify their subject is being used against them by the very secular intellectual traditions with which they had sought to ally themselves. Certainly there was evidence reviewed which showed the international rise of religious content in citizenship education, charting clear incursion of secular subjects on to the formerly exclusive territory of religious education.

Using Thomas Kuhn's notion of paradigm shift, Chapter 5 analysed six pedagogies of religious education amidst the intellectual currents of post-Enlightenment thinking: (1) the scriptural-theological; (2) the phenomenological; (3) the philosophical-conceptual; (4) the psychological-experiential; (5) the socio-cultural; and (6) the historical-political. It concludes that in the breakage between religious education and the religious life, represented by a shift from the scriptural-theological, the epistemological foundations of subsequent pedagogies of religious education emerge directly from those new 'scientific' disciplines which had their very origins in the critique of religion.

Chapter 6 examined the relation of religion and religious education to the arts, humanities, and sciences through the lens of the two cultures debate engendered by C. P. Snow. Though rich in material possibilities for the curriculum, no other curricula subject asks as much breadth of knowledge of its teachers – knowledge of world religions in and of itself is a task, mastering knowledge of one tradition is to set a lifetime achievement. When added to the religious effects on culture, the breadth of knowledge required of religious education teachers is daunting. But some practical recognition of the limitation of the aims and objectives is critical.

When confronted with the vast demands of religious education, one simple, practical corrective is the recognition that curriculum time for religious education in the school life of a child is limited. Time allocated to the subject is usually limited to an hour a week, and allowing for a 40-week school year, roughly calculated. Over a 5-year period, religious education in primary or secondary schools may be taught for around 200 hours, more if taken as an examination class in the later years of secondary education, but all the same, around 200 hours. Thinking of these 200 hours in such terms may be a rather down to earth way of managing some of the subject's otherwise daunting complexity, an aide memoire which, on the one hand, realistically checks overly ambitious aims, and on the other, nevertheless provides a holistic structure for the enrichment of children's knowledge of religion.

For structure is needed on so grand a canvass. Nevertheless, what so often provides the subject with its vibrancy is understanding the ways in which religion has moved from a civilizational core to an arguable periphery in the past few centuries, and that from the supposed intellectual margins and the borderland of political power, religion in all its plurality now exerts a far more complex and nuanced effect on so many aspects of human life.

Yet the seeking of public space for religion, often by religions themselves, has had the doubtful benefit of (ironically) *limiting* the educational scope of religion to the (broadly conceived) public and political face of religion. This risks becoming, if we are not already at this stage, of limiting, not widening of horizons in regard to teaching and learning in religion. Religious education risks representing religion as simply another socio-political instrument to manage life in this world; evidence here is that European researchers and

European political agencies in fact use the term 'diversity management' in treating of religion in education.

To configure the core of this debate back to the text – Bede's *History* – with which I opened, religions have of course legitimate concerns with the politics of nations and the relations between nations, and as well as morality on the smaller scale of the person. Christian tradition remains in all less concerned with the politics of this world; otherwise it would be politics and not religion. Christianity must ultimately be concerned with this world only insofar as action here ensures salvation, this life in other words as preparation for the judgement, punishment and rewards of the next. Despite the vast intellectual, sceptical currents to which state religious education has been subject, the fundamentals of Christianity have remained unchanged: they remain unchanged from the time of Bede's *History*, and the salvation history in which human history is set. I will allow others to draw conclusions from their own traditions, secular and other, but I can see no argument to counter this basic premise. To reiterate: Christian tradition concerned only with the politics would be politics and not religion; the *ultimate* concern of religion is not this world is not temporal but eternal.

Naturally, preparation for the next world is not something for which state-governed religious education is well equipped as children begin their lives in this one. Yet of all its features the answers to this existential question remains the most critical. The mystery of the brief span of individual human life and death, and the meaning of human history, its purpose and direction, no less than the meaning of life, *are* still asked in religious education, but the answers are uncertain, ambivalent, sceptical, the characteristics of an age of scepticism where systematic doubt has more political influence than faith.

Doubt too, though, has always been an integral aspect of faith:

> This is how the present life of man on earth, King, appears to me in comparison with that time which is unknown to us. You are sitting feasting with your ealdermen and thegns in winter time; the fire is burning on the hearth in the middle of the hall and all inside is warm, while outside the wintry storms of rain and snow are raging; and a sparrow flies swiftly through the hall. It enters in at one door and quickly flies out through the other. For the few moments it is inside, the storm and wintry tempest cannot touch it, but after the briefest moment of calm, it flits from your sight, out of the wintry storm and into it again. So this life of man appears but for a moment; what follows or indeed what went before, we know not at all. (Bede, 1999: 95)

Religious education which limits its perspective to 'the fire' which 'is burning on the hearth in the middle of the hall' closes the horizons to so much else.

References

AAR (2010) *American Academy of Religion Guidelines for Teaching about Religion in K-12 Public Schools in the United States.* Atlanta, GA: American Academy of Religion.

— (2012) www.aarweb.org/, accessed 29 May 2012.

Ackroyd, P. (2006) *Isaac Newton.* London: Chatto and Windus.

AHRC/ESRC (2012) *Religion and Society,* www.religionandsociety.org.uk/, accessed 29 May 2012.

Ainsworth, J. (2011) 'Church of England Schools', in L. Gearon (ed.), *The Religious Education Handbook,* re-handbook.org.uk/, accessed 29 May 2012.

Ajegbo, K. (2006) *Diversity and Citizenship Curriculum Review.* London: Department for Education.

Aldrich, D. (2012) 'Schemes of Work and Lesson Planning', in L. P. Barnes (ed.), *Debates in Religious Education,* 194–204. London: Continuum.

Alexander, H. A. (2001) *Reclaiming Goodness: Education and the Spiritual Quest.* Notre Dame, IN: University of Notre Dame Press.

— (ed.) (2004) *Spirituality and Ethics in Education: Philosophical, Theological and Radical Perspectives.* Brighton: Sussex Academic Press.

Alexander, L. G. (ed.) (1991) *Western State Terrorism.* Cambridge: Polity.

Amor, A. (2001) 'The Role of Religious Education in the Pursuit of Tolerance and Non-Discrimination', UN: International Consultative Conference on School Education in Relation with Freedom of Religion and Belief, Tolerance and Non-Discrimination. UN: Geneva.

Anon (2009) [c. ninth century onwards] *The Anglo-Saxon Chronicle: A History of England from Roman Times to the Norman Conquest.* St Petersburg, FL: Red and Black Books.

Anthony, M. J. and Benson, W. S. (2003) *Exploring the History of & Philosophy of Christian Education.* Grand Rapids, MI: Kregel.

AoC (2009) *United Nations' Alliance of Civilizations, Second Forum,* Istanbul, Turkey, 6–7 April 2009, www.unaoc.org/images/ws1.pdf, accessed 29 May 2012.

— (2012) *Education about Religions and Beliefs,* erb.unaoc.org/about/overview-of-erb/, accessed 31 May 2012.

Arendt, H. (2004) [1951] *The Origins of Totalitarianism.* New York: Schocken Books.

Arnold, M. (1974) [1882] 'Literature and Science', in R. H. Super (ed.), The *Complete Prose Works of Matthew Arnold,* 53–73. Ann Arbor: University of Michigan Press.

— (2009) [1869] *Culture and Anarchy.* Oxford: Oxford University Press.

Aron, R. (2001) [1955] *The Opium of the Intellectuals.* Piscataway, NJ: Transaction Publishers.

Arthur, J. and Davies, I. (eds) (2008) *Citizenship Education,* SAGE Library of Educational Thought & Practice. London: Sage.

Arthur, J., Davies, I. and Hahn, C. (eds) (2008) *SAGE Handbook of Education for Citizenship and Democracy.* London: Sage.

Arthur, J. Gearon, L. and Sears, A. (2010) *Education, Politics and Religion: Reconciling the Civic and the Sacred in Education.* London and New York: Routledge.

Arweck, E. and Nesbitt, E. (2010) 'Plurality at Close Quarters: Mixed-Faith Families in the UK', *Journal of Religion in Europe,* 3(1): 155–82.

Ashcroft, B., Griffith, G. and Tiffin, H. (2005) *The Post-Colonial Studies Reader*. London: Routledge.

Asser, J. (1908) [*c.* 888] *Life of Alfred*. London: Chatto and Windus; San Francisco. Internet Archive, archive.org/details/asserslifekinga00janegoog, accessed 29 May 2012.

Astley, J. (1994) *The Philosophy of Christian Religious Education*. Birmingham, AL: Religious Education Press.

Astley, Jeff and Francis, L. J. (eds) (1992) *Christian Perspectives on Faith Development: A Reader*. Leominster: Gracewing.

— (eds) (1994) *Critical Perspectives on Christian Education: A Reader on the Aims, Principles and Philosophy of Christian Education*. Leominster: Gracewing.

— (eds) (1996) Christian *Theology and Religious Education: Connections and Contradictions*. London: SPCK.

Astley, J., Francis, L. J. and Crowder, C. (eds.) (1996) *Theological Perspectives on Christian Formation: A Reader on Theology and Christian Education*. Leominster: Gracewing.

Augustine (1983a) *The Confessions of Saint Augustine*, translated by E. M. Blaiklock. London: Hodder and Stoughton.

— (1983b) *City of God*, translated by H. Bettenson. London: Penguin.

— (1998) *Confessions*, translated by H. Chadwick. Oxford: Oxford University Press.

— (1999) *On Christian Teaching*, translated by R. P. H. Green. Oxford: Oxford World Classics.

Avest, I. ter, Bakker, C., Bertram-Troost, G. and Miedema, S. (2007) 'Religion and Education in the Dutch Pillarized and Post-Pillarized Educational System: Historical Background and Current Debates', in R. Jackson, S. Miedema, W. Weisse and J.-P. Willaime (eds), *Religion and Education in Europe: Developments, Contexts and Debates*, 203–220. Münster: Waxmann.

Avis, P. (2002) *Anglicanism, and the Christian Church: Theological Resources in Historical Perspective*. New York: T&T Clark.

Axtell, J. L. (ed.) (1968) *The Educational Writings of John Locke*. Cambridge: Cambridge University Press.

Bagguley, P. and Hussain, Y. (2008) *Riotous Citizens: Ethnic Conflict in Multicultural Britain*. Aldershot: Ashgate.

Ball, T. and Bellamy, P. (eds) (2003) *The Cambridge History of Twentieth-Century Political Thought*. Cambridge: Cambridge University Press.

Barnes, L. P. (2001) 'What Is Wrong with the Phenomenological Approach to Religious Education?' *Religious Education*, 96(4): 445–61.

— (2006) 'The Misrepresentation of Religion in Modern British (Religious) Education', *British Journal of Educational Studies*, 54(4): 395–411.

— (2008) *Religious Education: Taking Religious Difference Seriously*. Salisbury: Impact, Philosophy of Education Society of Great Britain.

— (ed.) (2012) *Debates in Religious Education*. London: Continuum.

Barnes, L. P., Wright, A. and Brandom, A.-M. (eds) (2008) *Learning to Teach Religious Education in the Secondary School: A Companion to School Experience*. London: Routledge.

Barr, J. (1995) *Biblical Faith and Natural Theology: The Gifford Lectures for 1991: Delivered in the University of Edinburgh*. New York: Oxford University Press.

Bates, D. (1994) 'Christianity, Culture and Other Religions (Part 1): The Origins of the Study of World Religions in English Education', *British Journal of Religious Education*, 17(1): 5–18.

— (1996) 'Christianity, Culture and Other Religions (Part 2): F. H. Hilliard, Ninian Smart and the 1988 Education Reform Act', *British Journal of Religious Education*, 18(2): 85–102.

— (ed) (2005) *Education, Religion and Society: Essays in Honour of John M. Hull*. London: Routledge.

Bauman, Z. (2000) *Modernity and the Holocaust*. Cambridge: Polity Press.

Baumfield, V. M. (2003) 'Democratic RE: Preparing Young People for Citizenship', *British Journal of Religious Education*, 25(3): 173–84.

— (2012) 'Pedagogy', in L. P. Barnes (ed.), *Debates in Religious Education*, 205–12. London: Continuum.

Baumfield, V. M., Conroy, J. C., Davis, R. A. and Lundie, D. C (2012) 'The Delphi Method: Gathering Expert Opinion in Religious Education', *British Journal of Religious Education*, 4(1): 5–19.

BBC (2012) 'Richard Dawkins Supports School Bible Plan', BBC, www.bbc.co.uk/news/uk-18224114, accessed 29 May 2012.

Bede (1999) [*c.* 731] *The Ecclesiastical History of the English People*. Oxford: Oxford World's Classics.

Benedict, St (1952) *The Rule of Saint Benedict*, translated by Justin McCann. London: Sheed and Ward.

Bellah, R. (1967) 'Civil Religion in America', *Daedalus*, 96(1): 1–21.

— (1970) *Beyond Belief: Essays on Religion in a Post-Traditionalist World*. Berkeley, CA: University of California Press.

Bankston III, C. L. and Caldas, S. J. (2009) *Public Education – America's Civil Religion: A Social History*. Columbia: Teachers College Press.

Bennett, M. N. and Finnemore, M. (2004) *Rules for the World: International Organizations in Global Politics*. Ithaca, NY: Cornell University Press.

BERA (2012) British Educational Research Association, www.bera.ac.uk, accessed 29 May 2012.

Berger, P. (1967) *The Sacred Canopy: Elements of a Sociological Theory of Religion*. New York: Doubleday.

— (1970) *A Rumor of Angels: Modern Society and the Rediscovery of the Supernatural*. New York: Doubleday.

— (ed.) (1999) *The Desecularization of the World: Resurgent Religion and World Politics*. Washington, DC: Ethics and Public Policy Center.

Berger, P., Davie, G. and Fokas, E. (2008) *Religious America, Secular Europe? A Theme and Variations*. Aldershot: Ashgate.

Berger, P. and Luckmann, T. (1967) *The Social Construction of Reality: A Treatise in the Sociology of Knowledge*. New York: Anchor.

Berlin, I. (2002) *Isaiah Berlin: Liberty*, edited by H. Hardy. Oxford: Oxford University Press.

Best, R. (ed.) (1999) *Education, Spirituality and the Whole Child*. London: Cassell.

BFSS (2012) *The British and Foreign School Society*, www.bfss.org.uk/, accessed 29 May 2012.

Bible Gateway (2012) *Bible Gateway Searchable Online Bible*, www.biblegateway.com/, accessed 29 May 2012.

Bird, A. (2011) 'Thomas Kuhn', in E. N. Zalta (ed.), *Stanford Encyclopedia of Philosophy*, plato.stanford.edu/entries/thomas-kuhn/, accessed 29 May 2012.

Bird, G. (ed.) (2006) *A Companion to Kant*. Oxford: Blackwell.

Blaylock, L. (2012) in L. P. Barnes (ed.), 'Assessment', *Debates in Religious Education*, 235–46. London: Continuum.

Blunkett, D. (2000) 'Influence or Irrelevance: Can Social Science Improve Government?' Secretary of State's ESRC Lecture Speech, 2 February 2000. London: ESRC/DfEE.

Boulden, J. and Weiss, T. G. (eds) (2004) *Terrorism and the UN: Before and After September 11*. Bloomington, IN: Indiana University Press.

Bowker, J. (2007) *Oxford Dictionary of World Religions*. Oxford: Oxford University Press.

Bowles, N. R. (2004) *The Diplomacy of Hope: The United Nations since the Cold War*. London: I.B. Tauris.

Bragg, M. (2011) *The Book of Books*. London: Hodder and Stoughton.

Bridges, D. (2006) 'The Disciplines and Discipline of Educational Research', *Journal of Philosophy of Education*, 40(2): 259–72.

Bronfenbrenner, U. (1972) *Two Worlds of Childhood: U.S. and U.S.S.R.* New York: Simon and Schuster.

Brooke, J. H. (1993) *Science and Religion: Some Historical Perspectives*, Cambridge Studies in the History of Science. Cambridge: Cambridge University Press.

Brooke, J. and Maclean (eds) (2005) *Heterodoxy in Early Modern Science and Religion*. Oxford: Oxford University Press.

Brooks, V. and Fancourt, N. (2012) 'Is Self-Assessment in Religious Education Unique?' *British Journal of Religious Education,* 34(2): 123–37.

Brown, C. G. (2006) *Religion and Society in Twentieth-Century Britain.* London: Pearson.

— (2009) *The Death of Christian Britain* (2nd edn). London: Routledge.

Brown, K. and Fairbrass, S. (2011) *The Citizenship Teacher's Handbook.* London: Continuum.

Bruce, S. (2002) *God Is Dead: Secularization in the West.* Oxford: Blackwell.

— (2003) *Politics and Religion.* Cambridge: Polity.

Bryan, C. (2005) *Render to Caesar: Jesus, the Early Church, and the Roman Superpower.* New York: Oxford University Press.

Buchanan, A. (2000) 'Rawls's Law of Peoples: Rules for a Vanished Westphalian World', *Ethics,* 110(4): 697–721.

Burleigh, M. (2006) *Earthly Powers: Religion and Politics in Europe from the Enlightenment to the Great War.* London: Harper Perennial.

— (2007) *Sacred Causes: The Clash of Religion and Politics from the Great War to the War on Terror.* London: HarperCollins.

Cahn, S. M. (ed.) (2009) *Philosophy of Education: The Essential Texts.* London: Routledge.

Callon, E. (1997) *Creating Citizens: Political Education and Liberal Democracy.* Oxford: Oxford University Press.

Campbell, G. (2011) *Bible: The Story of the King James Version.* Oxford: Oxford University Press.

Carnegie (1997) *Carnegie Commission on Preventing Deadly Conflict.* New York: Carnegie Corporation.

Carr, D. (1995) 'Towards a Distinctive Conception of Spiritual Education', *Oxford Review of Education,* 21(1): 83–98.

— (1996) 'Rival Conceptions of Spiritual Education', *Journal of Philosophy of Education,* 30(2): 159–78.

Carr, D. and Haldane, J. (eds) (2003) *Spirituality, Philosophy and Education.* London: Routledge.

Casanova, J. (1994) *Public Religions in the Modern World.* Chicago, IL: Chicago University Press.

CES (2012) Catholic Education Service of England and Wales, www.cesew.org.uk/index.asp?id=1, accessed 29 May 2012.

Chadwick, H. (1990) *The Early Church.* London: Penguin.

Chadwick, P., Ainsworth, J., Gwynne, R., O'Reilly, L. and Brown, D. (2012) *The Church School of the Future Review.* London: Church of England Archbishops' Council and the National Society.

Chapman, R. (ed.) (2010) *Culture Wars: An Encyclopedia of Issues, Viewpoints and Voices.* New York: M.E. Sharpe.

Chazan, B. (1972) '"Indoctrination" and Religious Education', *Religious Education,* 67(4): 243–52.

Chesterman, S., Franck, T. M. and Malone, D. M. (2007) *Law and Practice of the United Nations.* Oxford: Oxford University Press.

Chomsky, N. (2003) *Power and Terror: Post-9/11 Talks and Interviews,* edited by J. Junkerman and T. Takei Masakazu (eds). New York: Seven Stories Press; Tokyo: Little More.

— (2006) *Failed States: The Abuse of Power and the Assault on Democracy.* New York: Metropolitan Books/Henry Holt.

— (2007) *What We Say Goes: Conversations on U.S. Power in a Changing World: Interviews with David Barsamian.* New York: Metropolitan Books.

Churchill, W. (1999) [1956–8] *A History of the English-Speaking Peoples,* one volume abridgement originally four volumes. London: Cassell.

CIA (2012a) Central Intelligence Agency, www.cia.gov/, accessed 29 May 2012.

CIA (2012b) 'Political Islam Strategic Analysis Program (PISAP)', www.cia.gov/, accessed 29 May 2012.

CIC (2007) *Our Shared Future.* London: Commission on Integration and Cohesion.

Clack, B. (1999) 'The Theologian as Artist: Exploring the Future of Religion', in L. Gearon (ed.), *English Literature, Theology and the Curriculum,* 313–26. London: Continuum.

CoE (2008) *White Paper on Intercultural Dialogue 'Living Together as Equals'*. Strasbourg: Council of Europe.

Coleridge, S. T. (2005) *Literaria Biographia*, digitized version, http://books.google.co.uk/books, accessed 22 September 2012.

Coles, R. (1986) *The Moral Life of Children*. New York: Atlantic Monthly Press.

— (1990) *The Spiritual Life of Children*. London: HarperCollins.

— (2011) *The Moral Intelligence of Children*. New York: Random House.

Collini, S. (1998) 'Introduction', C. P. Snow's *The Two Cultures*, vii–lxxi. Cambridge: Cambridge University Press.

Commonwealth (2007) *Civil Paths to Peace: Report of the Commonwealth Commission on Respect and Understanding*. London: Commonwealth.

Commonwealth (2009) 'Civil Society to Explore Interaction between Faith and Education', www.thecommonwealth. org/news/190663/163077/186933/210109faithineducation.htm.

Conroy, J. (2011a) *Does Religious Education Work? A Three-year Investigation into the Practices and Outcomes of Religious Education: A Briefing Paper*, www.gla.ac.uk/schools/education/research/currentresearchprojects/doesreligiouseducationwork/#d.en.153511, accessed 29 May 2012.

Conroy, J. (2011b) *Does Religious Education Work? A Three-year Investigation into the Practices and Outcomes of Religious Education: A Briefing Paper*, www.gla.ac.uk/schools/education/research/currentresearchprojects/doesreligiouseducationwork/#d.en.153511, accessed 29 May 2012.

Conroy, J. and Davis, R. (2010) 'Religious Education', in R. Bailey, R. Barrow, D. Carr and C. McCarthy (eds), *The SAGE Handbook of Philosophy of Education*, 451–66. London: SAGE.

Cooling, T. (2009) *Doing God in Education*. London: THEOS, also at www.canterbury.ac.uk/education/docs/doing-god-education.pdf, accessed 31 May 2012.

Copley, T. (1998) *Echo of Angels: The First Report of the Biblos Project*. Exeter: University of Exeter.

— (2000) *Spiritual Development in the State School: A Perspective on Worship and Spirituality in the Education System of England and Wales*. Exeter: University of Exeter Press.

— (2005) *Indoctrination, Education and God*. London: SPCK.

— (2008) 'Non-Indoctrinatory Religious Education in Secular Cultures', *Religious Education*, 103(1): 22–31.

Copley, C., Copley, T., Freathy, R., Lane, S. and Walshe, K. (2004) *On the Side of the Angels: The Third Report of the Biblos Project*. Exeter: University of Exeter.

Copley, T., Lane, S., Savini, H. and Walshe, K. (2001) *Where Angels Fear to Tread: The Second Report of the Biblos Project*. Exeter: University of Exeter.

Cox, E. (1967) *Sixth Form Religion*. London: SCM.

—. (1971) 'Changes in Attitudes towards Religious Education and the Bible among Sixth Form Boys and Girls', *British Journal of Educational Psychology*, 41(3): 328–41.

Crick, B. (1998) *Education for Citizenship and the Teaching of Democracy in Schools: Final Report of the Advisory Group on Citizenship*. London: QCA.

— (2004) 'Introduction', in D. Heater (ed.), *Citizenship: The Civic Ideal in World History, Politics and Education*. Manchester: Manchester University Press.

Cross, F. L. and Livingstone, E. A. (eds) (1997) *The Oxford Dictionary of the Christian Church* (3rd edn). Oxford: Oxford University Press.

Crozier, W. R. (2010) 'The Psychology of Education', in J. Furlong and M. Lawn (eds), *Disciplines of Education*, 31–49. London: Routledge.

Cush, D. (1999) 'The Relationships between Religious Studies, Religious Education and Theology: Big Brother, Little Sister and the Clerical Uncle?' *British Journal of Religious Education*, 21(3): 137–46.

— (2007) 'Should Religious Studies Be Part of the Compulsory State School Curriculum?' *British Journal of Religious Education*, 29(3): 217–27.

Crick, B. (1998) *Education for Citizenship and the Teaching of Democracy in Schools: The Final Report of the Advisory Group on Citizenship*, DfEE.

Daniels, H. and Edwards, A. (eds) (2004) *The RoutledgeFalmer Reader in Psychology of Education*. London: Routledge.

Darder, A., Torres, R. D. and Baltodano, M. (eds) (2008) *The Critical Pedagogy Reader* (2nd edn). London: Routledge.

Darwin, C. (2008) *Evolutionary Writings, Including Autobiographies*. Oxford: Oxford World's Classics.

Davie, G., Berger, P. and Fokas, E. (2008) *Religious America, Secular Europe: A Theme and Variations*. Aldershot: Ashgate.

Davies, L. (2006) *Educating against Extremism*. Stoke-on-Trent: Trentham.

Davis, C., Milbank, J. and Zizek, S. (eds) (2005) *Theology and the Political: The New Debate*. Durham, NC: Duke University Press.

Dawkins, R. (2006) *The God Delusion*. New York: Bantam.

— (2007) *The Greatest Show on Earth*. London: Transworld.

— (2007a) 'Dawkins: I'm a Cultural Christian', BBC, newsvote.bbc.co.uk/1/hi/uk_politics/7136682.stm, accessed 29 May 2012.

DawkinsFoundation(2010)'DawkinsDenouncesReligiousEducationas"WickedPractice"',TheRichardDawkinsFoundation,rich-arddawkins.net/articles/501585-dawkins-denounces-religious-education-as-%E2%80%98wicked-practice%E2%80%99, accessed 29 May 2012.

Dearing, R. (2001) *The Way Ahead: Church of England Schools in the New Millennium*. London: Church House Publishing, www.churchofengland.org/media/1118777/way%20ahead%20-%20whole.pdf, accessed 29 May 2012.

Desmond, A. (1997) *Huxley: From Devil's Disciple to Evolution's Priest*. London: Perseus.

Desmond, A. and Moore, J. R. (1992) *Darwin*. London: Penguin.

DeSouza, M., Francis, L. J., O'Higgins-Norman, J. and Scott, D. G. (eds) (2009) *International Handbook of Education for Spirituality, Care and Wellbeing*. Dordrecht: Springer.

Dewey, J. (1916) *Democracy and Education*, online www.ilt.columbia.edu/Publications/Projects/digitexts/dewy/, accessed 29 May 2012.

— (2011) [1916] *Democracy and Education*. London: Simon and Brown.

Dierenfield, B. J. (2007) *The Battle over School Prayer: How Engel V. Vitale Changed America*. Kansas: University Press of Kansas.

Dixon, T. (2008) *Science and Religion: A Very Short Introduction*. Oxford: Oxford University Press.

Dixon, A. C. and Torrey, R. A. (1910–15) *The Fundamentals*, twelve volumes, www.ntslibrary.com/PDF%20Books%20II/Torrey%20-%20The%20Fundamentals%201.pdf, accessed 29 May 2012.

Dorian, G. (1998) *The Remaking of Evangelical Theology*. Louisville, KY: Westminster John Knox Press.

Duffy, E. (2005) *The Stripping of the Altars* (2nd edn). New Haven, CT: Yale University Press.

Durkheim, E. (2001) [1912] *The Elementary Forms of the Religious Life*. Oxford: Oxford World Classics.

Eisenstadt, S. N. (2000) 'Multiple Modernities,' *Daedalus*, 129 (Winter): 1–30.

Eliade, M. (1957) *The Sacred and the Profane: The Nature of Religion*. Orlando, FL: Harcourt.

Eliot, T. S. (1938) *The Idea of a Christian Society*. London: Faber and Faber.

Emden, C. J. (2006) *Carl Schmitt. Political Theology: Four Chapters on the Concept of Sovereignty*. Chicago, IL: University of Chicago Press. Reviewed by C. J. Emden, www.h-net.org/reviews/showpdf.php?id=12384, accessed 29 May 2012.

Enger, T. (1992) 'Religious Education between Psychology and Theology', *Religious Education*, 87(3): 435–45.

EPPI (2005) *An International Review of Citizenship Education Research. The Evidence for Policy and Practice Information and Co-ordinating Centre*. London: EPPI.

EPPI (2012) 'The Evidence for Policy and Practice Information and Co-ordinating Centre', www.eppi.ioe.ac.uk, accessed 29 May 2012.

Erricker, C. and Erricker, J. (2000) *Reconstructing Religious, Spiritual and Moral Education*. London: RoutledgeFalmer.

Estep, J. R. and Kim, J. H. (2010) *Christian Formation: Integrating Theology and Human Development*. Nashville, TN: B&H Publishing.

EERA (2012) European Educational Research Association, www.eera-ecer.de, accessed 29 May 2012.

Fair, C. C. (2008) *Madrassah Challenge: Militancy and Religious Education in Pakistan*. Washington: United States Institute of Peace Press.

Fancourt, N. (2005) '"I'm Less Intolerant": Reflexive Self⊠Assessment in Religious Education', *British Journal of Religious Education*, 32(3): 291–305.

— (2012) 'Differentiation', in L. P. Barnes (ed.), *Debates in Religious Education*, 213–22. London: Continuum.

Felderhof, M., Thompson, P. and Torevell, D. (eds) (2007) *Inspiring Faith in Schools*. Aldershot: Ashgate.

Fenn, R. (1978) *Towards a Theory of Secularization*. Storrs, CT: Society for Scientific Study of Religion.

Ford, D. (ed.) (2000) *The Modern Theologians* (2nd edn). Oxford: Blackwell.

— (ed.) (2011) *The Modern Theologians Reader*. Oxford: Blackwell.

Forest, J. de (ed.) (2004) 'Editor's Review of The Human Rights Handbook: A Global Perspective for Education by Liam Gearon', *Harvard Educational Review*, 340–5, www.hepg.org/her/abstract/47, accessed 29 May 2012.

Fordham (2012) *Medieval Sourcebook*, Fordham University www.fordham.edu/halsall/sbook.asp, accessed 29 May 2012.

Fowler, J. W. (1981) *Stages of Faith: The Psychology of Human Development and the Quest for Meaning*. San Francisco, CA: Harper & Row.

Francis, L. and Astley, J. (eds) (1992) *Christian Perspectives on Faith Development: A Reader*. Leominster: Gracewing.

Francis, L. J. (2005) *Faith and Psychology: Personality, Religion and the Individual*. London, Darton, Longman and Todd.

— (2009) 'Understanding the Attitudinal Dimensions of Religion and Spirituality', in M. De Souza, L. J. Francis, J. O'Higgins-Norman and D. G. Scott (eds), *International Handbook of Education for Spirituality, Care and Wellbeing*, 147–168. Dordrecht: Springer.

Francis, L. J., Kay, W. K. and Campbell, W. S. (1996) *Research in Religious Education* Leominster: Gracewing.

Francis, L. J., Robbins, M. and Astley, J. (eds) (2005) *Religion, Education and Adolescence: International Empirical Perspectives*. Cardiff: University of Wales Press.

Freathy, R. J. K. (2006) 'Gender, Age, Attendance at a Place of Worship and Young People's Attitudes towards the Bible', *Journal of Beliefs and Values*, 27(3): 327–39.

Freire, P. (1996) *Pedagogy of the Oppressed* (2nd edn). London: Penguin.

Friedrich, C. J. and Brzezinski, Z. (1967) *Totalitarian Dictatorship and Autocracy* (2nd edn). New York: Praeger.

Fukuyama, F. (2006) *The End of History and the Last Man*. New York: Free Press.

Furedi, F. (2009) 'Re-reading C. P. Snow and His Elusive Search for Authority', in F. Furedi, R. Kimball, R. Tallis and R. Whelan (eds), *From Two Cultures to No Culture: C. P. Snow's Two Cultures Lecture Fifty Years On*, 61–76. London: Civitas: Institute for the Study of Civil Society.

Furedi, F., Kimball, R., Tallis, R. and Whelan, R. (2009) *From Two Cultures to No Culture: C. P. Snow's Two Cultures Lecture Fifty Years On*. London: Civitas: Institute for the Study of Civil Society.

Furlong, J. and Lawn, M. (2009) 'The Disciplines of Education in the UK: Between the Ghost and the Shadow', *Oxford Review of Education*, 35(5): 541–52.

— (eds) (2010) *Disciplines of Education*. London: Routledge.

Gay, P. (2009) 'Afterword', in S. M. Cahn (ed.), *Philosophy of Education*. London: Routledge.

Gearon, L. (ed.) (1999) *English Literature, Theology and the Curriculum*. London: Continuum.

— (2002a) 'Religious Education and Human Rights: Some Postcolonial Perspectives', *British Journal of Religious Education*, 24(2): 140–51.

— (ed.) (2002b) *Religion and Human Rights: A Reader*. Brighton and Portland: Sussex Academic Press.

— (2008) 'Religion, Politics and Pedagogy: Historical Contexts', *British Journal of Religious Education*, Special Issue: Religion, Human Rights and Citizenship, 30(2): 83–102.

— (ed) (2011) *The Religious Education Handbook*, re-handbook.org.uk/ accessed 29 May 2012.

— (2012a) 'European Religious Education and European Civil Religion', *British Journal of Educational Studies*, 60(2): 1–19.

— (2012b) 'The Securitization of Religion in Education', in T. van der Zee and T. Lovat (eds), *New Perspectives in Religious and Spiritual Education*, 215–33. Munster: Waxmann.

— (2013a, forthcoming) 'The King James Bible and the Politics of Religious Education', *Religious Education*, 108(1).

— (2013b, forthcoming) 'The Counter Terrorist Classroom: Religion, Education, Security', *Religious Education*, 108(2).

Geertz, C. (1975) *The Interpretation of Cultures*. New York: Basic Books.

Gibbon, E. (2000) *The History of the Decline and Fall of the Roman Empire*, abridged. London: Penguin.

Gildas (2012) [*c.* 547] *Concerning the Ruin of Britain*, Fordham University, www.fordham.edu/halsall/source/gildas.asp, accessed 29 May 2012.

Gillard, D. (2011) *Education in England*. www.educationengland.org.uk/, accessed 29 May 2012.

Goldman, R. J. (1964) *Religious Thinking from Childhood to Adolescence*. London: Routledge and Kegan Paul.

— (1969) *Readiness for Religion*. London: Routledge.

Goldstein, W. S. (2009) 'Secularization Patterns in the Old Paradigm', *Sociology of Religion*, 70(2): 157–78, first published online: 1 January 2009.

Gombrich, E. H. (1995) *The Story of Art* (16th edn). London: Phaidon.

Goodman, G. S. (ed.) (2010) *Educational Psychology Reader: The Art and Science of How People Learn*. New York: Peter Lang.

Grant, E. (2006) *Science and Religion, 400 BC to AD 1550: From Aristotle to Copernicus*. Baltimore, MD: John Hopkins University Press.

Gray, J. (2007) *Black Mass: Apocalyptic Religion and the Death of Utopia*. London: Penguin.

Greenawalt, K. (2007) *Does God Belong in Public Schools?* Princeton, NJ: Princeton University Press.

Grigg, R. (2009) 'What Did Wilberforce Really Say to "Darwin's Bulldog"? Huxley's Debate with Wilberforce', *Creation Ministries International*, creation.com/wilberforce-huxley-debate, accessed 29 May 2012.

Grimmitt, M. (ed.) (2000) *Pedagogies of Religious Education: Case Studies in the Research and Development of Good Pedagogic Practice in RE*. Great Wakering: McCrimmon.

— (ed.) (2010) *Religious Education and Social and Community Cohesion*. Great Wakering: McCrimmon.

Habermas, J. and Ratzinger, J. Cardinal (2007) *The Dialectics of Secularization*. San Francisco, CA: Ignatius.

Halstead, M. (2012) 'Faith Schools', in Barnes (ed.), *Debates in Religious Education*, 98–108. London: Continuum.

Hamlin, H. and Jones, H. W. (eds) (2010) *The King James Bible after Four Hundred Years: Literary, Linguistic, and Cultural Influences*. Cambridge: Cambridge University Press.

Hammersley, M. (2005) 'Countering the "New Orthodoxy" in Educational Research: A Response to Phil Hodkinson', *British Educational Research Journal*, 31(2): 139–55.

Hammond, J. and Hay, D. (1992) ' "When You Pray, Go To Your Private Room": A Reply to Adrian Thatcher', *British Journal of Religious Education*, 14(3): 145–50.

Hammond, J., Hay, D., Moxon, J., Netto, B., Raban, K., Straugheir, G. and Williams, C. (1990) *New Methods in R.E. Teaching: An Experiential Approach*. London: Oliver & Boyd.

Hand, M. (2003) 'The Meaning of "Spiritual Education" ', *Oxford Review of Education*, 29(3), 391–401.

Hayes, M. and Gearon, L. (eds) (2002) *Contemporary Catholic Education*. Leominster: Gracewing.

Hargreaves, D. H. (1996) *Teaching as a Research-Based Profession: Possibilities and Prospects*. London: Teacher Training Agency.

Hansard (1944) *Education Bill,* HC Deb, 19 January 1944, volume 396, cc207–322.

Harlow, B. and Carter, M. (eds) (1999) *Imperialism & Orientalism: A Documentary Sourcebook*. Oxford: Wiley-Blackwell.

Harrison, J. (1983) *Attitudes to Bible, God, Church*. London: Bible Society.

Harrison, P. (2010) *The Cambridge Companion to Science and Religion*, Cambridge Companions to Religion. Cambridge: Cambridge University Press.

Hawking, S. and Mlodinow, L. (2011) *The Grand Design*. New York: Bantam.

Haynes, J. (ed.) (2009) *Religion and Politics*. London, Routledge.

— (ed.) (2008) *The Handbook of Religion and Politics*. London: Routledge.

Heater, D. (2004) *Citizenship: The Civic Ideal in World History, Politics and Education*. Manchester: Manchester University Press.

Hedges, C. (2008) *American Fascists: The Christian Right and the War on America*. New York: Simon and Schuster.

Hefner, R. W. (1998) 'Multiple Modernities: Christianity, Islam, and Hinduism in a Globalizing Age', *Annual Review of Anthropology*, 27: 83–104.

Henningsen, M. (ed.) (2000) *Modernity without Restraint: The Political Religions* (Collected Works of Eric Voegelin). Columbia: University of Missouri.

Hick, J. (1989) *An Interpretation of Religion*. New Haven, CT: Yale University Press.

Hillage, J., Pearson, R., Anderson, A. and Tamkin, P. (1998) *Excellence in Schools*. London: Institute for Employment Studies.

Himmelfarb, G. (2005) *The Roads to Modernity: The British, French and American Enlightenments*. London: Vintage.

Hirst, P. and Peters, R. S. (1970) *The Logic of Education*. London: Routledge.

HMSO (1988) *Education Reform Act 1988*. London: Her Majesty's Stationary Office.

Hobsbawn, E. (1962) *The Age of Revolution: 1789–1848*. London: Abacus.

— (1988) *The Age of Capital: 1848–1875*. London: Abacus.

— (1989) *The Age of Empire: 1875–1914*. London: Abacus.

— (1995) *The Age of Extremes: 1914–1991*. London: Abacus.

Hodkinson, P. (2004) 'Research as a Form of Work: Expertise, Community and Methodological Objectivity', *British Educational Research Journal*, 30(1): 9–26.

Holmes, R. (2008) *The Age of Wonder: How the Romantic Generation Discovered the Beauty and Terror of Science*. London: Harper.

Homan, R. (2012) 'Constructing Religion', in L. P. Barnes (ed.), *Debates in Religious Education*, 183–93. London: Continuum.

Home Office (2002) *Community Cohesion*. London: HMSO.

— (2005) *Preventing Extremism Together*, www.aml.org.uk/pdf_files/PET_Report.pdf, accessed 29 May 2012.

— (2011a) 'New Prevent Strategy Launched', Tuesday, 7 June 2011, www.homeoffice.gov.uk/media-centre/news/prevent-strategy, accessed 29 May 2012.

— (2011b) *Review of Counter-Terrorism and Security Powers*. London: Home Office, www.official-documents.gov.uk/document/cm80/8005/8005.pdf, accessed 29 May 2012.

— (2011c) *Select Bibliography of Terrorism Sources*, www.parliament.uk/briefing-papers/SN05866.pdf, accessed 29 May 2012.

Hull, J. (1989) *The Act Unpacked*. Birmingham: CEM.

— (2003) 'The Blessings of Secularity: Religious Education in England and Wales', *Journal of Religious Education*, 51(3): 51–8.

Hull, J. M. (1992) 'The Transmission of Religious Prejudice', *British Journal of Religious Education*, 14(2): 69–72.

Hunter, J. D. (1991) *Culture Wars: The Struggle to Control the Family, Art, Education, Law, And Politics in America*. New York: Basic Books.

Huntington, S. (2002) *The Clash of Civilizations*. New York: Free Press.

Huxley, T. (1870) 'The School Boards', *Contemporary Review*, 16: 1–15.

— (2011) [1880] 'Science and Culture' in *Collected Essays*, 134–59, made available online by C. Blinderman and D. Joyce at aleph0.clarku.edu/huxley/bib1.html, accessed 29 May 2012.

Hyde, K. E. (1990) *Religion in Childhood and Adolescence: A Comprehensive Review of the Research*. Birmingham, AL: Religious Education Press.

Ilyich, I. (1995) *De-schooling Society* (new edn). London: Marion Boyars Publishers Ltd.

Isaac, J. C. (2003) 'Critics of Totalitarianism', in T. Ball and P. Bellamy (eds), *The Cambridge History of Twentieth Century Thought*, 181–201. Cambridge: Cambridge University Press.

Jackson, R. (1997) *Religious Education: An Interpretive Approach*. London: Hodder and Stoughton.

— (2003) *International Perspectives on Citizenship, Education and Religious Diversity*. London: Routledge.

— (2004) *Rethinking Religious Education and Plurality: Issues in Diversity and Pedagogy*. London: Routledge.

— (2009) The Contribution of Teaching about Religions and Beliefs to Education for Democratic Citizenship in Europe and Beyond: Consequences of the REDCo-project', in Weisse (ed.), *Religion in Education: Contribution to Dialogue Policy Recommendations of the REDCo Research Project*, 32–6. Hamburg, www.redco.uni-hamburg.de/cosmea/core/corebase/mediabase/awr/redco/research_findings/REDCo_policy_rec_eng.pdf, accessed 29 May 2012.

— (2011a) 'Religion, Education, Dialogue and Conflict: Editorial Introduction', *British Journal of Religious Education*, 33(2): 105–10.

— (2011b) 'The Interpretive Approach as a Research Tool: Inside the REDCo Project', *British Journal of Religious Education*, 33(2): 189–208.

Jackson, R., Julia Ipgrave, J., Hayward, M., Hopkins, P., Fancourt, N., Robbins, M., Francis, L. and McKenna, U. (2010) *Materials Used to Teach about World Religions in Schools in England*. London: DCSF.

Jackson, R., Miedema, S., Weisse, W. and Willaime, J.-P. (eds) (2007) *Religion and Education in Europe: Developments, Contexts and Debates*. Münster: Waxmann.

Jackson, R., Murphy, E. and Poynting, S. (eds) (2010) *Contemporary State Terrorism*. London: Routledge.

Jackson, R. and O'Grady, K. (2007) 'Religious Education in England: Social Plurality, Civil Religion and Religious Education Pedagogy', in R. Jackson, S. Miedema, W. Weisse and J.-P. Willaime (eds), *Religion and Education in Europe: Developments, Contexts and Debates*, 181–202. Münster: Waxmann.

James, W. (1983) [1902] *The Varieties of Religious Experience* (new edn). London: Penguin.

Jawoniyi, O. (2012) 'Children's Rights and Religious Education in State Funded Schools: An International Human Rights Perspective', *International Journal of Human Rights*, 16(2): 337–57.

Kant, I. (1784) *What Is Enlightenment?*, Fordham University, www.fordham.edu/halsall/mod/kant-whatis.asp, accessed 29 May 2012.

Kay, W. K. (1996) 'Historical Context: Loukes, Goldman, Hyde, Cox and Alves', in W. K. Kay and W. S. Campbell (eds) *Research in Religious Education*, 31–46. Leominster: Gracewing.

Keast, J. (2007) *Religious Diversity and Intercultural Education: A Reference Book for Schools*. Strasbourg: Council of Europe.

Kimball, R. (2009) 'The Two Cultures Today', in F. Furedi, R. Kimball, R. Tallis and R. Whelan (eds), *From Two Cultures to No Culture: C. P. Snow's Two Cultures Lecture Fifty Years On*, 31–43. London: Civitas Institute for the Study of Civil Society.

Kirkpatrick, S. (2002) *Education and Social Mobility in the Soviet Union 1921–1934*. Cambridge: Cambridge University Press.

Knauth, T. (2007) 'Religious Education in Germany', in R. Jackson, S. Miedema, W. Weisse, and J.-P. Willaime (eds), *Religion and Education in Europe: Developments, Contexts and Debates*, 243–65. Münster: Waxmann.

Knight, K. (ed.) (2012) *New Advent*. New York: New Advent, www.newadvent.org/, accessed 29 May 2012.

Kohlberg, L. (1981) *The Philosophy of Moral Development*. San Francisco, CA: Harper & Row.

Kozyrev, F. (2011) 'Russian REDCo Findings in Support of Dialogue and Hermeneutics', *British Journal of Religious Education*, 33(2): 257–70.

Kozyrev, F. and Federov, V. (2007) 'Religion and Education in Russia', in R. Jackson, S. Miedema, W. Weisse, and J.-P. Willaime (eds), *Religion and Education in Europe: Developments, Contexts and Debates*, 133–58. Münster: Waxmann.

Kuhn, T. (1996) *The Structure of Scientific Revolutions* (3rd edn). Chicago, IL: University of Chicago Press.

Laats, A. (2012) *Fundamentalism and Education in the Scopes Era: God, Darwin, and the Roots of America's Culture Wars*. New York: Palgrave Macmillan.

Lakhani, J. (2011) 'Hindu Schools', in L. Gearon (ed.), *The Religious Education Handbook*, re-handbook.org.uk/, accessed 29 May 2012.

Larson, E. J. (1998) *Summer for the Gods: The Scopes Trial and America's Continuing Debate over Science and Religion*. Boston, MA: Harvard University Press.

Lawton, C. (2011) 'Jewish Schools', in L. Gearon (ed.), *The Religious Education Handbook*, re-handbook.org.uk/, accessed 29 May 2012.

Leavis, F. R. (1983) [1948] *The Great Tradition*. London: Penguin.

— (1962) *Two Cultures? The Significance of C. P. Snow*. London: Chatto and Windus.

Lee, J. M. (1996) 'Religious Education and Theology', in J. Astley (eds), *Theological Perspectives on Christian Formation*, 45–68. Leominster: Gracewing

Leeuw, G. van der (1938) *Religion in Essence and Manifestation*. London: George Allen & Unwin.

Limbaugh, D. (2004) *Persecution: How Liberals Are Waging War against Christianity*. New York: Perennial.

Lippe, M. von der (2011) 'Young People's Talk about Religion and Diversity: A Qualitative Study of Norwegian Students Aged 13–15', *British Journal of Religious Education*, 33, 127–42.

Locke, J. (2009) 'Some Thoughts Concerning Education', in S. M. Cahn (ed.), *Philosophy of Education*, 179–199. London: Routledge.

Lofaso, A. M. (2009) *Religion in the Public Schools: A Road Map for Avoiding Lawsuits and Respecting Parents' Legal Rights*. Washington: Americans United for Separation of Church and State.

Loomba, A. (2005) *Colonialism/Postcolonialism*. London: Routledge.

Loukes, H. (1961) *Teenage Religion*. London: SCM.

— (1963) *Readiness for Religion*. Wallingford, PA: Pendle Hill.

Luckmann, T. (1966) *The Invisible Religion*. New York: Macmillan.

Lundie, D. (2010) 'Does RE Work? A Research Report', *British Journal of Religious Education*, 32(2): 163–70.

Luxon, T. H. (ed.) (2012) *The Milton Reading Room*. Dartmouth, New Hampshire: Dartmouth College, www.dartmouth.edu/~milton/reading_room/contents/index.shtml, accessed 29 May 2012.

McAfee (1998) *Religion, Race and Reconstruction: Public School in the Politics of the 1870s*. New York: State University of New York Press.

McAndrews, L. J. (2008) *Era of Education: The Presidents and the Schools, 1965–2001*. Champaign, IL: University of Illinois Press.

MacCulloch, D. (2010) *A History of Christianity: The First Three Thousand Years*. London: Penguin.

McGrath, A. (2007a) *Christian Theology: An Introduction* (5th edn). Oxford: Wiley-Blackwell.

— (2007b) *The Dawkins Delusion: Atheist Fundamentalism and the Denial of the Divine*. London: SPCK.

— (2010) *Mere Theology: Christian Faith and the Discipleship of the Mind*. London: SPCK.

— (2011) *Science and Religion: A New Introduction*. Oxford: Wiley.

MacIntyre, A. (1981) *After Virtue: A Study in Moral Theory*. London: Duckworth.

— (1988) *Whose Justice? Which Rationality?* London: Duckworth.

— (2011) *God, Philosophy, Universities: A Selective History of the Catholic Philosophical Tradition*. Lanham, MD: Rowman & Littlefield.

McLaughlin, T. H. (1992) 'Citizenship, Diversity and Education: A Philosophical Perspective', *Journal of Moral Education*, 21(3): 235–50.

McLaughlin, T. H. (2002) 'Citizenship Education in England: The Crick Report and Beyond', *Journal of Philosophy of Education*, 34(4): 541–70.

Marples, R. (ed.) (1999) *The Aims of Education*. London: Routledge.

Marshall, P. (ed.) (2000) *Religious Freedom in the World: A Global Report on Freedom and Persecution*. London: Broadman and Holman.

Marshall, T. H. (1950) *Citizenship and Social Class and Other Essays*. Cambridge: Cambridge, University Press.

Martin, D. (1978) *A General Theory of Secularization*. Oxford: Blackwell.

Mazower, M. (2009) *No Enchanted Palace: The End of Empire and the Ideological Origins of the United Nations*. Princeton, NJ: Princeton University Press.

Meehan, C. (2002) 'Resolving the Confusion in the Spiritual Development Debate', *International Journal of Children's Spirituality*, 7(3): 291–308.

Milbank, J. (2006) *Theology and Social Theory* (2nd edn). Oxford: Blackwell.

Mill, J. S. (2008) [1859] *On Liberty*, edited by A. Kahan. Boston, MA: Bedford/St Martins.

Moore, A. (ed.) (2006) *Schooling, Society and Curriculum*. London: Routledge.

Moore, D. L. (2007) *Overcoming Religious Illiteracy: A Cultural Studies Approach to the Study of Religion in Secondary Schools*. New York: Palgrave.

— (2010) 'Constitutionally Sound, Educationally Innovative', *Harvard Divinity Bulletin*, 38(3–4), www.hds.harvard.edu/news-events/harvard-divinity-bulletin/issues/summerautumn-2010-vol-38-nos-3-4, accessed 29 May 2012.

Moore-Gilbert, B., Stanton, G. and Maley, W. (eds) (1997) *Postcolonial Criticism*. London: Longman.

Morgan, M. L. (ed.) (2005) *Classics of Moral and Political Philosophy* (4th edn). Indianapolis, IN: Hackett.

Moulin, D. (2011) 'Giving Voice to "the Silent Minority": The Experience of Religious Students in Secondary School Religious Education Lessons', *British Journal of Religious Education*, 33(3): 313–26.

Murray, S. (2004). *Post-Christendom: Church and Mission in a Strange New World*. London: Paternoster.

Munsey, B. (ed.) (1980) *Moral Development, Moral Education, and Kohlberg: Basic Issues in Philosophy, Psychology, Religion, and Education*. Birmingham, AL: Religious Education Press.

Nakhleh, E. (2008) *A Necessary Engagement: Reinventing America's Relations with the Muslim World*. Princeton, NJ: Princeton University Press.

National Society (2012) National Society for Promoting Religious Education, www.churchofengland.org/education/national-society.aspx, accessed 29 May 2012.

Nelson, J. (2010) 'The Evolving Place of Research on Religion in the American Educational Research Association', *Religion and Education*, 37(1): 60–86.

Nesbitt, E. and Arweck, E. (2010) 'Issues Arising from an Ethnographic Investigation of the Religious Identity Formation of Young People in Mixed-Faith Families', *Fieldwork in Religion*, 5(1): 7–30.

Newby, M. (1996) 'Towards a Secular Concept of Spiritual Maturity', in R. Best (ed.), *Education, Spirituality and the Whole Child*, 93–107. London: Cassell.

Nicolson, A. (2011) *When God Spoke English: The Making of the KJV*. London: Harper.

Nord, W. (1995) *Religion and American Education*. Chapel Hill, NC: University of North Carolina Press.

NRP (2012) 'Remembering the Scopes Monkey Trial', National Public Radio, www.npr.org/templates/story/story.php?storyId=4723956, accessed 29 May 2012.

Oancea, A. (2005) 'Criticisms of Educational Research: Key Topics and Levels of Analysis', *British Educational Research Journal*, 31(2): 157–83.

— (2011) *Interpretations and Practices of Research Impact across the Range of Disciplines*, Final Report. Oxford University.

Oancea, A. and Pring, R. (2008) 'The Importance of Being Thorough: On Systematic Accumulations of "What Works" in Education Research', *Journal of Philosophy of Education*, 42(1): 4–15.

Ofsted (2010) *Transforming Religious Education*. London: HMSO.

Ortolano, G. (2009) *The Two Cultures Controversy: Science, Literature and Cultural Politics in Postwar Britain*. Cambridge: Cambridge University Press.

OSCE (2007) *Toledo Guiding Principles on Teaching about Religions and Beliefs in Public Schools*, www.oslocoalition.org/documents/toledo_guidelines.pdf, accessed 29 May 2012.

Osler, A. and Starkey, H. (2006) Education for Democratic Citizenship: A Review of Research, Policy and Practice 1995–2005. *Research Papers in Education*, 24, 433–66, eprints.ioe.ac.uk/4698/1/Starkey_2006BERAreview433.pdf, accessed 29 May 2012.

Oslo Coalition (2012) www.oslocoalition.org/html/project_school_education/final document_madrid.html, accessed 29 May 2012.

Pace, E. (1909) 'Education', K. Knight (ed.), *The Catholic Encyclopedia*, 2012. New York: New Advent, www.newadvent.org/cathen/05295b.htm, accessed 29 May 2012.

Pals, D. L. (2008) *Eight Theories of Religion* (2nd edn). Oxford: Oxford University Press.

Parsons, G. (ed.) (1994) *The Growth of Religious Diversity: Britain from 1945*. London: Routledge.

Pater, W. (2010) [1873] *Studies in the History of the Renaissance* (new edn). Oxford: Oxford World's Classics.

Philips, C., Tse, D. and Johnson, F. (2011) *Community Cohesion and Prevent: How Have Schools Responded?* London: DfE.

Phillips, M. (2008) 'Secular Inquisition at the Royal Society', *The Spectator*, Wednesday, 17 September 2008, www.spectator.co.uk/melaniephillips/2086801/secular-inquisition-at-the-royal-society.thtml, accessed 29 May 2012.

Piaget, J. (1997) *The Moral Judgement of the Child*. New York: Free Press.

Pike, M. A. (2009) 'Religious Freedom and Rendering to Caesar: Reading Democratic and Faith-Based Values in Curriculum, Pedagogy and Policy', *Oxford Review of Education*, 35(2): 133–46.

Pilgrim, W. E. (1992) *Uneasy Neighbours: Church and State in the New Testament*. Kitchener: Augsburg Fortress.

Polkinghorne, J. (2011) *Science and Religion in Quest of Truth*. London: SPCK.

Poole, M. (2011) 'Science and Religion', in L. Gearon (ed.), *The Religious Education Handbook*, re-handbook.org.uk/, accessed 29 May 2012.

— (2012) 'Science and Religion' in L. P. Barnes (ed.), *Debates in Religious Education*, 258–67. London: Continuum.

Popper, K. (1946) *The Open Society and Its Enemies*. London: Routledge.

— (1963) *Conjectures and Refutations: The Growth of Scientific Knowledge*. London: Routledge.

— (2002) *Unended Quest: An Intellectual Autobiography*. London: Routledge.

Porges, M. L. and Stern, J. (2010) 'Getting Deradicalisation Right', *Foreign Affairs*, May/June, www.foreignaffairs.com/articles/66227/marisa-l-porges-jessica-stern/getting deradicalization-right?page=2, accessed 29 May 2012.

Power, S. (2007) *A Problem from Hell: America and the Age of Genocide*. New York: Harper Collins.

Price, E. and Schmid, A. P. (2010) 'Selected Literature on Radicalization and De-radicalization from Terrorism', *Perspectives on Terrorism*, www.terrorismanalysts.com/pt/index.php/pot/article/view/102/html, accessed 29 May 2012.

Pring, R. (2004) *Philosophy of Educational Research* (2nd edn). London: Continuum.

PRIO (2010) *Teaching Religion, Taming Rebellion? Religious Education Reform in Afghanistan*, www.prio.no/sptrans/1917695848/PRIO%20Policy%20Brief_Teaching%20Religion%20Taming%20Rebellion_%20Afghan%20madrasa%20reform.pdf, accessed 29 May 2012.

QCA (1998a) *Model Syllabuses for Religious Education*. London: Schools Curriculum and Assessment Authority.

QCA (1998b) *Model Syllabuses for Religious Education: Faith Communities Working Group Reports*. London: Schools Curriculum and Assessment Authority.

QCA (2010) *Religious Education in English Schools*. London: DCSF.

Rahe, P. A. (2008) *Against Throne and Altar: Machiavelli and Political Theory Under the English Republic*. Cambridge: Cambridge University Press.

Rahner, K. (1992) *Church and State in Early Christianity*. San Francisco, CA: Ignatius Press.

Ramsey, I. T. (1970) *The Fourth R: Durham Report on Religious Education. Commission on Religious Education in Schools*. London: SPCK.

Rawls, J. (1996) *The Law of Peoples* (new edn). Cambridge, MA: Harvard University Press.

— (1999) *A Theory of Justice*. Cambridge, MA: Harvard University Press.

— (2005) *Political Liberalism*. New York: Columbia University Press.

REDCO (2012) 'Religion in Education: A Contribution to Dialogue or a Factor of Conflict in Transforming Societies of European Countries' (REDCo), www.redco.uni-hamburg.de/web/3480/3497/3503/index.html, accessed 29 May 2012.

REA (2012) Religious Education Association, www.religiouseducation.net/, accessed 29 May 2012.

Ricoeur, P. (1970) *Freud and Philosophy: An Essay on Interpretation*, translated by D. Savage, New Haven: Yale University Press.

Robbins, C. B. (1963) *The Robbins Report. Higher Education: Report of the Committee appointed by the Prime Minister under the Chairmanship of Lord Robbins*. London: HMSO.

Roberts, D. D. (2006) *The Totalitarian Experiment in the Twentieth Century: Understanding the Poverty of the Great Politics*. London: Routledge.

Rousseau, J. J. (1968) [1762] *The Social Contract*. London: Penguin.

— (2007) (1762) *Emile, or On Education.* Sioux Falls: NuVision.

Rudduck, J. and McIntyre, D. (eds) (1998) *Challenges for Educational Research.* London: Paul Chapman.

Rudge, J. (2008) 'Assessment in Religious Education', in L. P. Barnes et al. (eds), *Learning to Teach Religious Education in the Secondary School*, 96–111. London: Routledge.

Ruthven, M. (2007) *Fundamentalism: A Very Short Introduction.* Oxford: Oxford University Press.

Sayed, Y., Davies, L., Hardy M., Arani, A. M., Kakia, L. and Bano, M. (2011) 'Global Security, Religion and Education Development: A Crisis for the Field of Comparative Education?' *Compare: A Journal of Comparative and International Education*, 41(3): 415–31.

Schapiro, L. (1972) *Totalitarianism.* London: Pall Mall Press.

Schleiermacher, F. (1799) *On Religion: Speeches to Its Cultured Despisers*, www.ccel.org/ccel/schleiermach/religion.iii.i.html, accessed 29 May 2012.

Schmid, A. P. (ed.) (2011) *The Routledge Handbook of Terrorism Research.* London and New York: Routledge.

Schmidt, V. H. (2006) 'Multiple Modernities or Varieties of Modernity?' *Current Sociology*, 54(1): 77–97.

— (2010) 'Modernity and Diversity: Reflections on the Controversy between Modernization Theory and Multiple Modernists', *Social Science Information*, 59(4): 511–38.

Schmitt, C. (2005) [1922] *Political Theology: Four Chapters on the Concept of Sovereignty*, translated by G. Schwab. Chicago, IL: Chicago University Press.

Schools Council (1971) *Working Paper 36: Religious Education in Secondary Schools.* London: Evans/Methuen.

Scott, P. and Cavanaugh, W. T. (eds) (2004) *The Blackwell Companion of Political Theology.* Oxford: Wiley-Blackwell.

Seiple, C., Hooper, D. and Otis, P. (eds) (2011) *Routledge Handbook of Religion and Security: Theory and Practice.* London and New York: Routledge.

Seymour, J. (1996) 'Contemporary Approaches to Christian Education', in J. Astley et al. (eds), *Theological Perspectives on Christian Formation: A Reader on Theology and Christian Education*, 1–13. Leominster: Gracewing.

Skeie, G. (2007) 'Religion and Education in Norway', in R. Jackson, S. Miedema, W. Weisse, and J.-P. Willaime (eds), *Religion and Education in Europe: Developments, Contexts and Debates*, 221–42. Münster: Waxmann.

Smart, N. (1969a) *The Religious Experience of Mankind.* London: Macmillan.

— (1969b) 'The Comparative Study of Religions and the Schools', *Religious Education*, 64(1): 26–30.

— (1973) *The Science of Religion & the Sociology of Knowledge: Some Methodological Questions.* Princeton, NJ: Princeton University Press.

— (1979) *The Phenomenon of Christianity.* London: Collins.

— (1998) *The World's Religions*, second edition. Cambridge: Cambridge University Press.

— (1999) *Dimensions of the Sacred: An Anatomy of the World's Beliefs.* Berkeley, CA: California University Press.

Snow, C. P. (1951) *The Masters.* Kelly Bray, Cornwall: House of Stratus.

— (1964) *Corridors of Power.* Kelly Bray, Cornwall: House of Stratus.

— (1993) [1959] *The Two Cultures*, Introduction by S. Collini. Cambridge: Cambridge University Press.

Souza, M. de, Durka, G., Engebretson, K. and Gearon, L. (2010) *International Handbook for Inter-Religious Education.* Amsterdam: Springer.

Souza, M. de, Durka, G., Engebretson, K. and Jackson, R. (eds) (2007) *International Handbook of the Religious, Moral and Spiritual Dimensions in Education.* Amsterdam: Springer.

Spens (1938) *The Spens Report on Secondary Education.* London: HMSO.

Spencer, N. and Chaplin, J. (eds) (2009) *God and Government.* London: SPCK.

Stark, R. (1999) 'Secularization, RIP', *Sociology of Religion*, 60(3): 249–73.

Stern, J. (2006) *Teaching Religious Education.* London: Continuum.

— (2007) *Schools and Religions.* London: Continuum.

Stevens, J. W. (2010) *God-Fearing and Free: A Spiritual History of America's Cold War.* Cambridge, MA: Harvard University Press.

Storrar, W. F. and Morton, A. R. (2004) (eds) *Public Theology for the 21st Century.* London: Continuum.

Sunker, H. and Otto, H.-U. (eds) (2000) *Education and Fascism: Political Formation and Social Education in German National Socialism* (2nd edn). London: Routledge.

Swaine, L. (2006) *The Liberal Conscience: Politics and Principle in a World of Religious Pluralism.* New York: Columbia University Press.

Swann, M. (1985) *The Swann Report: Education for All Report of the Committee of Enquiry into the Education of Children from Ethnic Minority Groups.* London: HMSO.

Swierlein, A.-J. (ed.) (2005) *Unmapped Countries: Biological Visions in Nineteenth Century Literature and Culture.* London: Anthem Press.

Tallis, R. (2009) 'The Eunuch at the Orgy: Reflections on the Significance of F. R. Leavis', in F. Furedi, R. Kimball, R. Tallis and R. Whelan (eds), *From Two Cultures to No Culture: C. P. Snow's Two Cultures Lecture Fifty Years On,* 44–60. London: Civitas Institute for the Study of Civil Society.

Talmon, J. L. 1961 [1952] *History of Totalitarian Democracy.* London: Mercury Books.

Taylor, C. (2007) *A Secular Age.* Boston, MA: Harvard University Press.

— (2010) 'The Meaning of Secularism', *The Hedgehog Review,* 12(3): 1.

Taylor, F. (2010) *Exorcising Hitler: The Occupation and Denazification of Germany.* London: Bloomsbury.

Teece, T. (2010) 'Is It Learning about and from Religions, Religion or Religious Education? And Is It Any Wonder Some Teachers Don't Get It?' *British Journal of Religious Education,* 32(2): 93–103.

Thanissaro, P. N. (2012) 'Measuring Attitude towards RE: Factoring Pupil Experience and Home Faith Background into Assessment', *British Journal of Religious Education,* 34(2): 195–212.

Thatcher, A. (1991) 'A Critique of Inwardness in Religious Education', *British Journal of Religious Education,* 14(1): 22–7.

— (ed.) (1999) *Spirituality and the Curriculum.* London: Continuum.

The 9/11 Commission (2004) *The 9/11 Commission Final Report,* www.gpoaccess.gov/911/index.html, accessed 29 May 2012.

Thompson, P. (1993) 'Religionism: A Response to John Hull', *British Journal of Religious Education,* 16(1): 47–50.

TLRP (2011) Teaching and Learning Research Programme, www.tlrp.org/.

Thompson, P. (2004) *Whatever Happened to Religious Education?* London: James Clark & Co.

Tocqueville, A. de (2003) [1836] *Democracy in America,* translated by G. E. Bevan, introduction by I. Kramnick. London: Penguin.

Tooley, J. with Darby, D. (1998) *Education Research: An OFSTED Critique.* London: OFSTED.

Trevathan, A. (2011) 'Islamic Schools', in L. Gearon (ed.), *The Religious Education Handbook,* re-handbook.org.uk/, accessed 29 May 2012.

Trigg, R. (2007) *Religion in Public Life: Must Faith Be Privatized?* Oxford. Oxford University Press.

Trilling, L. (2001) 'The Leavis/Snow Controversy', in L Wieseltier (ed.), *The Moral Obligation to Be Intelligent,* Selected Essays by Lionel Trilling, 402–26. London: Farrar, Straus and Giroux.

Tschannen, O. (1991) 'The Secularization Paradigm', *Journal for the Scientific Study of Religion,* 30(4): 395–415.

USCIRF (2012) United States Commission on International Religious Freedom, www.uscirf.gov/, accessed 29 May 2012.

UN (1948) *Universal Declaration of Human Rights*. UN: Geneva.

— (2010) *Human Rights Council, Sixteenth session, Agenda item 3, Report of the Special Rapporteur on freedom of religion or belief, Heiner Bielefeldt United Nations General Assembly document A/HRC/16/53*. Geneva: UN.

— (2012) Office of the Special Rapporteur on Freedom of Religion or Belief, www.ohchr.org/EN/Issues/FreedomReligion/Pages/FreedomReligionIndex.aspx, accessed 29 May 2012.

UNESCO (2006) *Guidelines on Intercultural Education*. Paris: UNESCO.

— (2011) *Contemporary Issues in Human Rights Education*. Paris: UNESCO.

Urban, W. J. and Wagoner Jr. J. L. (2008) *American Education: A History* (4th edn). New York: Routledge.

Valk, P. (2007) 'Religious Education in Estonia', in R. Jackson, S. Miedema, W. Weisse, and J.-P. Willaime (eds), *Religion and Education in Europe: Developments, Contexts and Debates*, 159–80. Münster: Waxmann.

Vatican (1965) *Declaration on Christian Education, Gravissimum Educationis*, www.vatican.va/archive/hist_councils/iI_vatican_council/documents/vat-ii_decl_19651028_gravissimum-educationis_en.html, accessed 29 May 2012.

— (1997) *The Religious Dimension of Education in a Cath olic School*, www.vatican.va/roman_curia/congregations/ccatheduc/documents/rc_con_ccatheduc_doc_19880407_catholic-school_en.html, accessed 29 May 2012.

— (1998) *The Catholic School on the Threshold of the Third Millennium* www.vatican.va/roman_curia/congregations/ccatheduc/documents/rc_con_ccatheduc_doc_27041998_school2000_en.html, accessed 29 May 2012.

Vatican II (1975) *Vatican II: The Conciliar and Post Conciliar Documents*, edited by A. Flannery. Dublin: Dominican Publications.

Vries, H. de and Sullivan, L. E. (eds) (2006) *Political Theologies: Public Religions in a Post-secular World*. New York: Fordham.

Ward, K. (2008) *The Big Questions in Science and Religion*. West Conshohocken, PA: Templeton Press.

Ward, P. (2010) 'Roman Catholic Schools', in L. Gearon (ed.), *The Religious Education Handbook*, re-handbook.org.uk/, accessed 29 May 2012.

Waskey, A. J. L. (2006) 'Religion and Education in American Constitutional Law', *International Journal of Scholarly Academic Intellectual Diversity*, 1(1): 1–23.

Watson, J. (2003) 'Preparing Spirituality for Citizenship', *International Journal of Children's Spirituality*, 8(1): 9–24.

Weiss, T. G. and Daws, S. (eds) (2008) *The Oxford Handbook on the United Nations*. Oxford: Oxford University Press.

Weisse, W. (2009a) 'Overview of the EC REDCo-Project and Impulses for Interreligious Dialogue in Europe', www5.quvion.net/cosmea/core/corebase/mediabase/awr/redco/research_findings/REDCo_Brussels_Doc_2.pdf, accessed 29 May 2012.

— (ed.) (2009b) *Religion in Education: Contribution to Dialogue Policy Recommendations of the REDCo research project*, www.redco.uni-hamburg.de/cosmea/core/corebase/mediabase/awr/redco/research_findings/REDCo_policy_rec_Eng.pdf, accessed 29 May 2012.

— (2011) 'Reflections on the REDCo Project', *British Journal of Religious Education*, 33(2): 111–25.

Wells, H. G. (1938) 'The Informative Content of Education', onlinebooks.library.upenn.edu/webbin/book/lookupname?key=Wells%2C%20H.%20G.%20(Herbert%20George)%2C%201866–1946, accessed 29 May 2012.

Whelan, R. (2009) 'Any Culture At All Would Be Nice', in F. Furedi, R. Kimball, R. Tallis and R. Whelan (eds), *From Two Cultures to No Culture: C. P. Snow's Two Cultures Lecture Fifty Years On*, 1–30. London: Civitas Institute for the Study of Civil Society.

White, J. (2004) 'Should Religious Education Be a Compulsory School Subject?' *British Journal of Religious Education*, 26(2): 151–64.

— (2005) 'Reply to Andrew Wright', *British Journal of Religious Education*, 27(1): 21–3.

Whitmarsh, G. (2012) 'The Two Cultures Controversy: Science, Literature and Cultural Politics in Postwar Britain', *History of Education: Journal of the History of Education Society*, 41(1): 130–2.

Willaime, J.-P. (2007) 'Different Models of Religion and Education in Europe', in R. Jackson, S. Miedema, W. Weisse, and J.-P. Willaime (eds), *Religion and Education in Europe: Developments, Contexts and Debates*, 57–66. Münster: Waxmann.

Willaime, J.-P. (2007a) 'Teaching Religion in French Schools', in R. Jackson, S. Miedema, W. Weisse, and J.-P. Willaime (eds), *Religion and Education in Europe: Developments, Contexts and Debates*, 87–102. Münster: Waxmann.

Wilson, B. R. (1966) *Religion in Secular Society*. London: C.A. Watts.

Wilson, J. P. (ed.) (2011) *The Routledge Encyclopedia of UK Education, Training and Employment: From the Earliest Statutes to the Present Day*. London: Routledge.

Witham, L. A. (2002) *Where Darwin Meets the Bible: Creationists and Evolutionists in America*. Oxford: Oxford University Press.

Wolin, S. S. (2008) *Democracy Inc: Managed Democracy and the Specter of Inverted Totalitarianism*. Princeton, NJ: Princeton University Press.

Woodhead, L. (2011) *Report on Recent Research on Religion, Discrimination and Good Relations*, www.religionand-society.org.uk/uploads/docs/2011_05/1306247842_LINDA_WOODHEAD_FINAL_REPORT_MAY_2011.pdf, accessed 29 May 2012.

Woodhead, L., Kawanami, H. and Partridge C. (eds) (2009) *Religions in the Modern World: Traditions and Transformations*. London: Routledge.

Wright, A. (2000) *Spirituality and Education*. London: Routledge.

— (2003) 'The Contours of Critical Religious Education: Knowledge, Wisdom, Truth', *British Journal of Religious Education*, 25(4): 279–91.

— (2004) *Religion, Education and Postmodernity*. London: Routledge.

— (2007) *Critical Religious Education, Multiculturalism and the Pursuit of Truth*. Cardiff: University of Wales Press.

— (2008) 'Learning to Teach Religious Education at Key Stage 4', in L. P. Barnes et al. (eds), *Learning to Teach Religious Education in the Secondary School*, 112–26. London: Routledge.

Yale (2012) *Avalon Project Documents in Law, History and Diplomacy*, Yale University avalon.law.yale.edu/, accessed 29 May 2012.

Yates, P. (1999) 'The Bureaucratization of Spirituality', *International Journal of Children's Spirituality*, 4(2): 179–93.

Zalta, E. N. (ed.) *Stanford Encyclopedia of Philosophy*, plato.stanford.edu/, accessed 29 May 2012.

Zizek, S. (2004) *Did Somebody Say Totalitarianism?* London: Verso.

Index